THE OLD AND NEW WORLD ROMANTICISM OF WASHINGTON IRVING

THE OLD AND NEW WORLD ROMANTICISM OF WASHINGTON IRVING

Edited by
STANLEY BRODWIN

With an Introduction by William L. Hedges

Prepared under the auspices of Hofstra University

Greenwood Press
New York • Westport, Connecticut • London

Library of Congress Cataloging-in-Publication Data

The Old and New World romanticism of Washington Irving.

"Prepared under the auspices of Hofstra University."
Bibliography: p.
Includes index.
1. Irving, Washington, 1783-1859—Criticism and interpretation. 2. Romanticism. I. Brodwin, Stanley. II. Hofstra University.
PS2092.R6304 1986 818′.209 86-3168
ISBN 0-313-25441-9 (lib. bdg. : alk. paper)

Library of Congress Catalog Card Number: 86-3168
ISBN 0-313-25441-9

First published in 1986

Greenwood Press, Inc.
88 Post Road West, Westport, Connecticut 06881

Printed in the United States of America

The paper used in this book complies with the Permanent Paper Standard issued by the National Information Standards Organization (Z39.48-1984).

10 9 8 7 6 5 4 3 2 1

Copyright Acknowledgment

Chapter three, "Washington Irving: The Growth of a Romantic Writer," by Joy S. Kasson amplifies and focuses the author's earlier discussions of Irving's search for a literary vocation in " 'The Citadel Within': Washington Irving and the Search for a Literary Vocation," *Prospects* 3 (1977): 371-417, which formed the basis for the Irving chapter in *Artistic Voyagers: Europe and the American Imagination in the Works of Irving, Cooper, Hawthorne, Allston, and Cole* (Westport, Conn.: Greenwood Press, 1982).

Contents

THE OLD AND NEW WORLD ROMANTICISM OF WASHINGTON IRVING

1. Introduction

WILLIAM L. HEDGES

The essays assembled in this volume were, with one exception, originally presented at Hofstra University in October 1983, in a three-day series of symposia entitled "Romanticism in the Old and New World: International Conference in Celebration of Washington Irving, Stendhal and Vasilii Andreevich Zhukovskii." All three authors born in 1783, the bicentennial of their births was the occasion for the conference. It was sponsored by the Hofstra University Cultural Center under the directorship of Joseph G. Astman. The conference coordinators were Natalie Datlof and Alexej Ugrinsky. The director of the section on Irving was Stanley Brodwin.

Although American and European writers were explicitly brought together in a number of the papers given at Hofstra, the conference sessions on Irving were sufficiently detached from those on the other two principals to justify separate publication of these essays on Irving. A glance at the table of contents will indicate the considerable variation in scope and focus to be found in this collection. Certain aspects of Irving's career are freshly illuminated, as are a number of individual Irving texts. At the same time, the essays rather strikingly amplify and complement one another. Collectively they offer a more thorough and precise understanding than we have had of Irving as a romantic. This is something that one might have thought before the conference, could hardly be achieved. There can be no doubt that the conference justified itself in this accomplishment.

The agreement among these papers as to the nature and extent of Irving's romanticism is probably more fundamental than the disagreement. There are, however, some interpretations that at least on the surface sharply conflict with one another. The concluding sentence of Ralph Aderman's essay on Irving as a "Purveyor of Old and New World Romanticism" outlines one view. As the author "grew older," Aderman says, "romantic attitudes began more and more to dominate his writing, and . . . his literary material . . . was 'colored and toned,' often unconsciously, by the prevailing literary style in Europe and America in the first half of the nineteenth century." This sounds familiar enough, perhaps almost standard, but Aderman seems more skeptical of Irving's romanticism than a number of other conference participants. The substance of his view is that Irving was essentially a popular writer or "popularizer," that he began under the influence of "the neoclassical attitudes and practices found in his beloved Goldsmith and *The Spectator*," that he increasingly displayed romantic tendencies as they became more fashionable, that "there is little evidence that he was much concerned about the theoretical aspects of romanticism," and that, as Aderman says of *The Sketch Book*, one looks in vain in Irving for "profound statements or penetrating insights about life, setting, or character. Rather, romantic impressionism dominates."

For Aderman, Irving the romantic is subordinate to Irving the professional writer. Irving was the first American to be successful in this calling, his achievement coming significantly at the beginning of the age in which commercialization came to dominate literature. Though Irving had some personal emotional investment in what he wrote, what Aderman stresses is his social role as author. He amused large audiences, made them feel good, appealed to their sentimentality, or validated other standard attitudes and emotions. And for American readers in particular, whether in story, sketch, essay, or history, he satisfied a craving for information about the Old World in a way that featured novelty of setting, custom, and character.

Probably no student of Irving would deny that this view has considerable validity. Certainly Stanley T. Williams, Irving's most thorough biographer, would have endorsed it. Dissatisfaction with much of Irving's later work is fairly widespread even among those who find a good deal more originality and literary substance in his writing than Aderman seems to. Strategies of containment have been attempted. In 1965, for instance, I argued that Irving reached an intellectual dead end some time after 1825 and gradually settled into the role of glorified hack following his return to the United States in 1832.(1) A few years later Martin Roth pushed the cutoff point up much earlier. He maintains that there is a profound critique of American society and culture implicit in *Knickerbocker's History*, but he is willing to write off the rest of Irving, beginning with *The Sketch Book*--except for "Rip Van Winkle" and "The Legend of Sleepy Hollow"--as largely self-betrayal.(2) *Knickerbocker's* stock has risen a good deal lately, a number of scholars now seeming to consider it the highlight of Irving's career. In encouraging a reassessment of his mature work, therefore, the Hofstra conference has served a useful purpose.

For Jeffrey Rubin-Dorsky and Joy S. Kasson, Irving's romanticism is by no means reducible to a set of fashionable literary themes, attitudes, and devices adopted with an eye to what would sell. They see his personal involvement in his writing as crucial, no matter what his concern for his audience. The writing is a projection of himself, they argue, or a form of self-exploration which relates him generally to the great tradition of romantic self-consciousness and specifically to such writers as Wordsworth, Byron, Emerson, and Thoreau. Irving's self-preoccupation, however, according to both Rubin-Dorsky and Kasson, is somewhat disguised, filtered through the persona of Geoffrey Crayon, an unsettled bachelor like his creator, semi-retiring and self-effacing, slightly voyeuristic, a soft-spoken ruminator and man of feeling. It figures or is figured in the sights Crayon sees, the stories he hears or reads and tells the imagery and melody of his prose.

Kasson relates The Sketch Book to the "extraordinarily turbulent period in Irving's life" beginning in 1815, the lonely years in England when the Liverpool branch of the family business collapsed under him and he had "to reassess his personal and professional identity." The Sketch Book, one of the chief concerns of which is the writing, making, and meaning of books, becomes the visible proof that he has finally transformed himself, in spite of the social pressures he had long felt against so doing, into a full-time author. The book of course is not autobiography, not even Crayon's, but it shadows forth Irving's ordeal in its persistent dwelling on themes of "loss, a search for identity, and an expectation of redemption through suffering."

Rubin-Dorsky also sees The Sketch Book as "positive assertion of Irving's own individuality" and refers it to complications in the writer's life "in the years between 1815 and 1819." But in this view there are implications that are more far-reaching. For Rubin-Dorsky, Irving is "caught between two worlds, two cultures, two modes of perception, one American, one European." To be a writer in this predicament means that he has to create a world of his own, spin it out of himself imaginatively from private subjective responses, because, as a somewhat disoriented transient, he can objectively know or be sure of very little.

The argument is daring but carefully constructed. According to Rubin-Dorsky, Irving (or Crayon) in England, intrigued by but feeling half-alienated in the Old World past, paradoxically anticipated the dazzled but bewildered response to nature which the British critic Tony Tanner discerns in major American writers in the next generation. What those writers sought was intimacy, but Tanner maintains that the vast terrain of the New World, however sublime, remained awesomely distant even to the transcendental mind and spirit as long as nature was in no essential way transformed by culture. As an Emerson or a Whitman, in Tanner's view, was to occupy open space -- so to speak -- by imaginative self-expansion, by imposing on himself and his readers a spectacular verbal construct, a private but meaning-full "nature" or "America," so, for Rubin-Dorsky, does Irving create his own old England, a substitute past, out of private and personal associations and impressions, a snug refuge from real time which, like space to the later American writer, both stimulates and intimidates by its endless extension.

Irving's self-confidence does not approach that of the transcendentalists. Crayon may create a private time, but he risks self-obliteration in his desire to withdraw into it. Rubin-Dorsky does not say so, but his essay hints at a hidden death wish in Irving's preoccupation with antiquities, a morbidity which Emerson, Thoreau, and Whitman, however solipsistic, largely avoid through their cosmic optimism. Nonetheless, Irving emerges from Rubin-Dorsky's analysis a more thoroughgoing and more "American" romantic than he has previously been claimed to be.

As assessments of the depth of Irving's commitment to romanticism, the remaining conference papers occupy a middle position somewhere between Aderman's on the one hand and Kasson's and Rubin-Dorsky's on the other. Implicitly, if not explicitly, they all see Irving as a halfway figure. Forming a subgroup, however, are three papers which, concentrating on drawing the line between Irving and high romanticism, are somewhat more negative than positive in their appraisals of Irving. The first of these, by Peter Christensen relying on Tzvetan Todorov's structuralist definition of the genre of "the fantastic," argues that the stories and tales in The Sketch Book, Bracebridge Hall, Tales of a Traveller, and The Alhambra represent a "denial" of the genre. With one exception, "The Story of the Young Italian," in Tales of a Traveller, Irving, according to Christensen, does not encourage or tempt readers to take seriously the possibility that a supernatural agency is operative in his fiction. Instead, his talent is for what Todorov calls "the uncanny" or "the marvelous." In "the uncanny," seemingly or possibly supernatural occurrences are finally perceived by the reader to be the consequence of natural causes. In "the marvelous," by contrast, the laws of nature are suspended altogether, action has to be taken as supernatural, and we are forced to suspend disbelief too readily for a sense of "the fantastic" to be induced. For Christensen, Irving's denial of the fantastic is a "psychological and imaginative liability" associated with his general avoidance of "romantic passion" and with his political conservatism. It also serves to distinguish him from his (presumably more romantic) heirs in American fiction, Poe and Hawthorne.

Judith G. Haig's approach and terminology in the second of the three essays in the subgroup are more traditional, but her detailed reading of Tales of a Traveller places Irving in an almost identical position on the romantic scale. And her measuring device is as finely calibrated as Christensen's. The unifying theme that she finds running through the stories in the book bears directly on the issue of romanticism. Irving, she argues, is in the last analysis trying in Tales of a Traveller to come to terms with "imagination." Drawn to it for its power of alleviating or transforming the dullness of the world of common sense, he cannot divest himself of preromantic suspicions or fears of being deceived and led astray by what may prove to be mere dream or illusion. He flirts with imagination but does not use it as a means of discovering or creating a more fundamental reality. In denying the fantastic, then, Irving seems to be denying imagination as well. Haig, however, tends to see the divided or ambivalent artistic sensibility as possessing its own intrinsic interest and significance.

Haig's position is not unlike that of William Owen in the third paper of the subgroup, an analysis of "Abbotsford," Irving's reminiscence, written in 1834, of his visit to Sir Walter Scott in 1817. Owen maintains that the American author (as Crayon) in this text is distancing himself from Scott and Scott's romanticism in spite of being drawn forcefully toward them. They represent for Irving, at least in retrospect, the "mingling" of "imagination with superstition," the creation of a risky "dream world." Ironically, in Owen's view, there is something more "real" in Scott's dream than in Irving's denial of imagination. The dream grows out of Scott's native landscape and a culture that is fully integrated with the terrain. Totally at home in his surroundings, Scott can write in accordance with the "romantic claim that images must arise out of deeply-rooted feeling." He also has the power to "create individuality" in character. This is something Irving lacked because of his inability to "trust his own responses." Physically, emotionally, and artistically unsettled, remaining abroad too long, his inner eye turned more toward the past than the present, Irving never achieves a fullness of passion or vision. As a writer, he "offers an eclecticism that depends on the writer's craft to create unity out of diverse elements."

Obviously, Owen's interpretation of Irving stands as a direct challenge to Rubin-Dorsky's. Yet curiously the two essays confirm each other. Looking at them together we see differences diminishing in assessment of Irving. An undercurrent running through Owen's interpretation is the notion that Irving had a fairly clear sense of who he was (or was not) and of his talents and limitations as a writer. Further, we see that he more or less consciously and with considerable skill exploited his own uncertainties and ambivalences by projecting them through the figure of Geoffrey Crayon, the displaced person, and making them the half-acknowledged underlying theme of "Abbotsford," as they had been of much of his work since *The Sketch Book*. Several of the papers convey a strong sense of the enthusiasms that were a part of international romanticism. Thriving on novelty and an appetite for the exotic, it offered new sights and sensations, even if it often fell short of the totally transforming vision or totally transporting passion. Eclecticism -- the artist's drawing on a variety of inspirations and resources, styles and subject matter, ideas and impressions -- was pretty much the order of the day. Viewed in this context, no matter how tentative, skeptical, playful, even self-mocking his romanticism was, Irving commands a good deal of respect. Indeed in an age of overwriting his uncertainties were perhaps an asset. Presumably they helped him to develop a rather sophisticated, "knowing" craft, in which illusion entices the reader in the very process of proclaiming itself to be mere make-believe.

"Irving indulges in romance in full awareness of its duplicity," says Michael R. Katz in his essay, which traces through romantic literature the career of a ghostly lover -- born in an old Scottish ballad; gothicized in Burger's "Lenore"; brought back into English by, among others, Scott; parodied by Zhukovsky; prosified by Irving; and finally given its most sophisticated rendition by Pushkin. Irving's particular talent, Katz asserts, was for engaging in "mystery and parody" simultaneously.

John Frey and Loretta Sharon Wyatt, comparing and contrasting Irving with, respectively, Chateaubriand and the Brazilian writer Antonio Gonçalves Dias, examine Irving's romance with Spanish-Moorish Granada and its crowning jewel, the palace of Alhambra. Frey provides a particularly useful analysis of Irving's narrative (and nondescriptive) technique in _A Chronicle of the Conquest of Granada_. In both comparisons Irving, as usual, comes off as the less passionate romantic. But together Frey and Wyatt acknowledge an artistic authenticity in Irving's literary method in the _Conquest_ and also _The Alhambra_. He writes history which reads like romance, like a story-teller's inventions. He also preserves legends in which actual, if anonymous, storytellers have fictionalized or romanticized the past. He is willing to juxtapose the two sorts of narratives, complicating things still further by retelling the legends in his own style. Illusion and deception are omnipresent but easily seen through. Whimsy, humor, and mild satire insure the transparency.

One is reminded of Christensen's contention that _The Alhambra_ is Irving's best collection of fiction because it relies almost exclusively on "the marvelous," the genre in which "he coped most successfully with his aversion to the fantastic." Lee Fontanella's paper, contrasting the Alhambra as imaginatively depicted in Irving's prose with more objective representations in early photography, makes a similar point. The daguerreotype having come into use about 1840 during the early stirrings of realism in literature and photographs taken about 1860, some of them reproduced in this book, generally deromanticize the Moorish palace. But the romantic-realistic polarization is far from absolute. Fontanella sees the complexities of _The Alhambra_: Irving, though lured toward the inmost recesses of the palace as into a realm of pure romance, is yet unable to resist the backward look over his shoulder, as it were, at the actual world outside. Conversely, we see lingering romantic associations (to some extent, no doubt, derived from Irving himself) sometimes distracting photographers from their quasi-scientific detachment.

Irving's books on Spain, particularly _The Alhambra_, have always had their admirers. The strategy he had devised for introducing Americans to Old World cultures by converting them into exotic adventures in reading worked well. But his efforts after 1832 to do much the same thing with the American West have drawn heavy fire from modern critics. Thus John Joseph's defense of the artistry of "A Tour on the Prairies" in an essay on "The Romantic Lie" is a welcome minority report. It is also a major contribution to the conference's considerable effort to understand Irving's contribution to romanticism in terms of style and craft. Contemporary fiction's acute consciousness of itself as fiction may have a good deal to do with this interest. But be that as it may, we are consistently encouraged in this collection to keep in mind that Irving was first and foremost a fictionalizer.

What this means, I think, needs further study in the context of Irving's uneasiness in his own culture. But we can begin with his boredom with the humdrum routines of the American bourgeois culture into which as a young man he was more or less expected to fit. In one sense he never got away from that culture altogether, even in Europe, but he began early as a writer to rise above it by making fun of it, mocking typical behavior, distorting it, often quite senselessly. Without dissociating himself from the society in which he grew up -- he always wrote as a loyal New Yorker in his early years -- he burlesqued its politics, cultural institutions, and history, and he parodied its manners of speaking and writing as well as what it read. He must have begun to be conscious at some point -- while writing Knickerbocker's History, if not sooner -- of the power of his talent, of his ability to create worlds of words more interesting, however grotesque, than the real one. Eventually writing became his refuge both emotionally and vocationally, as romanticism gave sanction to his impatience with commercial culture and gave him license as a professional storyteller to indulge to a certain degree his fantasizing proclivity. He could give himself to bookmaking even if not abandon himself altogether to imagination or the fantastic.

His literary craft centered on holding fiction and reality, illusion and common sense more or less plausibly together. By the time of "A Tour on the Prairies" the craft had become largely instinctive or automatic. Joseph shows how Irving's account of a relatively routine bee hunt in the Oklahoma Indian territory became "a wholly different way of seeing" it. The technique used in this instance Irving had aptly described in 1825 in a letter to Henry Brevoort as "the play of thought, and sentiment, and language." Such play half pulls the reader of "A Tour" away from the bees in the direction of what they are whimsically but tellingly made to analogize: "merchantment in a money making metropolis, little suspicious of impending bankruptcy and downfall" (a not uncommon theme in Irving, as Kasson shows). The conventional criticism of Irving's treatment of the West is just this, that he is distracted from the "real" frontier by what it reminds him of back East or in Europe. Joseph's defense is that Irving is arousing interest in experience that might otherwise be scarcely worth reporting. If he is distorting reality, not showing the West as it really is, he is nonetheless living up to an implied contract with his readers, who buy the book as much for Geoffrey Crayon's special way of seeing things as for factual information about the prairies.

And as Irving wrote, so he built. Among the author's eclectic and quaintly exotic works of art, David R. Anderson suggests, was Sunnyside, the old Dutch house on the Hudson in Tarrytown, bought after his return from Europe and romantically and picturesquely remodeled into the modest mansion of his middle and old age. Reading this architectural fantasy as a symbolic text, Anderson makes one wonder if Sunnyside was not the major achievement of Irving's later years. Reflecting values and traditions handed down from a remote past, it was nonetheless a private retreat, not a public monument. Viewers clearly understood, Anderson shows, that they were looking at a material replica of Geoffrey Crayon himself. In a bit of devil's advocacy while commenting on the papers at one of the conference sessions, I suggested that _Knickerbocker's History_ might be looked upon as Irving's most romantic text. Christensen's references to Todorov were what sparked this notion. I have noticed that Todorov speaks of a sort of subgenre or variation of the genre of the fantastic in which readers (and characters) have to hesitate between accepting happenings as real and taking them as imaginary. This is an ambiguity slightly different from that of the fantastic proper, in which the issue is whether happenings are natural or supernatural. The nagging question in the subgenre is, Did this really happen or was it only imagined or dreamed?(3)

Knickerbocker of course does not fit Todorov's definition of the fantastic even in its varied form. But I am struck by what seems to be a related effect repeatedly induced by Irving's mock-history. This is the eerie feeling that comes with our inability to decide how seriously to take Diedrich Knickerbocker. Is he the earnest antiquarian he claims to be or is he idiot or madman? Is he a deliberate falsifier of the past or an ingenious ironist -- or is he somehow all of these? Whatever the peculiar persona is, it seems that the reader is continually thrown off balance by wanting or trying to believe him even when what he is saying is absurd.

The papers at Hofstra had neglected the early Irving, falling in too readily perhaps with the conventional view that his romanticism does not begin until the period of his visit to Walter Scott and the inspiration for _The Sketch Book_. The textbooks and anthologies still picture him as essentially a neoclassicist in his amateur years, even though we know that his early humor consistently mocks the eighteenth-century attitudes and forms of which it makes use. The more I thought about Irving after the conference, the more it seemed to me that the deliberate disorientation in which his early nonsensical humor revels has, as Martin Roth has argued, a significant affinity with romanticism.

My reading of _Knickerbocker_ has altered over the years. The book now seems to me more positively charged than it used to. I think we have not yet learned how to respond to Irving's mock-history because we have been trying too hard to grasp what it means. My conviction that the _History_ is a proto-romantic text has been strengthened by the papers and discussions at Hofstra. Whether there is more behind the view than post-conference euphoria, however, the reader may judge. My paper on _Knickerbocker's History_ has been included as a postscript at the end of this collection. In it I am not primarily arguing the romanticism of Irving's text. But the relevance of the paper to the theme of this book will be apparent.

I am deeply grateful to Stanley Brodwin for encouraging me to make this belated contribution to the Hofstra conference.

NOTES

1. William L. Hedges, *Washington Irving: An American Study, 1802-1832* (Baltimore: Johns Hopkins University Press, 1965).
2. Martin Roth, *Comedy and America: The Lost World of Washington Irving* (Port Washington, N.Y.: Kennikat Press, 1976).
3. Tzvetan Todorov, *The Fantastic: A Structural Approach to a Literary Genre* (Cleveland: Case Western Reserve, 1973), p. 36.

Part I

Washington Irving as Romantic: The Issue Joined

2.

Washington Irving as a Purveyor of Old and New World Romanticism

RALPH M. ADERMAN

Washington Irving is regarded as one of the earliest and strongest voices of romanticism in America, but what is often overlooked is his close connection with English and Continental romanticism. His role as popularizer of such romantic elements as early American history, the scenery of the Hudson River and the Catskills, and the Indian has long been acknowledged, but his exploitation of European materials has not been fully explored, or so it seems to me. In the ensuing remarks I hope to suggest something of the range and intensity of Irving's romanticism, both in its use of native materials and in its exploitation of a variety of European elements. Indeed, Irving's work in acquainting Europeans with American romantic topics was counterbalanced by his introduction of European romantic materials to American readers. Until his _Sketch Book_ took England by storm and soon made its way into the hands of Continental readers in translation as well as in English, readers on the eastern side of the Atlantic had only limited acquaintance with American writers of any sort. The condescending verdicts of English critics effectively curbed circulation of American fiction, drama, and essays, and most readers abroad were not inclined to sample American writing, even if they could find it. Although Sir Walter Scott had expressed delight with _Knickerbocker's History_, it was only when _The Sketch Book_ appeared that Irving was recognized as a writer with a felicitous style, touching emotional appeal, and a sensitive appreciation of the culture and traditions of England. Thus a new awareness of American literary potential manifested itself.

Before exploring this problem further, I would like to examine Irving's own background to ascertain the elements which were shaping his literary outlook. His earliest writing reflected many of the neoclassical attitudes and practices found in his beloved Oliver Goldsmith and in _The Spectator_ of Addison and Steele. Character types, humor, parody, and satire in the letters of Jonathan Oldstyle and in the sketches and social commentary of _Salmagundi_ had a strong eighteenth-century flavor, as did many of the passages in *Knickerbocker's History*, but by the time Irving was writing for the *Analectic Magazine* and editing its pages a few years later he revealed increasingly romantic attitudes toward his material. Although Irving reflected many of the romantic tendencies of the early nineteenth century, there is little evidence that he was much concerned about the theoretical aspects of romanticism or reflected upon them. His was a kind of intuitive, emotional reaction to impressions derived from his travels, his conversation, and his reading. That these impressions coincided with the prevailing attitudes of the times was largely fortuitous. It must be emphasized that Irving was not a theoretician or a philosopher; he was only a sensitive individual recording his reactions in a manner which readers of the time found appealing.

His romantic attitudes were nurtured as a result of his grand tour to France, Italy, and England from 1804 to 1806. Repeatedly in his journals and letters he remarked about romantic scenery, especially in the mountains with their varied and spectacular wildness. Like his English and Continental counterparts, he expressed his emotional reaction to the spectacle which unfolded before him. Irving's travels in southern France and Italy exposed him to the colorful activities and customs of the natives, and his encounters with mouldering ruins and his explorations of the old churches and their vaults filled with skeletons made him aware of the past and the long-established traditions and also gave him a firsthand glimpse of some of the macabre elements he had encountered in Mrs. Radcliffe and other Gothic writers. To a young, impressionable mind the sights of southern Europe opened new romantic vistas which were later reflected in his writing.

In his early writings Irving frequently used the word "romantic" to convey his sense of wonder and awe. Variants and embellishments of the phrase "romantic scenery" appeared regularly in his journals, letters, and published writings, and the romantic outlook seems firmly fixed in his imagination, to appear in various ways for the next half century. Without doubt Irving's youthful exposure to European scenery and attitudes conditioned and strengthened his romantic predisposition.

When he returned to New York in 1806, he plunged almost immediately into the writing of *Salmagundi*, a literary venture which he carried out with his brother, William, and with James Kirke Paulding. As a literary miscellany, *Salmagundi* was too narrow and provincial in scope to attract the attention of overseas readers. However, it provided Irving with a training ground in which to introduce romantic elements to offset the dominant neoclassical tone of the sketches, essays, and poems. Emotion and sentiment counterbalanced crude satire and carping criticism. The same mixture can be found in *Knickerbocker's History of New York* with its strokes of broad humor and caricature along with the individualism, iconoclasm, petulance, and emotionalism of some of the Dutch leaders.

Further manifestations of romanticism appear in his

contributions to the Analectic Magazine. Appearing during the struggle with the British in the period from 1812 to 1815, many of these pieces, either written or selected by Irving, emphasized nationalism, patriotism, and indigenous elements of the American scene. They represent a skirmish in the "paper war" or literary nationalism which complements the economic and military battles fought in other segments of American society. They show Irving's growing dedication to the romantic outlook.

When Irving went to England in 1815 to assist in the overseas operation of the faltering family importing business, he had the opportunity to develop and extend his romantic proclivities. Upon his arrival he observed that "[t]he country is enchanting."(1) His travels through the English, Welsh, and Scottish countrysides enabled him to savor the picturesque scenery and untamed vistas. For him Kenilworth Castle was a "magnificent wreck of feudal grandeur" with an air "of opulence, and power and lordly superiority,"(2) and "the valleys or rather glens of Derbyshire are beautifully romantic."(3) As he sailed along the eastern coast of Scotland on one occasion, he spoke of "the excitement of my feelings in this romantic part of my voyage,"(4) and he found Edinburgh "the most picturesque romantic place I have ever seen except Naples."(5) Wherever he traveled in Britain, the scenery stirred his romantic spirit.

Visits to John Murray's drawing room and to London publishers provided him with further opportunities to expand and intensify his romantic disposition. As he listened to Isaac D'Israeli's anecdotes and read a letter of Lord Byron's which Murray showed him, he became more aware of the manifestations of the romantic mood in the English literary establishment, a feeling which was enhanced by the talk of Thomas Moore's Lalla Rookh and the speculation about Scott's authorship of the Waverley novels.(6) Such heady gossip stirred Irving's feelings and caused him to study these writers with added interest. Later, when economic circumstances forced him to turn to his pen for his livelihood, he could emulate the techniques and draw upon the ideas and feelings which brought these writers fame, if not fortune.

In The Sketch Book, Irving produced a literary work, a miscellany, which displayed many facets of the romantic temperament. The satire, parody, and burlesque of Knickerbocker's History had been dropped; instead, Irving introduced humor, sentiment, strong appeals to the emotions, Gothic elements, reverent appreciation of the past, admiration of the beauties of nature, New World elements like the Indian, topographical descriptions of both Old and New World settings, and sensitive reactions to local customs and folklore. These elements were greatly admired by popular readers, and Irving's felicitous style appealed to sophisticated readers not ordinarily attracted to the sentimental and sensational. Consequently, through his happy combination of subjects and methods Irving was able to attract and engage a body of transatlantic readers who ordinarily would not converge on the same body of reading material.

Although in later prefaces to The Sketch Book Irving disclaimed any intention of writing the pieces solely for British readers, the early numbers published in New York soon made their way to England and were received so favorably that he arranged for their publication in London. Thus it happened that while American readers were entranced by his descriptions of rural England, or vignettes of the Boar's Head Tavern in Eastcheap, or impressions of Westminster Abbey and Stratford-on-Avon, or vivid accounts of an English Christmas and its customs British readers warmed to his sympathetic response to English life and scenery and to his clear presentation of Indian life and character in America. Moreover, his engaging descriptions of the Hudson River valley provided a pleasanter, more positive picture of the United States than those found in the travel accounts of jaundiced British visitors like Charles William Janson, John Melish, and Isaac Weld. Furthermore, the aura of romance which Irving threw over his American subjects tempered the harsh, negative impressions which most English readers had acquired from their biased, illiberal countrymen. Irving's romanticizing did not conceal the plainness, even ugliness, which he found in the environs of the Sleepy Hollow or the Hudson River, but it helped to offset the defamatory misrepresentations of ill-natured British travelers. His treatment of the American scene in The Sketch Book, then, blended the real and the ideal, suffused the details with an air of mystery and feeling, and conveyed his impressions in a gracious style which even the most discriminating British reader could not object.

It should be emphasized that Irving's purpose in writing The Sketch Book was neither a defense of his native land nor an appreciation of Britain. His basic motive for writing was to earn money to sustain himself away from home, and he was also expressing an emotional reaction to scenes, stories, and people he encountered on British soil. In true romantic fashion he let his feelings and impressions dictate the nature of his response. Nowhere in The Sketch Book are there any profound statements or penetrating insights about life, setting, or character. Rather, romantic impressionism dominates. As he observed at the beginning of "The Broken Heart,"

> It is a commom practice with those who have outlived the susceptibility of early feeling, or have been brought up in the gay heartlessness of dissipated life, to laugh at all love stories and to treat the tales of romantic passion as mere fictions of novelists and poets. My observations on human nature have induced me to think otherwise. . . . I believe in broken hearts and the possibility of dying of disappointed love.(7)

Then Irving illustrated by telling the story of an Irish girl who gives all to love, lost her beloved, sank into melancholy, wasted away, and died of a broken heart.

These sentiments, repeated in such stories as "The Widow and Her Son" and "The Pride of the Village," had great popular appeal.

Other romantic impressions appeared in Irving's descriptions of revered landmarks like Westminster Abbey and Stratford-on-Avon, where he could allude to historical and literary events and evoke a sense of England's rich past in a way that could be enjoyed by both the English and their American cousins. The feeling of kinship and commonality superseded the bitterness and recrimination of recent economic struggles and military conflicts. With geniality and sentiment Irving used his romantic approach to efface and heal old wounds and misunderstandings. Throughout the collection of materials Irving's emphasis was always positive and restrained.

The popular acclaim and financial success of The Sketch Book on both sides of the Atlantic induced Irving to repeat the literary formula with the focus on strictly English material in Bracebridge Hall. His mental exhaustion and physical distress after its completion led him to Germany, Vienna, Prague, and Dresden, where he absorbed Continental scenery, folklore, and ideas. Earlier at Walter Scott's suggestion, he had studied the German language and read German literature and was able to fashion new materials on German models in his next work, the Tales of a Traveller. As Henry Pochmann observed many years ago, "Buckthorne" is an imitation of Wilhelm Meister; "The Devil and Tom Walker" is a New England Faust done up in sportive style; "The Adventure of My Aunt" and "The Adventure of the German Student" are filled with Gothic elements; and "The Bold Dragoon," "The Adventure of My Uncle," and "The Story of the Young Italian" all draw upon German writing.(8) Although the vigor of the style and the originality of the material were somewhat diminished in this collection, Irving succeeded in giving his readers a variety of romantic stories and sketches from a fresh perspective. American writing gained greater variety and respectability with these literary pieces, and American readers were exposed to the permutations and adaptations of European styles and models with Irving's sensitive, imaginative treatment.

Irving next conceived a group of American essays and sketches in his continuing series, but this project never reached fruition. Perhaps he had written himself out in this vein, or perhaps his long absence from his native land had cut him off from the inspiration he needed. After an extended period of desultory socializing in Paris and Bordeaux, he accepted the invitation of Alexander Hill Everett, the American minister, to go to Madrid and translate some documents compiled by the Spanish historian and antiquary Navarette relating to the explorations of Christopher Columbus. Although Irving regarded the project as a way of earning money by publishing his translation with John Murray, he found that the prosaic documents lacked drama and human interest. Soon he adapted them into a colorful narrative highlighting the exploits of Columbus in his quest for new lands and new riches. The result was not a conventional biography but rather a gripping story with moving episodes combining documented facts and imaginative dramatic details created and presented in Irving's smooth, effortless style. In Columbus and other historical and biographical works that followed in Spain, Irving romanticized his materials and made them palatable and enjoyable for his readers in England and America.

Perhaps his handling of the material in this vivid way was not a deliberate decision but rather an instinctive approach with colorful and dramatic details which would appeal to the ordinary reader and enable him to feel and appreciate the events and situations. As he observed to a friend in Paris concerning the biography of Columbus, "This was a trial of skill in an entirely new line in which I had to satisfy both the public and myself. I determined . . . that I would enter minutely into every research and investigation & in short execute every thing to the best of my abilities."(9) Another assessment, written after the completion of the manuscript, shows his high regard for the biography: "It is a link in history that every complete library must have, and I know one thing for certain, that from the materials which have been furnished me and which have been generally withheld from Strangers, I have been able to furnish a more ample and correct Statement of facts relative to Columbus and his voyages than has as yet been presented to the world."(10) Irving's turning to the biographical mode, dramatizing it, and making it available to a wide readership show that he recognized that novelty was an important element in his continuing success as a writer. Moreover, he recognized that the abundance of new facts that he had found made the biography particularly appealing to his countrymen across the sea, for heretofore they had been dependent upon European historians and biographers who could not appreciate and exploit European historians and biographers who could not appreciate and exploit American interest in an exhaustive account of Columbus's work. Probably without fully realizing it, through his use of romantic techniques and attitudes, Irving was bringing new ideas and values to American and English readers.

Irving's writing on Spanish subjects continued with his account of the conquest of Granada and the end of Moorish rule in Spain. His interest in this subject was enlivened by a visit in March 1828 to Granada and the Alhambra and by his firsthand observations of the ruined palace. Stories about the building and its earlier occupants stimulated his imagination and induced him to read more widely about Ferdinand and Isabella and to review his notes for details about their military campaigns against the Moors. By August 31, 1828, he reported that he had completed part of his chronicle of the conquest of Granada,

> which I have endeavoured to work up into an entertaining and popular form, without sacrificing the intrinsic truth of history. I have been over most of the scenes of the history, so as to give graphical force to the descriptions. With

> all its romantic colouring I really believe it will give a more full and correct idea of that rugged and singular war than any work extant; many of the details having hitherto existed in manuscript - and all being dressed up with an eye to the scenery of the country and the customs of the times. It is an attempt, not at historical romance but a romantic history.(11)

Two weeks later, writing to Alexander Hill Everett, Irving described his new work as

> a Chronicle, made up from all the old Spanish historians I could lay my hands on, colored and tinted by the imagination so as to have a romantic air, without destroying the historical basis or the chronological order of events. I fancy it is as near the truth as any of the chronicles from which it is digested, and has the advantage of containing the striking facts and achievements, true or false, of them all. Of course it will have no pretensions as a grave historical production, or a work of authority, but I cannot help thinking it will present a lively picture of the war, and one somewhat characteristic of the times, so much of the materials having been drawn from contemporary historians.(12)

This description amplifies Irving's ideas about romantic history. He will use the old chronicles, even though they may be untrustworthy or inaccurate, because they provide an aura of verisimilitude and a sense of contemporaneity even as they evoke the mood of a historical period in the past. The combination of factual detail and imaginative coloring appealed to Irving's fancy and provided him with materials that he could shape into romantic history with his unique stamp upon it.

Later, while waiting to see a copy of the published book, which Murray had delayed issuing because of the furor in England over the Catholic question, Irving reiterated the point, calling the work "something of an experiment" which was made "out of the old chronicles, embellished, as well as I was able, by the imagination, and adapted to the romantic taste of the day. Something that was to be between a history and a romance."(13) He felt that the success of his experiment should not be judged too quickly because the effect of his novel approach might not be accepted by the first readers of the book. He alluded to the case of *The Sketch Book*, which Murray had at first rejected and only later purchased when he recognized the financial benefits deriving from its popular acceptance by a broad readership.

Irving's statements here are significant in the consideration of his later development as a romantic writer using both European and American materials. His sense of "romantic history" was to permeate his sequel on the companions of Columbus, as well as his later biographies of

John Jacob Astor, Captain Bonneville, Oliver Goldsmith, Mahomet, and George Washington. With The Conquest of Granada Irving seems to have found the proper combination of factual detail and romantic coloring to attract readers in large numbers. In most instances he was able to recreate a remote or exotic setting with an imaginative overlay of color and drama. Although these works were neither strict history and biography nor fancifully imaginative sketches, they appealed to readers in both areas and enhanced Irving's popularity as an entertaining writer.

Just as Irving was disturbed by Murray's cautious hesitation in issuing The Conquest of Granada, he was annoyed by what he considered Murray's tampering with the details on the title page. Irving had instructed that the work be called "A Chronicle of the Conquest of Granada by Fray Antonio Agapida" so that he as author could hide behind the persona of the Spanish friar and avoid responsibility for any errors or distortions. Instead, Irving noted, Murray "has inserted my name; I presume to make the work more immediately salable, but it is an unwarrantable liberty, and makes me gravely, in my own name, tell many round untruths. I here openly make myself responsible as an author for the existence of the manuscript of Agapida, &c., &c. Literary mystifications are excusable when given anonymously or under feigned names, but are impudent deceptions when sanctioned by an author's real name."(14) His letter to Murray is equally pointed:

> I must protest against the alteration you have made in the title page. I do not concieve [sic] that the purchase of the work gave you any right to make such alteration. I put in the title page the name of Fray Antonio Agapida as author of the chronicle. You must have percieved [sic] that this was a Nom de Guerre to enable me to assume greater freedom & latitude in the execution of the work, and to mingle a tinge of romance and satire with the grave historical details. By inserting my name in the title page as the avowed author, you make me personally responsible for the verity of the facts and the soundness of the opinions of what was intended to be given as a romantic chronicle.(15)

And so because of Murray's intervention, Irving's experiment in imaginative romantic history did not have the protection of authorial anonymity.

These protests suggest that Irving had developed an approach to historical narration which enabled him to take factual details, even unreliable or dubious ones, and blend them with his own imaginative coloring to produce a piece of writing which, strictly speaking, is neither history nor romance. To protect himself, he used a mask or persona to relate the story, an approach which he had first adopted in his dramatic criticism for the Morning Chronicle in the guise of Jonathan Oldstyle. Diedrich Knickerbocker came next with his mock history of New York, and Geoffrey Crayon followed with The Sketch Book. But Fray Antonio Agapida is exposed as Irving's alter ego, much to his chagrin. Increasingly, Irving used the persona to avoid responsibility for his imaginative flights in his romanticizing of history. But Irving's distress was soon replaced in the spring of 1829 by a romantic excursion through the picturesque scenery of Andalusia and a return to Granada. Here, through the kindness of the governor of the Alhambra, Irving was permitted to reside in his apartment in the paand steep himself in its exotic atmosphere. Here he had the leisure to review his notes on the activities of the associates of Columbus, to draft in rough form accounts of other Spanish heroes not included in The Conquest of Granada, to listen to and record the legends and folklore passed along to him by his housekeeper Dona Maria Antonia and his factotum Matteo Jimenez, and to continue his research in the library of the Duke of Gor. The charm and enchantment of the Moorish palace are vividly communicated in his subsequent sketches in The Alhambra. As he observed to his brother Peter, "It is a singular good fortune to be thrown in this most romantic and historical place, which has such a sway over the imaginations of readers in all parts of the world. . . . I am determined to linger here until I get some writings under way connected with the place, and that shall bear the stamp of real intimacy with the charming scenes described."(16)

Irving's plan to combine leisure and labor in the exotic setting of the Alhambra was disrupted in the summer of 1829 by letters informing him that he had been appointed secretary of the American Legation in London through the efforts of well-meaning relatives and friends who regarded his researches and travels in Spain as wasteful and unproductive for a man in the prime of his life. So he hurried to England and settled into the routine of a diplomatic functionary with little free time for personal literary projects. After serving conscientiously for two years, Irving resigned his post and resumed work on The Alhambra. By March 1832, before he had departed for the United States, he arranged for its subsequent publication by Colburn and Bentley. Since the book follows the romantic impressionism and Gothicism of his earlier collections of tales and sketches, we need not examine it in detail.

With his return home after a seventeen-year absence, Irving looked at American scenery and values through the eyes of a cultivated expatriate who had achieved literary fame with his deft literary handling of a variety of English and Spanish materials. Now he was ready to apply his method of romantic history and literary impressionism to native materials, and within five years he demonstrated the mastery of his approach in A Tour on the Prairies (1835), Astoria (1836), and The Adventures of Captain Bonneville (1837).

When offered the opportunity to visit the trans-Mississippi west with Henry Ellsworth, United States Indian commissioner, Irving readily accepted, for now he could observe firsthand "the remnants of those great Indian tribes, which are about to disappear as independent nations. . . . I should see those fine countries of the 'far west,' while still in a state of pristine wildness, and behold herds of buffaloes scouring their native prairies, before they are driven beyond the reach of a civilized tourist."(17) Once again Irving could convey the sense of transience, express his romantic feelings, and treat the Noble Savage, unsullied nature, the unsettled wilderness and its creatures, and the exhilaration of novel experiences in the mode which had served him so well in England and Spain. In short, Irving would apply his romantic sensitivity to the materials of his native land.

Opportunity for applying his "romantic history" approach came fortuitously when John Jacob Astor approached him and proposed that he compile an account of Astor's fur-trading activities in the Pacific Northwest from documents and narratives. Irving was interested: "I have felt aware that a work might be written on the subject, full of curious and entertaining matter, comprising adventurous expeditions by sea and land, scenes beyond the Rocky Mountains, incidents and scenes illustrative of Indian character, and of that singular and but little known class, the traders and voyageurs of the Fur Companies."(18) Since he was engaged at the time in preparing _A Tour on the Prairies_ for _The Crayon Miscellany_, with _Abbotsford and Newstead Abbey_ and _Legends of the Conquest of Spain_ as sequels, he turned the initial research over to his nephew Pierre Munro Irving. As Irving conceived of the project, Pierre would "collate the various documents, collect verbal information, and reduce the whole to such form that I might be able to dress it up advantageously, and with little labor, for the press."(19)

Irving's approach is clearly revealed in this statement. After Pierre had gathered and arranged the important details, Irving would "dress up" the material by applying his method of romantic history to it, even as he had with the Spanish materials and the numbers of _The Crayon Miscellany_. He intended to shorten the process for himself by having Pierre take care of the basic research, a step which he and his brother Peter had carried out together in the earlier projects. The end result, however, would be the same. He would produce a dramatic narrative based on documentary and firsthand evidence and embellished with colorful imaginative touches which would carry it beyond the usual prosaic accounts of such exploit. Although admitting in the introduction that the account was somewhat rambling and disjointed, Irving asserted that "the work, without any labored attempt at artificial construction, actually possesses much of that unity so much sought after in works of fiction, and considered so important to the interest of every history."(20) The plan was carried out as Irving had conceived, and he soon was established as one of the foremost chroniclers of the American frontier.

While working on _Astoria_, Irving met Captain Benjamin Bonneville, an army officer who had just returned from explorations west of the Rocky Mountains. When Bonneville failed to interest a publisher in his journal, Irving offered to purchase it for $1,000 and transform it into a romantic narrative in the style of _Astoria_. Thus, Irving was able to draw upon the knowledge and experience acquired during the preparation of the history of Astor's enterprise and add "a tone and coloring"(21) which placed Bonneville's account beside _Astoria_ in the romanticizing of the American West. When factual details were scanty, Irving drew upon his fancy and created stirring pictures of scenery and events, even as he had done in _The Conquest of Granada_. As he indicated to Colonel Thomas Aspinwall, his literary agent in England, the results pleased him: "It is full of striking scenes and adventures; characteristic of an immense and very interesting region, very little known and laying open a kind of wild life among the mountains of which the public have very little idea."(22) Irving's fascination with unusual adventures in remote, unfamiliar regions accorded with his purpose in writing romantic history.

Throughout the 1830s, then, Irving continued to follow his peculiar romantic approach, chiefly with respect to American materials. His own adventures in the Indian Territory under the watchful eyes of a band of army rangers were dressed up with imaginative details, and the characterizations of some members of the party were sketched with the skill of an experienced novelist. _Astoria_ and _The Adventures of Captain Bonneville_ display a similar narrative art. The exuberance and vitality presented in these accounts probably transcended the tiresome reality of the actual experiences. But in keeping with his romantic vision Irving wished to convey an idealized picture of life in the wilderness, a life which suggested America's potential for the future. The hardships and unpleasantness were glossed over, and the reader is left with a glowing, though distorted, impression of frontier life. Irving's romanticizing continued without pause in these American books.

With his treatment of the American West behind him, Irving turned to the Hudson River valley for a series of essays and sketches which were published in the _Knickerbocker Magazine_ between May 1839 and October 1841. Interspersed among these were articles drawn from notes and drafts left unused from earlier projects in Spain. By combining Old and New World materials Irving was able every month to turn out an entertaining piece which conveyed his romantic impressions about nature, society, literature, and history on both sides of the Atlantic. Much of this material reflected his feelings of an earlier period of his life, and it suggests that he was drawing upon nostalgic memories and capitalizing on his established reputation.

Two biographies appeared during this period, one a reworking of an earlier sketch of Oliver Goldsmith and the other a sentimental account of a fifteen-year-old comsumptive poetess, Margaret Miller Davidson. Neither work added to Irving's literary reputation or development, each being little more than a perfunctory potboiler.

As early as the 1820s Irving had contemplated a biography of George Washington, the soldier and patriot after whom he had been named. The press of other literary activities and the need for quick income forced him to postpone serious, extended work on the project until he returned from Spain in 1846. Even then he delayed concerted efforts on it until he had completed the revisions of his earlier writings for the new collected edition being published by George P. Putnam.

In connection with this venture Irving seized the opportunity to dust off the partially completed manuscript of his biography of Mohammed, "a work without pretension," and to revise it in keeping with the current attitudes toward the prophet.(23) He hoped that, in company with the other volumes in his revised edition, it would sell well enough to repay him for his efforts of toning and coloring. After a lapse of twenty years Irving could not recapture the enthusiasm which had gripped him as he wrote _The Conquest of Granada_, and the result was a pedestrian account of Mohammed's life as gleaned from the popular sources of the day. He did not seriously treat the philosophy and theology of Islam, and many of the dreary passages are mere paraphrases of the sources from which he borrowed.

In his life of Oliver Goldsmith (1849), Irving reworked his earlier sketches of 1825 and 1840 by drawing on the recent biography of John Forster and adding romantic touches. The sentimental appeal to the feelings of his readers shows that Irving had not lost his touch for coloring his material for maximum popular effect. The 382-page volume added impressively to his collected edition, but despite Irving's personal debt to Goldsmith's style, it contributed little to his reputation as a romantic biographer.

With the help of his nephew Pierre Munro, Irving devoted the last decade of his life to the biography of George Washington. As he continued his research in the archives of Washington and the libraries of New York, Irving amassed details which swelled the work to five volumes. Although his tendency to dramatize and romanticize was checked somewhat by his close adherence to fact, he nonetheless attempted to bring in colorful details to enliven it. As he acknowledged in the preface to the first volume, he wanted to combine the historical facts with "familiar anecdote, excursive digressions, and a flexible narrative."(24) In so doing, he continued to practice the method of the romantic historian and closed his writing career with a monumental biography which remained unchallenged until the twentieth century.

For over forty years Irving wrote in a mode dictated by the nature of the material and by his own personal inclinations. Preconceived theories or literary principles had little influence on his writing. What mattered was an instinctive, almost impulsive approach to which he gave free rein. For him writing was not a chore or burdensome activity; it was a pleasurable task in which he engaged, one stimulated by his imagination and by the materials around him. As he grew older, romantic attitudes began more and more to dominate his writing, and for the last half of his life his literary material, whether essay, sketch, tale, history, or biography, was "colored and toned," often unconsciously, by the prevailing literary style in Europe and America in the first half of the nineteenth century.

NOTES

1. Ralph M. Aderman, Herbert L. Kleinfield, and Jenifer S. Banks, ed., _Washington Irving, Letters, Volume I, 1802- 1823_ (Boston: Twayne Publishers, 1978), p. 398.
2. _Letters, Volume I_, p. 406.
3. _Letters, Volume I_, p. 454.
4. _Letters, Volume I_, p. 496.
5. _Letters, Volume I_, p. 497.
6. _Letters, Volume I_, p. 488-489.
7. Washington Irving, _The Sketch Book of Geoffrey Crayon, Gent._, ed. Haskell Springer (Boston: Twayne Publishers, 1978), p. 56.
8. Henry A. Pochmann, introduction to Washington Irving, _Representative Selections_ (New York: American Book Company, 1934), p. lxvii.
9. Ralph M. Aderman, Herbert L. Kleinfield, and Jenifer S. Banks, ed., Washington Irving, Volume II, 1823-1838 (Boston: Twayne Publishers, 1979), p. 207.
10. _Letters, Volume II_, p. 251.
11. _Letters, Volume II_, p. 330-331.
12. _Letters, Volume II_, p. 347.
13. _Letters, Volume II_, p. 396.
14. _Letters, Volume II_, p. 400.
15. _Letters, Volume II_, pp. 414-15.
16. _Letters, Volume II_, p. 436.
17. _Letters, Volume II_, pp. 733-34.
18. _Letters, Volume II_, p. 798.
19. _Letters, Volume II_, p. 798.
20. Washington Irving, _Astoria, or Anecdotes of an Enterprise beyond the Rocky Mountains_, ed. Richard Dilworth Rust (Boston: Twayne Publishers, 1976), p. 4.
21. Washington Irving, _The Adventures of Captain Bonneville_, ed. Robert A. Ries and Alan Sandy (Boston: Twayne Publishers, 1977), p. 6.
22. _Letters, Volume II_, p. 902.
23. Ralph M. Aderman, Herbert L. Kleinfield, and Jenifer S. Banks, eds., _Washington Irving, Letters, Volume III, 1839-1845_ (Boston: Twayne Publishers, 1982), p. 124.
24. Washington Irving, _Life of George Washington_, ed. Allen Guttmann and James A. Sappenfield (Boston: Twayne Publishers, 1982), I: p. 2.

3.
Washington Irving: The Growth of a Romantic Writer

JOY S. KASSON

In The Sketch Book Washington Irving found his voice as a writer. To be sure, his previous achievements had been substantial; Scott and Coleridge had both admired The History of New York, and Irving figured among the leaders of the New York literary world on the basis of his editorship of Analectic Magazine as well as the witty Salmagundi. But with the serial publication of The Sketch Book, beginning in 1819, Irving acquired a transatlantic reputation of a different order, striking a note so perfectly pitched that he would ever afterward strive with varying degrees of success to recapture it.

The voice of The Sketch Book identified Irving as a writer making the transition to a prose style that could be called romantic. Although he drew on such antecedents as the sentimental essay and the literature of travel, Irving infused these forms with his special blend of melancholy introspection, passionate concern for the human heart, and understated humor. To unify his diverse materials, Irving hit upon the perfect device in the persona of Geoffrey Crayon, whose sentimental, detached stance toward his material has been described by William L. Hedges as the viewpoint of the "alienated observer."(1) Characterizing himself as a desultory wanderer who longs to "escape...from the commonplace realities of the present, and lose myself among the shadowy grandeurs of the past," Crayon suggests a romantic traveler such as Lord Byron's Childe Harold in the service of the picturesque rather than the sublime. Explicating the book's title, Crayon compared himself to a landscape painter whose sketchbook was "crowded with cottages, and landscapes, and obscure ruins; but he had neglected to paint St. Peter's or the Coliseum; the cascade of Terni or the Bay of Naples; and had not a single Glacier or Volcano in his whole collection."(2) Not only did Crayon contribute a romantic authorial voice but he presented himself as a collector of romantic materials. Parts of The Sketch Book could be considered a sort of prose Lyrical Ballads, drawing on folklore and logical history, presenting sketches of rural village folk, tales of broken hearts, and just a hint of the supernatural. Although the more sentimental and anecdotal sketches tend to be dismissed by modern critics as the least interesting sections of The Sketch Book, these pieces can provide essential clues to the literary transformation Irving had undergone.

One could argue convincingly that Irving's new style, formulated in London soon after a visit to Walter Scott at Abbotsford, reflected a skillful assimilation of the best in the contemporary British romantic movement. Certainly Scott, to whom Irving respectfully dedicated the miscellany when it appeared in book form, exerted a considerable influence on the younger writer, urging him to study folklore and encouraging him in his literary ambitions. Literary predecessors and mentors lie behind almost every chapter, sometimes humorously personified as in "The Art of Bookmaking," the sketch in which outraged authors jump down from their portraits in the British Museum reading room to chastise modern scribblers who appropriate their works too freely. Numerous essays in The Sketch Book pay tribute to particular writers of the past, from Shakespeare to Izaak Walton.

In addition to these literary influences, however, more personal factors should also be considered in contemplating the change in Irving's literary strategy represented by The Sketch Book. The miscellany appeared at the close of an extraordinarily turbulent period in Irving's life, a period that caused him to reassess his personal and professional identity. The terms in which this reassessment took place anticipate to a remarkable extent the shift in his literary stance. Irving's emergence as a romantic writer, I would argue, represents at least partly a strategy for expressing the themes and conflicts of a period of great stress and self-examination.

In 1815 Irving was a man of letters receiving financial support from a business operated by his older brothers; within three years, the business had gone bankrupt and he found himself facing a financially uncertain future. Furthermore, Irving involved himself directly in the last desperate attempts to save the business from financial ruin. In 1815 he had embarked on a European voyage for the purposes of rest and relaxation. However, visiting his brother Peter in Liverpool, he soon found it necessary to take over some of the duties of his temporarily invalid brother. For more than two years, Washington Irving worked in the unfamiliar realm of business, keeping the company's books and trying to maintain its credit. He felt that he was taking on another identity, writing miserably to friends at home that he was "so much engrossed by the cares of this world" that he had "lost . . . all relish and aptitude for my usual pursuits." "I have never passed so anxious a time in my life--my rest has been broken & my health & spirits almost prostrated."(3) As he watched the company sink slowly into bankruptcy, he received word from home of his mother's death. Depressed and discouraged, he despaired of succeeding in his literature or any other field. The financial struggle not only removed his source of income but also eroded his self-confidence and sense of purpose. "When I do take hold of my pen, I feel so poverty struck, such mental sterility, that I throw it down again," he wrote to a friend.(4)

Years later Irving described this crucial period in his life in a long autobiographical letter to a trusted friend, Amelia Foster, written in April or May 1823. Although it was a retrospective formulation -- Irving could never write about himself without in some sense recasting himself as his own persona -- his description of his mood and concerns during the bankruptcy crisis corresponds with his statements in letters written at the time. Irving's triumphant emergence as a romantic writer in The Sketch Book proceeded directly out of a period of profound crisis -- financial, professional, and personal. The terms in which he described this crisis indicate the kind of romantic writer he became.

Three themes dominate the letter to Amelia Foster: themes of loss, questioning of identity, and justification through suffering. Trying to explain his melancholy temperament and account for the fact that he never married, Irving focused on two episodes of loss: the death in 1809 of Matilda Hoffman, and the bankruptcy crisis of 1816-1818. The fact that he compared the experience of bankruptcy to this earlier tragedy emphasizes the importance this reversal of fortunes held for him.

The death of Matilda Hoffman has been recognized as one of the turning points of Irving's life. When he wrote about it in the letter to Amelia Foster, the pain evoked by the illness and death of the young girl he had hoped to marry still seemed fresh: "I cannot tell you what I suffered," he wrote.(5) Matilda's death left Irving in "a horrid state of mind": "I seemed to care for nothing -- the world was a blank to me." His sense of loss continued to haunt him; he "tried to form other attachments; but my heart would not hold on; it would continually recur to what it had lost."

Interestingly enough, through Irving's discussion of his attachment to Matilda Hoffman runs a second theme, muted but significant: that of the search for his own professional identity. Matilda's father, Judge Hoffman, served as Irving's mentor in his short-lived law career, and his courtship was predicated upon his settling down to a life he was by no means certain he wanted. "I considered myself bound in honour not to make further advances with the daughter until I should feel satisfied with my proficiency in the Law -- It was all in vain. I had an insuperable repugnance to the study -- my mind would not take hold of it." Matilda's death, much as he lamented it, released him from bondage to a career he had grown increasingly to dislike. He experienced this newfound freedom as a loss of purpose, indeed a loss of indentity: "I went into the country, but could not bear solitude yet could not enjoy society -- There was a dismal horror continually in my mind that made me fear to be alone -- I had often to get up in the night & seek the bedroom of my brother, as if having a human being by me would relieve me from the frightful gloom of my own thoughts." From this abyss, Irving was able to escape at last by reasserting his identity as a writer: he completed The History of New York; "it took with the public & gave me celebrity. . . . I was noticed and carressed & for a time elated by the popularity I gained."

Although his crisis of identity had been resolved, Irving insisted, his suffering never abated completely. Matilda's death "seemed to give a turn to my whole character . . . her image was continually before me, and I dreamt of her incessantly." In a sense, Matilda's death had contributed to his success as a writer, and he could imagine that his suffering was redeemed by its transmutation into literary expression. His very description of Matilda's illness, though sorrowful, was also highly literary: "I saw her fade rapidly away beautiful and more beautiful and more angelical to the very last." In the expression of loss, suffering found its justification.

When he turned in the letter to Amelia Foster to the second major crisis of his life, the bankruptcy of his family's business, Irving described it in very much the same terms of loss, the questioning of identity and redemptive suffering. The experience of financial ruin was a kind of deathbed scene with himself as protagonist this time: "Good heavens what I suffered for Months and months and months -- I lost all appetite[.] I scarcely slept -- I went to my bed every night as to a grave." What he called the "horrible ordeal of Bankruptcy" inflicted upon him a sense of dreadful loss. "To me it was a cruel blow -- I felt cast down -- abased -- I had lost my _cast_," he wrote. His entire cast of mind, his appearance, manner, characteristic style, in short, his very identity seemed to be taken away. "I had always been proud of Spirit, and in my own country had been, as it were, a being of the air -- I felt the force of the text, a wounded spirit who can bear? I shut myself up from society -- and would see no one." His response to the bankruptcy crisis, then, recapitulated for him in many ways his earlier grief and self-questioning after the death of Matilda Hoffman. This conjunction of the two experiences perhaps explains in part the vehemence of his response. In the letter to Amelia Foster, Irving specifically compared the two events: "This new calamity seemed more intolerable even than that which had before overcome me. That was solemn and sanctifying, it seemed while it prostrated my spirits, to purify & elevate my soul. But this was vile and sordid and humiliated me to the dust."

Just as he had found relief in literature after the death of Matilda Hoffman, he was able to overcome his despair and isolation after the bankruptcy by resolving to reconstruct himself as a man of letters. "The idea suddenly came to return to my pen[,] not so much for support, for bread & water had no terrors for me, but to reinstate myself in the world[']s thoughts -- to raise myself from the degradation into which I considered myself fallen. I took my resolution -- threw myself a stranger into London -- shut myself up and went to work. . . . In this way, I produced the Sketch Book." Hugging to himself his sense of loss, seeking solitude (as he relates it in this letter), and above all reaffirming his identity as a writer, Irving thus came to the writing of _The Sketch Book_ with a strong sense of self-vindication, "to reinstate myself in the world[']s thoughts," and a melancholy sensibility.

In the letter to Amelia Foster, then, Irving described his frame of mind during the period that produced The Sketch Book. The distinctive voice of The Sketch Book was in many ways Irving's own. Geoffrey Crayon, a homeless bachelor, wanderer, frequenter of churchyards and libraries, literary pilgrim, observer of the emotions of others, reflected at least partially the mood of the melancholy, exiled Irving. The three themes that characterized Irving's reaction to the bankruptcy crisis, as he described it in the letter to Amelia Foster, surge through The Sketch Book: a sense of loss, a search for identity, and an expectation of redemption through suffering.

The turmoil of Irving's bankruptcy lies close to the surface in two sketches that were published in the very first number of The Sketch Book. Both "The Wife" and "Roscoe" deal explicitly with financial ruin and its threat to individual identity. The protagonist of "The Wife" dreads confessing his financial failure to his wife, fearing she will spurn him: "How am I to strike her very soul to the earth, by telling her that her husband is a beggar! . . . How can she bear poverty? . . . How can she bear neglect?"(6) The wife responds admirably, supporting her husband in his misfortune, "abiding," as Irving put it, "with unshrinking firmness, the bitterest blasts of adversity."(7) "Roscoe" sketches the career of a banker-scholar, William Roscoe, who was forced because of business failure to part with his mansion and ultimately even with his collection of books. But Roscoe, as Irving pictured him, was saved by his inner strength and his sense of identity as a scholar. Quoting Roscoe's sonnet to his lost books, Irving compared him to a giant whose armory was being rummaged by pigmies. "A man like Roscoe is not to be overcome by the mutations of fortune. They do but drive him in upon the resources of his own mind, to the superior society of his own thoughts..."(8) In the wake of his own bankruptcy, Irving had applied almost exactly the same image to himself, writing in his journal in 1817: "I have repeatedly applied for some paltry public situation but have been as often disappointed -- It has pleased heaven that I should be driven on upon my own strength -- and resort to the citadel within me."(9) Only from this citadel of inner resources, this stronghold where he could picture himself a scholar-giant rather than a pigmy man of the world (and a failed one at that) could Irving draw the strength to emerge from this crisis justified in the world's eyes and his own, his identity as a writer affirmed.

Themes of loss and redemptive suffering dominate large sections of The Sketch Book, especially in the sentimental, anecdotal pieces. "The Widow and Her Son," "The Pride of the Village," and "The Broken Heart" focus on the conventional theme of romantic death, but they can also be read as Irving's own sense of loss and neglect. The protagonist of "The Widow and Her Son" is a young man, torn from his parents by the evil of impressment, who returns, broken in body and spirit, to live out his last days tended like an infant by his solicitous mother, whose death follows his by only a few weeks. Is it too farfetched to see in this poor sufferer a projection of Irving himself, whose desire to fly home for comfort after the ordeal of bankruptcy was thwarted by his own mother's death? "In the midst of my distress," he wrote Amelia Foster, "I heard of my poor Mother's death. She died without a pang[;] she talked to me to the last, and would not part with a letter she had received a few days before from me. I loved her with all the affection of a son, and one of my most poignant griefs wa[s] that her latter days should be embittered by my reverses."(10) In the sketch it is the son who becomes childlike and will not let his mother out of his sight, clasping her hand in sleep and, finally, in death. The sketch projects both guilt (the son's ruined hopes hasten his mother's death) and self-pity, as Irving extolls the redemptive power of mother-love: "Who that has pined on a weary bed in the neglect and loneliness of a foreign land, but has thought on the mother 'that looked on his childhood,'" wrote Irving in the sketch. "If adversity overtakes him, he will be the dearer to her by misfortune; and if disgrace settle upon his name, she will still love and cherish him; and if all the world beside cast him off, she will be all the world to him"(11) Longing for affection and comfort, afflicted by a sense of loss, disgrace, and a separation from loved ones, Irving created a character who reacted to the assault on his identity by reverting to the most primitive source of his sense of self and justified his suffering through a pitiful death.

Two other sentimental sketches, "The Broken Heart" and "The Pride of the Village," concern beautiful young girls who die of romantic disappointment. In the pathos of these tales, Irving was both paying tribute to Matilda Hoffman, whose memory seemed fresh again after his recent woes (and we know from his journal entries that this connection was explicit for him) and projecting his own sense of victimization in the wake of the bankruptcy. Both heroines have been wronged and betrayed, one by a cruel government that executed her patriot lover, the other by a heartless soldier who trifled with her affections. In both cases the victim seeks solitude, grows more unworldly, and wins esteem in the eyes of the world through her sacrificial suffering. So too Irving pictured himself in the letter to Amelia Foster as withdrawn from the world and seeking redemption through his writing. Although love is literally thrown at the feet of Irving's heroines -- by the repentent betrayer in one story, a stalwart comforter in the other -- both women ultimately justify their suffering by making the supreme sacrifice of life itself. Similarly, Irving declined an offer of financial rehabilitation that came, belatedly, when _The Sketch Book_ was well under way. Refusing a political appointment in Washington, he insisted in a letter home that he was on the verge of achieving a new literary identity and described himself in a way that recalls his proud, suffering heroines: "I am living here in a retired and solitary way, and partaking in little of the gaiety of life, but I am determined not to return home until I have sent some writings before me that shall, if they have merit, make me return to the smiles, rather than skulk back to the pity of my friends."(12)

The Sketch Book's romantic emphasis on broken hearts, redemptive suffering, loneliness, and loss thus represented Irving's translation into literary form of his own struggle for identity after a period of personal crisis. Of course, the theme of literary identity runs like a thread through The Sketch Book.(13) One sketch in particular sums up Irving's growing sense that only literary achievement could redeem him from his suffering and loss of position: "A Royal Poet," first published in the third number of The Sketch Book. In this piece Irving paid homage to a writer of the past, James I of Scotland, describing the castle in which he was imprisoned for many years and where he did much of his writing. James's very character -- prince, poet, and prisoner -- embodies Irving's sense of his own precarious position following the bankruptcy crisis. Cast down, abased, a wounded spirit, as he described himself to Amelia Foster, Irving could well have seen himself in the young prince imprisoned by enemies, cut off from friends and family and from the pleasures of life. Irving quoted James's poetry, the lovepoems he wrote to his jailer's daughter (who eventually became his wife), his celebrations of nature, and his longing for freedom. But it was above all the character of James's mind and his response to his terrible deprivation that fascinated Irving. "Some minds corrode, and grow inactive, under the loss of personal liberty," wrote Irving, who had complained of mental sterility under the pressure of business cares, "others, morbid and irritable; but it is the nature of the poet to become tender and imaginative in the loneliness of his confinement. He banquets upon the honey of his own thoughts, and, like the captive bird, pours forth his soul in melody."(14) Like Roscoe being driven in upon the resources of his own mind, like Irving in his notebook vowing to resort to "the citadel within," the poet-prince drew strength from his isolation and suffering. In fact, Irving insisted, the literary genius could transform and transcend its own isolation: "It is the divine attribute of the imagination, that it is irrepressible, unconfinable -- That when the real world is shut out, it can create a world for itself, and, with a necromantic power, can conjure up glorious shapes and forms, and brilliant visions, to make solitude populous, and irradiate the gloom of the dungeon."(15)

With this triumphant description of the writer's powers (similar to the more elaborate statement in his essay on Shakespeare, "Stratford-on-Avon"), Irving declared his passionate allegiance to the concept of the romantic artist, the artist as magician, as molder of the human heart. In "A Royal Poet" he made clear the connection he saw between the writer's imaginative success and his personal suffering. For the royal poet, and by implication for the fallen man of business, literary identity redeemed his loss and justified his apparent worldly failure.

The Sketch Book thus chronicled the growth of a romantic writer. Both the development of a voice, in the persona of Geoffrey Crayon, and the exploitation of sentimental anecdote and local history enabled Irving to strike a note that readers on both sides of the Atlantic found highly congenial. Irving's passionate interest in the truths of the human heart proceeded at least partly from his own experience of loss and introspection following the drastic shift in his fortunes culminating with the bankruptcy of his family's business. Although Irving would experience other periods of melancholy and professional uncertainty, he never again suffered the agonies of doubt and loss that accompanied the bankruptcy crisis. The literary identity that emerged in The Sketch Book, the alienated observer with the tender heart and the twinkle in his eye, provided him a way to write about the subjects that gripped his imagination: loss, failure, isolation, and suffering -- in a way that charmed his readers and brought him the recognition he so passionately desired.

NOTES

1. William L. Hedges, Washington Irving: An American Study, 1802-1832 (Baltimore: Johns Hopkins University Press, 1965), pp. 128-63.

2. [Washington Irving], The Sketch Book of Geoffrey Crayon, Gent. (New York: C.S. Van Winkle, 1819), 1:8-9.

3. Washington Irving to Henry Brevoort, March 15, 1816, in Ralph M. Aderman, Herbert L. Kleinfield, and Jenifer S. Banks, eds., Washington Irving, Letters, Volume I, 1802-1823 (Boston: Twayne Publishers, 1978), pp. 432, 435.

4. Washington Irving to Henry Brevoort, November 6, 1816, in Letters, Volume I, p. 457.

5. This and subsequent quotations from Washington Irving to Amelia Foster, April-May 1823, in Letters, Volume I, pp. 737-45.

6. The Sketch Book, 1:46.

7. The Sketch Book, 1:40.

8. The Sketch Book, 1:32.

9. Walter A. Reichart and Lillian Schlissel, eds., Washington Irving, Journals and Notebooks, Volume II, 1807-1822 (Boston: Twayne Publishers, 1981), p. 11.

10. Washington Irving to Amelia Foster, April-May 1823, p. 742.

11. The Sketch Book, 3:213.

12. Washington Irving to Ebenezer Irving, March 3, 1819, in Letters, Volume I, p. 541.

13. I have elsewhere argued that books, bookmaking, and literary identity constitute a major theme in The Sketch Book. See Joy S. Kasson, Artistic Voyagers: Europe and the American Imagination in the Works of Irving, Allston, Cole, Cooper, and Hawthorne (Westport, Conn.: Greenwood Press, 1982), pp. 18-39.

14. The Sketch Book, 3: 180.

15. The Sketch Book, 3: 180.

4.
Washington Irving as an American Romantic

JEFFREY RUBIN-DORSKY

Not the least of the reasons for The Sketch Book's enormous success was the gentlemanly manner in which its vignettes of English life were presented. In the words of Francis Jeffrey, founder and editor of the Edinburgh Review, it was prose "written throughout with the greatest care and accuracy, and worked up to great purity and beauty of diction, on the model of the most elegant and polished of our native writers."(1) This judgment has tended to prevail, even into our own time.(2) But Washington Irving's writing was not in the vein of firm public speech based on communal values; lacking the moral purpose of the Addisonian essay, it instead was founded upon and dedicated to sentiment and deep feeling. The language of The Sketch Book is porous, far less weighty and substantial -- less rooted to a cultural milieu -- than that of The Spectator. In The Sketch Book, Irving created a kind of autobiographical fiction that is closer in spirit to the literature of the romantic period than to its predecessors in the eighteenth century. The particular, and indeed private or personal, way in which language operates in The Sketch Book reinforces the romantic quality of the text. Moreover, from his fiction we can trace what might be called the psychology of American style.

In addition, because Irving did not simply record impressions derived from the external world but measured that world against his responses to it, his prose is like that of the "personal" or romantic writer, who is often characterized by the utmost importance he allots to "subjective emotional experiences."(3) The Sketch Book is nothing if not a positive assertion of Irving's own individuality and of his own unique reactions to the phenomenal world -- habits of mind that are associated with the personal writer. According to Herbert Read, "the aim of the [personal] writer became the expression of the uniqueness of his personality, his individuality, or idiosyncrasy" (Read's emphasis). In his sketchbook he promises to look out upon a recognizable world and introduce to his readers either familiar scenes and objects or out-of-the-way places and settings; once he accomplishes this, however, the only identity and meaning these have derives solely from their relationship to him. The ordinary world exists, like his smooth and correct style, on the surface of his writing, but acting upon it, and making its impression felt through many levels, is the texture of his personality. In "The Voyage," for example, Crayon's debarkation is described, paradoxically, not as a movement into a real environment but as a projection back onto the self: "I stepped upon the land of my forefathers -- but felt that I was a stranger in the land." Stylistically, it was not Irving's manifest intention to create a personal, self-conscious, "expressionistic" rhetoric,(4) but in the years between 1815 and 1819 he was caught between two worlds, two cultures, two modes of perception, one American, one European. Tied to neither, yet requiring for his art some bond to a fixed and solid cultural / emotional environment, he sent out his words, attempting to stabilize himself while he determined and secured his position. In so doing, he anticipated the advice Emerson tendered at the conclusion of *Nature*: he built, therefore, his own world.

It is the contention of Tony Tanner that this particular relationship between the writer and his words -- art as a continuous building of a private edifice -- is a peculiarly American one, and in an essay entitled "Notes for a Comparison between American and European Romanticism," he undertakes an explanation of how and why it developed.(5) Though he begins with a familiar theme -- the American artist confronted with a sense of space as "vast unpeopled solitudes such as no European Romantic could have imagined" (p. 86) -- his formulation of the stylistic peculiarities of the American writer is a useful gauge of the Americanness of Irving's style. Unlike the European romantic, who was forced to create his own solitude, the American romantic found that solitude was all but imposed upon him. He need take only a few steps and he was facing those "measureless oceans of space" where Whitman (in "A Noiseless Patient Spider") found his soul both "surrounded" and "detached." As Tanner points out, "this gravitation towards empty space is a constant in American literature, even if it appears only in glimpses" (p. 86). But the American artist, "once he found himself at sea in space," needed some way of maintaining himself, and one instinctive response was to expand into the surrounding area. Emerson, for example, records in "Circles" how "the heart refuses to be imprisoned; in its first and narrowest pulses it already tends outward with a vast force and to immense and innumerable expansions . . . there is no outside, no inclosing wall, no circumference to us." Again, Emerson, writing about the appeal of stimulants to "The Poet," says, "These are auxiliaries to the centrifugal tendency of a man, to his passage out into free space, and they help him to escape the custody of that body in which he is pent up, and of that jail-yard of individual relations in which he is enclosed." In the three seminal American romantics -- Emerson, Thoreau, and Whitman -- a similar "centrifugal tendency" is present; it is as Tanner labels it, a "dilation of self," which can readily become an "abandoning of self, into the surrounding vastness" (p. 87). Such activity, however, cannot establish a literary heritage, "since words are not carefully strung together by a man in the process of being metamorphosed into the circumambient air" (p. 87). Emerson apparently recognized as much when he wrote to Samuel Gray Ward in July 1841: "Can you not save me, dip me into ice water, find me some girding belt that I glide not away into a steam or a gas, and decease in infinite diffusion?"

The American romantic, of course, did not "decease in infinite diffusion"; instead he found his support, his "girding belt," by producing a distinct and highly personal body of literature. Tanner adopts the image of the spider (as it is delineated in "A Noiseless Patient Spider") as an emblem of this writer. Isolated as he is, he secretes, out of himself, filament upon filament of words "to explore, to relate to, and to fill 'the vacant vast surrounding'" (p. 84). In this paradigm, America is Whitman's "measureless oceans of space"; the web is the "private creation of the writer, constructed with a view of attaching himself somehow to reality" (p. 84). Thus, he changes an unacceptable condition into one with which he can live, and he invariably manages to accomplish this with a sense of independence, appropriating from his environment whatever is necessary for his creation. That is why, paradoxically, the webs are often celebrated for being composed of numerous "concrete particulars and empirically perceived facts" (think of the whaling sections in Moby Dick); the piling up of solid details creates a sense of stability, or in Tanner's words, an "anchoring attachment." Thus, the literature of the American romantic becomes, in a way, a "stay against diffusion" (p. 87).

More precisely, then, the web is the writer's style; "the concrete details are the nourishing particles which the web ensnares and transforms" (p. 87). And the webs spun by the writers of the American Renaissance were in many ways far more stylistically distinctive than those of their European counterparts. One of the great differentiating factors between American and British romantics, between, say, Whitman and Wordsworth, is that, as Tanner argues, for the former there is a lack of psychological intimacy with the environment -- Wordsworth's sense of the "harmonious reciprocities between mind and landscape" is absent from Whitman's more forced and sometimes tortured strivings. "My mind lay open," says Wordsworth in The Prelude, "to Nature's finer influxes . . . to that more exact / And intimate communion which our hearts / Maintain with the minuter properties / Of objects which already are beloved" (II. 298-302). Whitman and the American romantics, on the other hand, pursue objects and words to fill a void that directly results from their experience of the world, and they engage in this pursuit with a zest and hardiness and a virtual frenzy that surpasses the more subdued utterances of the European romantics. Contrast Whitman's view, in "Song of Myself" (sec. 25), of how the writer devours his environment -- "My voice goes after what my eyes cannot reach, / With the twirl of my tongue I encompass worlds and volumes of worlds" -- with the calm and ease which, for Wordsworth, "in that silence while he hung / Listening, a gentle shock of mild surprise / . . . carried far into his heart the voice / Of mountain torrents; or the visible scene / Would enter unawares into his mind / With all its solemn imagery" (The Prelude, V: 406-11). The remarkable difference in tone flows from their dichotomous vantage points.

The American romantics maintained an especially visual relationship with nature. Beginning with Emerson's famous utterance in Nature about becoming a "transparent eyeball," the image of "man seeing" appears frequently in subsequent American writing. It is not that English romantics did not have visual rapport with nature; rather, more often than in America, the response of the English writer was also auditory, as in Wordsworth's "The Solitary Reaper," where the poet is nurtured by the woman's song: "The music in my heart I bore, / Long after it was heard no more." While it would be absurd to claim that there are no auditory responses in the works of the American romantics, overall these writers do not appear to value them, nor are they sustained by them, to the same degree as their English counterparts. But more important, as Tanner points out, "a purely visual relationship to the outside world" is indicative of a condition of "deprivation [and] a loss of intimacy" (p. 88). A predominantly visual relationship with nature implies, in fact, separation, "a state of alienation or detachment from it," since the very process of seeing emphasizes the space between the eye and the object. The American romantics, who relied so heavily on sight, did not make an emotional connection to the landscape. They were distant watchers, and when they sang their songs they brought into being their own worlds.

Of central importance in American romanticism, then, is the formulation of these "verbal web[s]" which offer protection while promoting self-expansion. It is the American poet's own voice, often in the form of a ritualistic chant, that recreates nature; rarely in his works do we find a concentration on specific and local sights and sounds. It is not nature, but "the metamorphosis of nature" which interests Emerson, and in a journal entry during the summer of 1841 he writes that this metamorphosis "shows itself in nothing more than this, that there is no word in our language that cannot become typical to us of Nature by giving it emphasis." Between Emerson and the world stands the word, as the continuation of the entry makes clear: "The world is a Dancer; it is a Rosary; it is a Torrent; it is a Boat; a Mist; a Spider's Snare; it is what you will; and the metaphor will hold, and it will give the imagination keen pleasure. Swifter than light the world converts itself to the thing you name, and all things find their right place under this new and capricious classification" (my emphasis). (It might be argued that Thoreau at Walden Pond is the glaring exception here, but he, too, can be strangely detached from his surroundings.) It is clear that, given an overwhelming, unreceptive, unyielding environment, the American romantic writer was forced to develop strategies for survival other than an attempted merger with that environment.

Wallace Stevens has written (in "The Irrational Element in Poetry") that "resistance to the pressure of ominous and destructive circumstances consists of its conversion, so far as possible, into a different, an explicable, an amenable circumstance";(6) this appears to have been the very program of the American romantic writer, who "converted" or attempted to transform his given surroundings and circumstances into something "amenable," not necessarily placid or "benevolent" (think of Poe, Hawthorne, and Melville) but submissive--in Tanner's words, "ductile to the weavings of [his] art" (p. 92). All romantic writers turned imagination onto the world to mediate and modify it, but the European romantic was able to draw upon resources such as "history, legend, memory," friends and lovers, "visions of future societies" (p. 103), and the landscape itself to combat isolation and despair. The American romantic depends more heavily on the intricacies of his own creations. The poetic flights and visions of the European romantics were not alien to their natural and human surroundings and interpenetrated with them. It is this feeling of "interpenetration" that is absent in the literature of the American romantics, and that is why the image of the spider "drawing the filament out of himself alone, weaving his private web" (p. 103), is such an apt one for the situation, and the responses to it, of the American writer.

It is clear that Irving was not technically an American romantic writer in the sense of the term as it has been applied here: he was neither preoccupied with nature nor alive to his surroundings in quite the way as those authors who make up our first great wave of national genius. Yet it requires no leap of faith to see that there are many affinities between Irving and the American romantics, especially in terms of the relationship between writer, word, and world, and the development of a personal, idiosyncratic style. During the years of his European sojourn, in which the three sketchbooks were produced, Irving did not have to confront vast oceans of American space; on the contrary, as much as the American romantic writer repudiated and fled the Past -- for example, Emerson describing himself in "Circles" as "an endless seeker with no Past at my back" -- that is the extent to which Irving embraced it. But it was as an idea only, for in actuality it became the equivalent of the American romantic's experience of space: vast, impenetrable, everywhere present but nowhere assimilable. For Irving, in The Sketch Book ("The Author's Account of Himself"), to "lose [him]self among the shadowy grandeurs of the past" was a mental formulation comparable to Emerson's "centrifugal tendency" and his "passage out into free space"; to Thoreau's celebration, in the chapter "Spring" of Walden, of the "ethereal flight" of a hawk which soared alone "in the fields of air" -- "It appeared to have no companion in the universe . . . and to need none but the morning and the ether with which it played"; and to Whitman's diffusion, in Canto 52 of "Song of Myself," back into the elements: "I depart as air, I shake my white locks at the runaway sun / I effuse my flesh in eddies, and drift it in lacy ags."

Irving in the midst of Westminster Abbey is as solitary and isolated a figure as Emerson in Nature or Thoreau at Walden Pond; the tombs, monuments, and memorials to the dead (and hence to the past) are all foreign objects which yield no mysteries except those which Irving's imagination imputes to them. Not only does he fail to assimilate them, but he actually turns away in fright, reconfirming his isolation. In the same way that Emerson (according to Tanner) interposed his version of "a ductile, transparent, fluid, apparitional nature between himself and the hard, opaque, refractory (and dazzling) otherness of the real American landscape" (p. 91), in order to bring nature into alignment with his purposes, Irving postulated a richly endowed and infinitely knowable antiquity, filled with "ruins [which] told the history of times gone by," "mouldering stone[s]" which were chronicles of "renowned achievement" -- in short, the "accumulated treasures of age" -- separating him from a past that had long since receded into history, legend and myth, custom, manner and tradition, essentially out of reach for one who was not native to the terrain, beyond the grasp of one who was not "to the manner born." Irving, unlike contemporary European Romantics, but very much akin to his American successors, could not rely on recollection to connect him to the nurturing past he sought (though he did at least try, like the former group, to cultivate an awareness and a sense of society's historical past). Having reached maturity in a country whose very distinction was to have repudiated the past, he had no accumulated consciousness of an extended cultural tradition, no deeply internalized sense of communal history. What Irving the traveler and pilgrim really wanted, therefore, was history as it existed (and as he could imagine it to exist) in the present moment, surrounding him with its wondrous and ever-arresting images, liberating him from the tyranny of his own oppressive insecurities.

When in "The Author's Account of Himself" Irving juxtaposes the "commonplace realities of the present" and "the shadowy grandeurs of the past," the implied linking comes at the conclusion of an intricate sentence which, if examined in its entirety, is quite revealing of motive and method:

> I longed to wander over the scenes of renowned achievement -- to tread, as it were, in the footsteps antiquity -- to loiter about the ruined castle -- to meditate on the falling tower -- to escape, in short from the common-place realities of the present, and lose myself among the shadowy grandeurs of the past [my emphasis] (*The Sketch Book*, 744).

This rhythmic repetition of infinitives demonstrates an implicit desire to expand the physical journey into a metaphysical encounter. He begins with the verb "wander" and then varies that term so as to achieve an alteration in his projected state of being: the initial action develops into one with both emotional and intellectual significance. The progression is from a physical action ("to wander") which gradually diminishes ("to tread," "to loiter") and gives rise to mental reflections ("to meditate") that reach a new spiritual level ("to escape," to "lose"). The action he describes commences in the outside world, moves into the world of the self, and then out of the self by way of an extension to a more amorphous realm. Therefore, to travel from "the commonplace realities of the present" into "the shadowy grandeurs of the past" is to achieve an imaginative construct that will replace the previously known reality: as he verbally transforms his experience, which his decreased physical activity makes possible ("loiter" becomes "meditate"), Crayon transcends the actual by attaining the imaginary.

American romantics have traditionally sought to move out of time altogether and into some sort of space. Time means history, and history means "traces of men" and society, which is precisely what interested and stimulated Irving. Yet in the midst of a dense London he often winds up, like his countrymen in the limitless space of America, strangely alone. As with Rip Van Winkle off in the Catskill Mountains, we are never sure whether people and places that populate Irving's pages have any real existence outside of their connection to him -- they sometimes seem only projections of his imagination. Thoreau emphasized that "we are as much as we see," and in Nature Emerson said of the soul: "It is a watcher more than a doer, and it is a doer, only that it may the better watch." In "Salut au Monde!" Whitman asks himself, "What do you see Walt Whitman?" and answers himself obsessively by responding "I see" eighty-three times. (Interestingly enough, when he asks himself in the same poem "What do you hear Walt Whitman?" he repeats "I hear" only eighteen times.) And in Canto 25 of "Song of Myself" he chanted, "Speech is the twin of my vision, it is unequal to measure itself, / It provokes me forever, it says sarcastically, / Walt you contain enough, why don't you let it out then?" (Whitman's emphasis). In The Sketch Book, Geoffrey Crayon begins the tradition of these great American watchers and creators, fusing his own visual perception and imaginative self-projection into a new, vital creative unit.

In his notebooks and essays, in several different forms, Emerson often makes the world vanish. "If there be one lesson more than another which should pierce his ear," he writes of "The American Scholar," "it is, The world is nothing, the man is all; in yourself is the law of all nature." His Idealism extends even beyond the denial (in Nature) of "the absolute existence of nature"; it is as if nature were saying to him, "Do with me what you will." In his journal for September 1, 1841, he makes the following entry: "Every gardener can change his flowers and leaves into fruit and so is the genius that today can upheave and balance and toss every object in Nature for his metaphor, capable in his next manifestation of playing such a game with his hands instead of his brain." Shakespeare, he claims in Nature, "possesses the power of subordinating nature for the purposes of expression"; he "tosses the creation like a bauble from hand to hand." The overwhelming solidity of the midnineteenth-century

American landscape has disappeared and in its place Emerson has substituted an image of nature as a series of "playthings"; this, Tanner would argue, is Emerson's "web," the creation by which he sustains himself (p. 91). Irving's web is style itself: that poetic, mellifluous, highly metaphoric and alliterative style (which is, after all, an embellished imitation of an approved British style) stands between himself and his experience, tentatively connecting him to a world and to a culture from which, by the very nature of that experience, he was alienated. The "nourishing particles" which the web "ensnares and transforms" are the concrete details of English life and landscape, past and present; through ironical humor and whimsical good-naturedness, Irving makes them "amenable" -- unthreatening to his sense of order and readily available for his artistic purposes. Thus, Irving, too, constructs a private network; the acts of building, of rearranging and reshaping, and, ultimately, reconstituting the visible scene are psychologically more important than the finished artifact. The specific contents of Irving's book may be mostly public and recognizable (or so it appears on the surface), but the deeper significance is private and cryptic. The meaningful link to early nineteenth-century England is often more apparent than real. That is why *The Sketch Book* has sometimes been thought of as presenting a dreamlike world of ethereal filaments (rather than solid structures)--sweet and harmonious, but amorphous, one that seems to dissolve if examined too closely. At the same time that Irving was exploring his surroundings, and "fill[ing] in the spaces between [him]self and the environment" (p. 87), he was also reconstructing, and therefore remaking and reordering the world in the web of his individual style.

If we examine that style in some detail, and if we view style broadly as all of the linguistic and narrative decisions a writer makes -- that is, not only as diction, syntax, and image patterns but also as tone, narrative technique, structure, and even choice of genre -- then we will see that, taken together, Irving's stylistic features add up to a psychology of style. They are all dictated by his needs: with his substance, Irving talks about English rural and urban landscapes, but with his style he sings an elaborate song of himself. That song, *The Sketch Book* itself, attempts to satisfy a deep longing for solace. In his sketch of "Rural Life in England," for example, Irving's diction generates a motif of order through patterned word choice. Through the guise of his persona, Geoffrey Crayon, he discloses the effect English park scenery creates upon him:

> Vast lawns that extend like sheets of vivid green, with here and there clumps of gigantic trees, heaping up rich piles of foliage: the solemn pomp of groves and woodland glades, with the deer trooping in silent herds across them; the hare, bounding away to the covert; or the pheasant, suddenly bursting upon the wing: the brook, taught to wind in natural meanderings, or

> expand into a glassy lake: the sequestered pool, reflecting the quivering trees, with the yellow leaf *sleeping* on its bosom, and the trout roaming fearlessly about its limpid waters; while some rustic temple or sylvan statue, grown green and dank with age, gives an air of *classic sanctity* to the *seclusion* [my emphasis] (*The Sketch Book*, 797).

The mood is one of serenity -- "classic sanctity"; the total picture projects a calm, refined, soothing state of nature. Unlike the natural grandeur of the American landscape, the subdued terrain of the English rural countryside has been created deliberately: the once free-flowing brook is "taught" to wind in what seems like, but are not, "natural meanderings" or is made to "expand into a glassy lake," which then reflects the sleepy quiet of the entire surroundings. This scene is particularly appealing to Crayon because he would like to be able to exert this kind of control over his environment. His tour in England thus reveals itself, through his stylistic choices, as both an "unconscious quest for order and stability"(7) and a release of imaginative energy.

Irving's pervasive use of womb imagery in *The Sketch Book* -- for nature, for architecture, even for the past -- is another distinctive feature of style related to the need for protection against a world of flux. The sketches of London experiences -- "The Boar's Head Tavern, Eastcheap," "A Sunday in London," "London Antiques," and "Little Britain"--follow a general pattern of penetration into a hidden corner of the city, as Crayon hopes to discover some facet of the English mythos and then lose himself in reverie as he meditates upon its significance. The search for a nurturing source -- a home for the spirit -- leads Crayon to explore London in "quest of relics of old times," as he says in "London Antiques." Here he "*Plunged*" into a "bye-lane," passes through "several obscure nooks and angles," and "emerges into a quaint and quiet court with a grassplot in the centre, overhung by elms, and kept perpetually fresh and green by a fountain with its sparkling jet of water." With this "oasis" situated in the "very centre of sordid traffic," again, diction becomes image pattern; the accumulation of word choices takes on metaphorical import as Crayon seeks a home "locked up in the heart of the city" (*The Sketch Book*, 963-4).

William L. Hedges has suggested that with his penchant for exploring dark, womblike passageways and hidden recesses, Crayon seems like a driven figure, trying to fight his way back into some protective cavern of the past. The search, however, becomes paradoxical when the representative of a living tradition, such as Westminster Abbey, is also a monument to the dead. Then, as might be expected of a man from the New World, "his subdued fear of old things" -- that persistent sense of being haunted -- "reflects the great American suspicion that the past is basically irrelevant to the present." Geoffrey Crayon may dream of "woman's devotion, the wife as guardian angel," or "home and marriage as [a] refuge from the vicissitudes of the world," but everywhere in The Sketch Book concrete images of the "vestiges of the past" surface, "remind [him] of the process of decay."(8) Eventually, as Irving eloquently stated in "Westminster Abbey," the "dilapidations of time" conquer all that is mortal and of this earth. Against the power of such reflection and realization, even the idea of "home" must give way.

The anxiety inherent in a sketch like "Westminster Abbey" -- the feeling of being unsettled -- leads Irving to other stylistic choices, most notable the creation of illusions and the reliance upon sentiment and romance, both of which smooth away all the nonductile, nonpliant qualities of the English landscape. Once Irving realized that the meaning he sought in English institutions and culture was not to be emotionally his, he fabricated an illusion of stability through the very design and construction of The Sketch Book. An illusion, of course, is a distortion of reality, a deception of sorts, wherein misleading appearance is perceived as the real or true nature of something. Crayon's commitment to an ideal, which he defined in "The Author's Account of Himself" as that of a romantic wanderer on a quest, drives him to weave a fabric of illusion around and through all of his experience. The appearance of a reposeful life, the glamorous antique past, the poeticized, romanticized landscape -- all appear to be contrivances of Geoffrey Crayon, palliatives for the truth that the sketches inevitably reveal.

Another equally excessive and recognizable strain in The Sketch Book is its sentimentalism. Aware of the danger of gratifying a feeble taste for pathos, Irving, as Hedges has pointed out, nonetheless "sentimentalized parts of The Sketch Book beyond anything that modern taste can bear."(9) In one instance, Crayon discourses on broken hearts and young women "dying of disappointed love." In another -- his sketch of "The Widow and Her Son" -- he anguishes over a bereaved mother. The cumulative effect of this outpouring of sentimentality is a blotting of the hard, crisp lines of differentiation between eager expectation and actual discovery -- an obscuring of the territory between the viewer and the world, the territory of obdurate fact. Enveloping Crayon's experience is a cloud of familiar, comfortable sentiment, affording him (and his readers) easy access to a safe emotional escape.

Even Irving's narrative technique has implications for the psychology of his style. One of the important advantages of sketching for Irving is that it enabled him to grapple with his personal preoccupations by imaginatively projecting himself, through Crayon, back into a variety of situations that he had already experienced in the world. What Crayon "sees" on his journeys is an overlay of the actual scene he encounters with his expectations and desires, the associations he brings with him from his vast literary heritage, and his romantic projections -- all part of his attempt to envision a world that functions according to his quixotic illusions. Irving indulges in the fiction but uses the mode of comic deflation (stylistically, another representation of the war between the real and the imagined) to pull himself away from it. Thus, he can laugh at Crayon's foibles as if they were not his own; in effect, he can tell his own story while appearing not to be talking about himself at all.

Finally, the very ordering of the sketches, essays, and stories within The Sketch Book not only composes its structure but is the summation of all other stylistic properties, and in this larger choice we see that, for Irving, style was directly correlated to personal needs. Each of the original seven numbers of The Sketch Book contained at least three types of sketches: a reverie, a comic piece, and a sentimental offering. As an outreach toward comfort and succor, Crayon dreams of inhabiting John Bull's "old castellated manor-house" and, on another level, of interpolating his random wandering and observation into the continuous flow of a valued literary inheritance; however, when the illusion of stability and permanence is destroyed by mutability ("the quest for a meaningful past constantly verges on graveyard rumination"(10), he turns to mockery and deflation, then to sentimentality, with its substitution of banal and "sympathetic" feeling for deep, painful emotion. Particular kinds of stories, then, compensate for the loss of the past, while the choice and ordering of genre afford protection and escape from threatened isolation.

Those American writers whom we generally associate with the New England Renaissance were isolated figures; neither political nor social commitment united them firmly to a community, nor were they secured in any stable, intimate way to the overpowering natural environment. Strangely enough, this state was often cherished and preferred: "To sport in fields of air," says Tanner, "could be the ultimate ecstacy" (p. 89). Yet this abandoned floating also posed the possibility of danger, a fear of "vanishing or diffusing altogether." The solution was to create something which would provide a home for the spirit at the same time that it allowed for an angle of vision onto the world. But even when they turned a critical eye on their environment and appropriated the necessary details "to weave into their webs of art" (p. 89), they tended to remain apart from it. This experience of failed connections recalls Irving's inability to engage the mythic England which seemed to be hovering everywhere. Irving, like the New Englanders, understood that a state of detachment could bring great joy and freedom; he was, let us not forget, a compulsive traveler. Yet he knew what it meant to be disconnected, for his personal tragedies had left him on the edge of a breakdown. He had experienced the emotional truth of the paradox that the other side of freedom is often intense loneliness and isolation. Keen perception has its pleasure, as does the movement away from concrete structures, but fear may set in when the people and places become unreal, "apparent, not substantial," as Emerson said in Nature, "wholly detached from all relation to the observer."(11) The romantic longing for fusion with the "Not Me," for the melding of mind and nature, is rarely achieved in American literature. Somewhere below the plane of visual ecstacy on which the American romantics prefer to exist lies the ever-present, consuming spatial void, which is fed by the writer's own words. While we do not tend to think of him in this way, Irving also spun out his web of words, filling in the gaps as he sought to ensnare a tradition and secure a culture.

Whatever else style does, it is certain that it manifests the writer's relationship to his time, place, and milieu and that it reveals, in subtle, seemingly nontangible ways, the personal, psychological contexts of his words. The very traditional nature of Irving's prose, its familiar grammatical and linguistic structures, its formalistic correctness, its smooth and fluid movement -- all apparently outward, impersonal qualities of style -- have covert meanings and ramifications which supersede any simplistic claims of their being linked to Irving's cultural aspirations. Beyond that, Irving's prose sustained him in a way that would become characteristic of the American romantic writers and the inheritors of their renaissance. Despite the fact that he did not wholly and consciously accept the making of fictions as the only true support in a universe of flux and instability, his style earned for him another, rather different world in which he could feel at home, however momentarily. After all, the very impetus to _imitate_ a British style was a symptom of an emotional, and ultimately linguistic, homelessness. Though he was claimed by the English as one of their own, and though he wrote as well as any Englishman, his style was, underneath its surface precision and attention to detail (and in a deeper, more profound sense), that of an American. Finally, like his American successors -- like Whitman with his catalogs and notations, like Emerson with his extended metaphors and analogies -- Irving's stylistic brilliance connected him not to society, and not to nature, but to his own web of words. In his psychological relationship to words, in the way in which word becomes world, he marks the beginning of an American tradition in prose.

NOTES

1. Review of _The Sketch Book_, _Edinburgh Review_ 34 (1820): 160. According to Jeffrey, Irving's style was "copied" from Addison and Goldsmith "in the humorous and discursive parts" and from Mackenzie "in the more soft and pathetic" (pp. 161, 162). The _Quarterly Review_ (25 [1821]: 67) declared that his work was "exclusively English." "He seems to have studied our language -- where alone it can be studied in all its strength and perfection -- in the writings of our old sterling authors; and in working these precious mines of literature, he has refined for himself the ore which there so richly abounds." In the _Edinburgh Monthly Review_ (4 [1820]: 304) he was compared, to the authors of _The Tatler_ and _The Spectator_, and the _Monthly Review_ (2d ser., 93 [1820]: 198-207) recognized him as an aspiring young imitator of British models. "He is not national, but English," was how the _Retrospective Review_ (9 [1824]:316) put it, and the _Monthly Maga-_

zine (50 [1820] :362) was lavish in its praise: "The Sketch Book," it said, "bids fair to rank high among the best classical writings of our own country." It then went on to say that Irving wrote in the "manner of Sterne" (p. 363).

2. Two examples of modern criticism must suffice: Lewis Leary acknowledges that Irving's style was recognized and admired as an "amalgam of the best English styles, those of Scott, Addison, and Sterne," and that his mood was "sentimentally and fashionable nostalgic, like that of Goldsmith" ("The Two Voices of Washington Irving," in From Irving to Steinbeck: Studies in American Literature in Honor of Harry R. Warfel, eds. Motley Deakin and Peter Lisca [Gainesville: University of Florida Press, 1972], p. 14); William L. Hedges comments that in "Westminster Abbey" Irving "suggests Goldsmith and Addison," and on a trip to the country he "slightly resembles the Spectator visiting Sir Roger de Coverly." "Indeed," continues Hedges, "his very sound has affinities with the language of Addison and Goldsmith. This is in part what it meant for Irving to be hailed as the first literate American -- that he had mastered a familiar English prose style." (See "Washington Irving: The Sketch Book of Geoffrey Crayon, Gent.," in Landmarks of American Writing, ed. Hennig Cohen [New York: Basic Books, 1969], pp. 58-59.) My text for The Sketch Book will be: Washington Irving, History, Tales, and Sketches, ed., James W. Tuttleton (New York: The Library of America, 1983. This volume prints texts from The Complete Works of Washington Irving, eds. Richard Dilworth Rust, Haskell Springer et al, published by Twayne Publishers.

3. For a discussion of the traits of the personal writer, see the chapter entitled "Expressionism," in Herbert Read's English Prose Style, rev. ed. (1952; reprint, Boston: Beacon Press, 1970), pp. 158-66.

4. "Two things," says Read, "are essential to an expressionistic rhetoric: *sensibility* enough to be aware of one's individual reactions, and *emotion* enough to enlarge this sensibility, to magnify and exploit it in the interests of self-projection, self-'creation'" (English Prose Style, p. 159; Read's emphasis).

5. Tanner's essay, which appeared in the Journal of American Studies (2 [1968]:83-103), is a preliminary hypothesis about the basic differences between the relationships of European and American romantics to their immediate environments, to nature, and to art. I find Tanner's elaborate emblem of the American writer in the midnineteenth century as a spider spinning his web in midair most helpful in my delineation of the predominant stylistic peculiarity which Irving shares with the American romantic writer. Much as Tanner considers his work here a tentative exploration of a vast topic, I view this essay as the introduction to a more extensive and exhaustive examination which the question demands and which my current project on Irving entitled "Representative American: Washington Irving as Psychological Pilgrim" undertakes. (Quotations from Tanner's essay are acknowledged in

parenthesis in the text; I have borrowed several of Tanner's examples of British and American Romantic writing and have added several of my own.)

6. _Opus Posthumous_ (New York: Knopf, 1957), p. 225.

7. Washington Irving: _The Sketch of Geoffrey Crayon, Gent._", in _Landmarks_, p. 61.

8. Washington Irving: _The Sketch of Geoffrey Crayon, Gent._", in _Landmarks_, pp. 63-64.

9. Washington Irving: _The Sketch of Geoffrey Crayon, Gent._", in _Landmarks_, p. 63.

10. Washington Irving: _The Sketch of Geoffrey Crayon, Gent._", in _Landmarks_, p. 62.

11. The American obsession with space is reflected in the current fascination with our space program, with the space shuttle, and, most emphatically, with walking in space. Floating weightless in the heavens, with no solid ground beneath the astronaut's feet, and tethered tenuously to a mother ship, the "space man" is another emblem for the American writer. Literally sporting in air (or more precisely, airlessness) is freedom personified, but at a tremendous risk: should the precarious connection be severed, the astronaut might very well vanish into the void.

Part II

Imagination and the Fantastic

5.

Washington Irving and the Denial of the Fantastic

PETER CHRISTENSEN

Revising The Alhambra for its re-publication in his collected works in 1850, Washington Irving reorganized his old material and added several sketches and stories, including two new "legends." The second of these legends, "The Enchanted Soldier," includes some folk traditions about the cave of St. Cyprian which was the meeting place of a sacristan and his students in the magic arts. It was decided by lot that one student should pay for the education of the entire group. If he did not pay, he had to remain inside the cave until funds were forthcoming.

In the first version of this story, the sacristan is really the devil, and the student cheats him through the use of necromancy, leaving his shadow, but not his body, in the cave. Of the second version, Irving writes:

> On one occasion the lot fell on Henry de Villena, son of the marquis of the same name. He, having perceived that there had been trick and shuffling in the casting of the lot, and suspecting the sacristan to be cognizant thereof, refused to pay. He was forthwith left in limbo. It so happened that in a dark corner of the sacristy was a huge jar or earthen reservoir for water, which was cracked and empty, In this the youth contrived to conceal himself. The sacristan returned at night with a servant, bringing lights and a supper. Unlocking the door, they found no one in the vault and a book of magic lying open on the table. They retreated in dismay, leaving the door open, by which Villena made his escape. The story went about that through magic he had made himself invisible.
>
> The reader now has both versions of the story, and may make his choice. I will only observe that the sages of the Alhambra incline to the diabolical one.(1)

It may at first glance seem that the two versions of the story exemplify one characteristic of nineteenth-century fantastic fiction discussed by Tzvetan Todorov in his book The Fantastic: A Structural Approach to a Literary Genre. This characteristic, alternate explanations of events which create a hesitation in the reader, appears in Todorov's definition of "the fantastic" as a genre. According to Todorov:

> The fantastic requires the fulfillment of three conditions. First, the text must oblige the reader to consider the world of living persons and to hesitate between a natural and supernatural explanation of the events described. Second, this hesitation may also be experienced as a character; thus the reader's role is so to speak entrusted to a character, and at the same time the hesitation is represented, it becomes one of the themes of the work - in the case of naive reading, the actual reader identifies himself with the character. Third, the reader must adopt a certain attitude with regard to the text; he will reject allegorical as well as "poetic" interpretations. These three requirements do not have equal value. The first and the third actually constitute the genre. The second may not be fulfilled. Nonetheless, most examples satisfy all three conditions.(2)

What is peculiar about Irving's legend of the cave of St. Cyprian is the way in which it fails to fulfill Todorov's third category. Although we, as readers, are aware that Irving does not have a properly fantastic attitude toward his story, it is not because of poetical or allegorical concerns, but rather because of his attitude toward history. Both versions of the story are equally valid as part of the tradition of the Alhambra, the enchanted castle in which Irving is temporarily residing. Although it may appear that we are supposed to choose between the two accounts, this is only a pretense. Irving does not want to discard any legend of the palace-fortress. He is not weighing alternative versions of the events, but preserving a precarious cultural heritage.

This specific case of a denial of the fantastic by Irving comes at the end of a brief career as a writer of collections of sketches and stories. This side of Irving's work as an author includes four works: The Sketch Book (1819-20), Bracebridge Hall (1822), Tales of a Traveller (1824), and, finally, The Alhambra (first version, 1832). The three earlier works are connected by the figure of Geoffrey Crayon, the nominal author. This persona is not used in The Alhambra, thus setting this later collection somewhat apart from the others.

The obvious superiority of The Sketch Book over Bracebridge Hall, the lack of inspiration in most of Tales of a Traveller, and the travelogue nature of The Alhambra often make us forget to examine these books as a group rather than as a repository of a few interesting set pieces. However, when we remember that Irving's considerably later volume of stories and sketches, Wolfert's Roost

(1855), was rather casually assembled long after its individual pieces had appeared in periodicals, we are justified in thinking of the four works as a unit marking one major stage in Irving's thought.

Irving's denial of the fantastic begins with *The Sketch Book*, and, although his strategy changes, the goal remains the same in all four works. John Clendenning has noted the debunking of the Gothic tradition in the three famous inserted stories of *The Sketch Book*: "Rip Van Winkle," "The Spectre Bridegroom," and "The Legend of Sleepy Hollow."(3) In addition, we must remember that these stories are found in a work which has for one of its main themes imaginative literature itself. In this respect, *The Sketch Book* differs in a major way from its three successors.

Among the "chapters" which concern literature are the following: "Roscoe," "English Writers on American," "The Art of Bookmaking," "A Royal Poet," "The Boar's Head Tavern, Eastcheap," "The Mutability of Literature," "Westminster Abbey," and "Stratford-on-Avon." Four of these sketches present Crayon's reminiscences on famous literary sites: Windsor Castle (for James I of Scotland, the "royal poet"); Poet's Corner; and the two Shakespearean locales, one made famous by his plays and one made famous by his origins. Not only is imaginative literature necessary to society, it is important, on a personal level, to Crayon himself. In his first sketch, "The Voyage," we best see this concern.

> There was a delicious sensation of mingled security and awe with which I looked down, from my giddy height, on the monsters of the deep at their uncouth gambols. Shoals of porpoises tumbling about the bow of the ship; the grampus slowly heaving his huge form above the surface; or the ravenous shark, darting like a spectre through the blue waters. My imagination would conjure up all that I had heard or read of the watery world beneath me; of the finny herds that roam its fathomless valleys; of all the shapeless monsters that lurk among the very foundations of the earth; and of those wild phantoms that swell the tales of fishermen and sailors.(4)

In the light of these reflections, we are not surprised that the three famous stories in *The Sketch Book* deal with uncommon and surprising events. None of these is written by Crayon himself. He is the dreamer, open to suggestion, not an imaginative writer.

In an excellent analysis of the first story, "Rip Van Winkle," Haskell S. Springer writes:

> "Rip Van Winkle," whose central events (a meeting with henry hudson, and a twenty-year sleep) Are clearly not rationally credible, is introduced by a headnote in which Crayon comments on Diedrich Knickerbocker's "scrupulous accuracy."

> Then, at the close of the narration, Knickerbocker himself adds an appendix attesting to Rip's truthfulness, and the actuality of his experiences. He concludes that "the story . . . is beyond the possibility of doubt." Crayon, who introduces it, feels that Knickerbocker's appendix proves the story "an absolute fact, narrated with his usual fidelity."(5)

Springer is correct in concluding that the literary imagination is validated over the demonstrability of historical event, as is further evidenced by the fact that Rip, like Knickerbocker and Crayon, becomes a storyteller.(6)

On this level, in Todorov's scheme, "Rip Van Winkle" represents the genre of "the marvelous," for the hesitation of the fantastic is absent. Instead, we are convinced that new laws of nature must be entertained to account for the unusual phenomena.(7) Nevertheless, the story's frame adds to its complexity. It is unfortunate that Christine Brooke-Rose did not discuss the frame in her analysis of the story's overdetermination of action and mystery codes included in her superb theoretical study, A Rhetoric of the Unreal.(8) The frame is clearly overdetermined also, since the information about the tale's veracity at both beginning and end goes beyond the need for pure information. Since so much protest is made about the veracity of the story, the reader begins to wonder if there is a more plausible explanation. However, in the context of the story, no nonmarvelous explanation can be imagined. Thus the frame story raises the possibility of the fantastic, only simultaneously to deny it. Obviously, the possibility need not have been raised at all. Ironically, the fantastic is present only as an absence, and this technique is what is central to the artistry of perhaps Irving's most popular story.

"The Legend of Sleepy Hollow" functions as a complementary piece to "Rip Van Winkle," since it is grounded in "the uncanny," the genre which flanks "the fantastic" on the opposite side from "the marvelous." In this genre, the reader decides that the laws of reality remain intact and permit an explanation of the phenomena described.(9) In this case, we know that it is really Brom Bones, not the Galloping Hessian, who has pursued Ichabod Crane. As is also the case with "The Spectre Bridegroom," the story's affirmation of local superstition, not the bizarre nature of the occurrences, creates a situation by which the story can be considered uncanny. Because there is already a legend about the Hessian, Ichabod's disappearance can be explained by recourse to the supernatural, although the schoolmaster's rivalry with Brom Bones over Katrina van Tassel is the obvious cause. Once again the possibility of the fantastic is raised for the sole purpose of being denied. Such a strategy indicates that Irving was not just parodying the excesses of contemporary Gothic and romantic fiction, which can be commended. He was also refusing a form of literature which provides a valid alternative vision of the human condition. In this area Irving can only appear narrow-minded or frightened.

"The Legend of Sleepy Hollow" is not similar to the famous tales in *The Alhambra*, which are also called "legends." There are six of these "legends" in the first version of *The Alhambra* and eight in the second version. Except for the "Three Beautiful Princesses," which tells of the escape of the two bravest princesses, all of these stories partake of the marvelous, primarily through the use of magic spells and objects, such as the weathercock in "The Arabian Astrologer" and the candle and scroll in "The Moor's Legacy." In addition, "The Legend of Prince Ahmed Al Kamel" is a fairytale complete with talking animals. Local beliefs are not treated as superstitions, as we find in "The Legend of Sleepy Hollow." Instead, the Alhambra safeguards the world of the marvelous as an architectural embodiment of Spain's historical debt to its great Moorish past.

It would be hard to think of an edifice more unlike the Alhambra than Bracebridge Hall, the home of a friend with whom Crayon spent Christmas in *The Sketch Book*. The four short stories included in *Bracebridge Hall* are all told or read aloud by one member of the house party to the others, whereas in *The Sketch Book* the three short stories were inserted with far less integration.

In the first three stories of *Bracebridge Hall*, "The Stout Gentleman," "The Student of Salamanca," and "Annette Delabre," Irving uses suspense to create within the reader a feeling that the story may take a fantastic turn. However, as it turns out, these expectations prove to be unfulfilled.

In "The Stout Gentleman" the "nervous gentleman" who tells the story finds no one in Room 13 when he finally goes to investigate.

> The mysterious stranger had evidently but just retired. I turned off, sorely disappointed to my room, which had been changed to the front of the house. As I went along the corridor, I saw a large pair of boots, with dirty, waxed tops, standing at the door of a bed-chamber. They doubtless belonged to the unknown; but it would not do to disturb so redoubtable a personage in his den; he might discharge a pistol, or something worse, at my head. I went to bed, therefore, and lay awake half the night in a terribly nervous state; and even when I fell asleep, I was still haunted in my dreams by the idea of the stout gentleman and his wax-topped boots.(10)

Here the motifs of dreams and hauntings make a departure toward the fantastic possible, but the story ends two paragraphs later, as the narrator finally catches a glimpse of the mysterious guest bending down to get into his coach.

In the longer, more complicated, story "The Student of Salamanca," a similar function is invested in the motif of alchemy. Antonio, the hero, falls in love with the daughter of the old alchemist, Felix de Varquez. All three characteristics are abducted mysteriously, but none of the disappearances prove to have anything to do with alchemy. (In contrast, in "The Legend of the Arabian Astrologer" the old alchemist, Ibrahim Ebn Abd Ayub, provides the marvelous elements in the narrative.) The protagonist in "Annette Delabre," the third story, suffers from hysteria after the supposed loss of her boyfriend, but the wanderings of her mind do not take us toward the fantastic.

The last and best story of Bracebridge Hall, "Dolph Heyliger," is introduced by a brief framing device called "The Haunted House: From the Manuscripts of the Late Diedrich Knickerbocker," which testifies to the reliability of the following account. "Dolph Heyliger" is the story of an unpromising youth, who, nevertheless, surprises those around him by gaining a fortune, a suitable bride, and a position in society. Before he could achieve these things, the ghost of an ancestor had to emerge from a picture on the wall and indicate to him the site of a concealed family fortune. this ghostly forefather had also previously visited Dolph in a haunted house which he had been assigned to watch. The atmosphere of the marvelous is created by reference to local legends, such as "The Storm-Ship," which is the title of an inserted tale. However, the ending of the story casts doubt on Dolph's truthfulness. He may have lied about his coming into his fortune. If the story is entirely fabricated, then there are no events that can suggest two different explanations. The account is simply true or false. There is no chance for a fantastic interpretation of events.

Related to the existence of ghosts and phantoms is the essay "St. Mark's Eve," earlier in the collection. The beliefs of the townsfolk, the parson, and Crayon himself do not generate a fantastic story. According to Crayon,

> There is, I believe, a degree of superstition lurking in every mind; and I doubt if anyone can thoroughly examine all his secret notions and impulses without detecting it, to be a part of our nature, like instinct in animals, acting independently of our reason. It is often found existing in lofty natures, especially those that are poetical and aspiring. A great and extraordinary poet of our day, whose life and writings evince a mood subject to powerful exaltation, is said to believe in omens and secret intimations. Caesar, it is well known, was greatly under the influence of such belief; and Napoleon had his good and evil days, and his presiding star.(11)

The reason why no tales of a fantastic nature are included has to do with the nature of the polite society hearing the stories. The group consciously or subconsciously censors material which would be too upsetting to have to face. The volume ends with a wedding, a symbol of the triumph of the social order in which all elements have their just place. Even Dolph Heyliger's experiences can be explained away by the lie that enables the young man to enter his equivalent of the Hall's polite society.

In *Tales of a Traveller* Irving once again changes his framing device. The book is divided into four sections, linked by the presence of Geoffrey Crayon. However, the nature of the stories in each section is different. The first group, "Strange Stories by a Nervous Gentleman" and the last, "The Money Diggers: Found among the Papers of the Late Diedrich Knickerbocker," contain stories which can be considered in the light of the fantastic.

Tales of a Traveller elaborates on the technique of stories that contain other stories. Not surprisingly, the stories are important *as* stories, not as works of the creative imagination as *in The Sketch Book*, nor as means of polite recreation as in *Bracebridge Hall*. As William L. Hedges astutely points out,

> The keynote of *Tales of a Traveller* is the recognition of a certain fraudulent quality in fiction. Crayon will not let his readers forget that he is only telling them stories: ". . . I am an old traveler. I have read somewhat, heard and seen more, and dreamt more than all. My brain is filled therefore, with all kinds of odds and ends . . . and I am always at a loss to know how much to believe of my own stories" (p. lx) The implication is that stories are not actualities; one needn't pretend that they really happened or be duped into taking them the wrong way.(12)

With this warning in mind we pass through three initial semicomical ghost stories, "The Adventure of My Uncle," "The Adventure of My Aunt," and "The Bold Dragoon; or the Adventure of My Grandfather," before arriving at Irving's first horror story, "The Adventure of the German Student." In this short tale, Gottfried Wolfgang arrives in Paris at the time of the French Revolution and falls in love with a mysterious woman whom he meets near the guillotine. They become lovers, and the next morning Gottfried leaves to look for better lodgings for them. When he returns, he finds his lover dead. Untying the black collar around her neck, he witnesses her severed head falling to the floor. The narrator claims, at the story's close, to have heard the story directly from the student in the madhouse in which he spent the remaining days of his life.

Walter A. Reichart, in his *Washington Irving and Germany*, locates the story's origin in a suggestion Irving received from Thomas Moore. Reichart indicates that the basic story was available in French in at least three collections. One version, "Le Revenant succube," was published in Paris in 1819, five years before Irving's adaptation. According to Reichart, the use of the madhouse motif was Irvins particular contribution.(13)

In reference to the madhouse, John Clendenning writes:

> We are left, as we often are left in Irving's stories with two possible explanations: either Gottfried met the transcendent lady truly incarnated, a ghost who became a corpse in the morning, or the woman was a corpse from the beginning. If the psychic condition of a Gottfried who, we are told, related the story to the narrator in a madhouse, is significant, then the second version has the great validity.(14)

Actually, it is more important to remember that the student's madness cast doubt on any version of the story he may give. The affirmation of veracity turns out to be inseparable from the questioning of the protagonist's sanity. Thus, Irving shifts the discussion away from whether or not the events actually happened in the way the student described to whether or not the story is "authentic." The events are marvelous if they actually happened. They are uncanny if they are explained away by the student's madness. The hesitation characteristic of the fantastic is not experienced. Within the marvelous there are two choices Clendenning points out, but that is all.

The next three stories are linked by a mysterious picture which the Baronet received from a mysterious stranger, who had, in turn, acquired it from a young Italian, Ottavio. "The Story of the Young Italian" is a first-person narrative, a form which Irving had avoided before this volume. It is the only story in the four collections which follows the pattern of the typical nineteenth-century fantastic story. At the end of his story, Ottavio tells the mysterious stranger what events befell him after he murdered his rival for the love of his sweetheart, Bianca.

> By degrees this frenzied fever of remorse settled into a permanent malady of the mind -- into one of the most horrible that ever poor wretch was cursed with. Wherever I went the countenance of him I had slain appeared to follow me. Whenever I turned my head, I beheld it behind me, hideous with the contortions of the dying moment. I have tried in every way to escape from this horrible phantom, but in vain. I know not whether it be an illusion of the mind, the consequence of my dismal education at the convent, or whether a phantom really sent by Heaven to punish me, but there it ever is -- at all times -- in all places. . . I once had recourse to my pencil, as a desperate experiment, I painted an exact resemblance of this phantom-face. I placed it before me, in hopes that by constantly contemplating the copy, I might diminish the effect of the original. But I only doubled instead of diminishing the misery.(15)

Most readers will want to know why Irving finally wrote this particular fantastic tale after so many attempts at avoiding the genre. Ottavio's story recounts at first hand the upsets of romantic passion which Irving either omitted from or sentimentalized in _The Sketch Book_ and _Bracebridge Hall_. Romantic obsession and murder create the background for this tale, as they do in the fantastic tales of many other writers.

In Part IV of _Tales of a Traveller_, "The Money Diggers," we are back in the world of the New Amsterdam stories, here represented by "The Devil and Tom Walker" and "Wolfert Webber." Both are humorous stories about greed: Tom is punished for it, and Wolfert is rewarded for it. "The Devil and Tom Walker" puts across an obvious message. Consequently, it is more of a moral tale than an example of the marvelous. "Wolfert Webber" is a realistic story with recourse to superstitions, but it fails to create the ambiguities and complications of "The Legend of Sleepy Hollow." Neither of the Dutch stories is as closely related to "The Story of the Young Italian" as "The Story of the Young Robber" from the "Italian Banditti" section. It is another story of love and murder, but without any recourse to the fantastic. The presence in the collection of this story indicates that Irving was probably more interested in the experience of passion than in the fantastic milieu of "The Story of the Young Italian." In addition, it is probable that Ottavio imagines the type of haunting that he undergoes, since psychology relates the two stories to each other.(16)

The passion which twice erupts in _Tales of a Traveller_ is nowhere present in the idealized love stories of _The Alhambra_. Even the purity of the good young lovers seems to reflect the marvelous enchantment of the place. The legends of the Alhambra reward the courageous (the two princesses who escape) and downtrodden (Peregil) and punish the greedy (Aben Habuz) and hypocritical (Fray Simon). In _The Alhambra_ the health of the literary imagination suggested in _The Sketch Book_ is reestablished on the level of collective authorship.

Irving's most successful volume of stories and sketches, _The Alhambra_, shows that he coped most successfully with his aversion to the fantastic through the marvelous. "The Legend of the Arabian Astrologer" and "The Legend of Ahmed Al Kemal" are, in my view, his only stories as enjoyable as "Rip Van Winkle" and "The Legend of Sleepy Hollow." Nevertheless, the denial of the fantastic represents a psychological and imaginative liabililty on Irving's part. As Rosemary Jackson notes:

> The fantastic is a literature which attempts to create a space for a discourse other than a conscious one and it is this which leads to its problematization of language, of the word, in its utterance of desire.(17)

Working in the tradition of Irene Bessiere and Helene Cixous, Jackson goes on to indicate that as a "literature of absences, fantasy throws back on to the dominant culture a constant reminder of something 'other.'" Irving, as the champion, first of the British gentry and later of the Moorish past, could not allow himself this literature of limits and transgression. Ironically, as the literary father figure to be denied and overthrown, he stood before Poe and Hawthorne, as they began the journeys which changed American literature for all time.

NOTES

1. Washington Irving, The Alhambra, rev. ed. (Chicago: E. A. Weeks & Co., n.d.), pp. 400-401.

2. Tzvetan Todorov, The Fantastic: A Structural Approach to a Literary Genre (Paris, 1970; reprintst. Ithaca: Cornell University. Press, 1973), p. 33.

3. John Clendenning, "Irving and the Gothic Tradition," Bucknell Review 12 (1964): ps. 90-98.

4. Washington Irving, The Sketch Book of Geoffrey Crayon, Esquire (Boston: Twayne Publishers 1978), p. 12.

5. Haskell S. Springer, "Creative Contradictions in Irving," American Transcendental Quarterly 5 no. 1 (1970): ps. 15.

6. "Creative Contradiction", p. 16.

7. Fantastic, p. 41.

8. Christine Brooke-Rose, A Rhetoric of the Unreal: Studies in Narrative and Structure, Especially of the Fantastic (Cambridge: Cambridge University. Press, 1981), pp. 106-12.

9. The Fantastic, p. 41.

10. Washington Irving, Bracebridge Hall (Boston: Twayne Publishers, 1977), p. 56.

11. Bracebridge Hall, p. 82.

12. William L. Hedges, Washington Irving: An American Study, 1802-1832 (Baltimore: Johns Hopkins University. Press, 1965), pp. 195-96.

13. Walter A. Reichart, Washington Irving and Germany (Ann Arbor: University of Michigan Press, 1957), p. 149.

14. "Irving and the Gothic Tradition", p. 97.

15. Washington Irving, Tales of a Traveller (New York: G. P. Putnam's Sons, 1965), p. 129.

16. I am indebted to Hedges' reading of the stories in Parts I and III of Tales of a Traveller.

17. Rosemary Jackson, Fantasy: The Literature of Subversion (London: Methuen, 1981), p. 62.

6.

Washington Irving and the Romance of Travel: Is There an Itinerary in *Tales of a Traveller*?

JUDITH G. HAIG

Most readers of Washington Irving's Tales of a Traveller, from its publication in 1824 until the present day, have found the work an unsatisfying conglomeration of stories and sketches patchworked together without coherence or unity.(1) They have looked to Tales of a Traveller for an itinerary, and they have found none. Such criticism persists in spite of William L. Hedges' identification of a consistency of narrative technique, of a pattern in "The Way the Story Is Told."(2) Two years later, Henry A. Pochmann, presumably unconvinced, labeled the book "a hodgepodge in four parts, none of which has any relationship to the others."(3) But the search for that relationship has not looked to the traditions of travel writing or to the significance which travel undoubtedly held for Irving personally as avenues into the tales. Such an investigation, however, is profitable, as much for what it suggests about Irving's attitude toward writing as for what it contributes to an understanding of the work's thematic unity.

If travel has any consistent pattern of association in Irving's works and career, it is with imagination. Travel was quite literally the goad to his own creativity. "It is not chance that each of his best books follows close on a prolonged season of wandering."(4) His tours filled his notebooks with lore and legends from foreign countrysides, the raw materials over which his imagination could work to produce the sketches and tales which made him famous. The reflections of his most congenial persona, Geoffrey Crayon, are filled with autobiographical accounts of the importance of travel to the exercise of bhis imagination. In "the holiday rovings of boyhood" he found amid his native landscape much to give impetus to his "incipient habit of day-dreaming and to a certain propensity to weave up and tint sober realities with [his] own whims and imaginings."(5) Later, his travels in England and on the Continent continued to be a way to elude or transform sober realities, a means of "escape . . . from the commonplace realities of the present" to journey in imagination "among the shadowy grandeurs of the past."(6) Travel, then, became a way of releasing and refreshing the imagination. The "glory of travel" for the mature Irving lay in the inducement of "'a kind of intoxication of the heart,'" a detachment from everyday reality and an immersion in imaginative "self-hypnotism."(7) The association of travel with imagination also exists in Tales of a Traveller and is linked from the start with what is perhaps the central enigma of the volume: the relationship between fact and fiction. "I am an old traveler," Geoffrey Crayon tells the reader; "I have read somewhat, heard and seen more, and dreamt more than all. My brain is filled, therefore, with all kinds of odds and ends. In traveling, these heterogeneous matters have become shaken up in my mind, as the articles are apt to be in an ill-packed traveling trunk; so that when I attempt to draw forth a fact, I cannot determine whether I have read, heard, or dreamt it; and I am always at a loss to know how much to believe of my own stories."(8) The question of credibility Crayon raises for himself and for us provides, in its prominence at the beginning of the volume, a basis for other questions we might ask of Tales of a Traveller. In particular it prompts us to examine to what extent travel and imagination constitute identifiable motifs that operate throughout the tales and therefore provide a form of unity. And, given what we know of the essentially positive association travel and imagination had in Irving's life, we might well ask to what extent that association was reinforced by or demonstrated in this work.

Tales of a Traveller embraces the narratives of two travelers; Geoffrey Crayon, the quintessential European wanderer, is joined in the final fourth section by his elderly counterpart Diedrich Knickerbocker, whose more circumscribed rambles about the Hudson River valley inspire reveries in the antiquarian bent on mining old legends from a new land. And within this large frame there are other travelers aplenty, interesting and entertaining in their variety and in their purposes for traveling. As one of them asserts, everyone travels nowadays. There are those who travel for traditional reasons: the Baronet embarked on "a grand tour"; the Popkins family enjoying the pleasures their wealth affords; the Polish count reduced by exile to a life of pleasant vagabondage; the Spanish Princess making a pilgrimage to Loretto to expiate a lifetime of indiscretion; the Venetian couple sharing a honeymoon journey. There are those who seek an escape in travel: the German Student attempting to find relief from his melancholy; the Young Italian attempting to "out-travel" the curse of Cain; or a Buckthorne or a Poor-Devil Author attempting to escape to environments better suited to the exercise of their poetical temperaments. There are the professional travelers: the merchant knights-errant of traveling, the solid middle-class figures at the various inns, the itinerant antiquarian, and the wandering outlaws and strolling players, drawn to the road or to the mountain trails by their vocations. There are mysterious travelers and successful ones: a buccaneer voyager laden with sea-chest; a "hot-pressed traveler in quarto with plates"

(p. 123), whose success warrants him a place about the salt at the literary dinner; and even a Bold Dragoon, whose most profitable travels, it is suggested, occur not on land or sea but "about inns at night" (p. 54).

Travel and travelers in their various forms virtually overpopulate the work and, in their repeated appearances, provide a unity which is more pronounced in the first and third sections than in thf other two. Where there are links between tales or among sections, it is partially the emphasis on travel and travelers that provides them. Clearly, travelers exist primarily to tell, hear, or figure in the stories which make up the volume. But beyond that, they frequently exist to serve as targets for Irving's amiable satire.

Although the pattern is by no means pervasive, there are many instances where travel, travelers, and their motives for traveling are spoofed. The Baronet's grand tour, to acquire the wisdom with which "my parents had tried in vain to inoculate me" (p. 73), is a case in point. What attracts him to Venice is not the education to be derived from a study of men and manners but rather the excitement of "a pair of languishing black eyes" (p. 73). Believing himself "profoundly instructed . . . in the ways of women," the Baronet returns home only to be plunged into a life of bachelorhood by "the Mortification of being jilted by a little boarding-school girl, . . . scarcely versed in the accidence of love(p. 17).

The Baronet's grand tour is one of three pointed but jovial jibes at the attitudes and expectations of the English traveler abroad. If what entices his imagination on the Continent fails to yield any practical benefits at home, the Baronet has at least enjoyed imaginative participation in and interaction with the lands he visits. The stereotypical rich Englishman and the equally famililar Alderman Popkins are, on the other hand, indicted for their lack of imaginative participation in their travels.

The Englishman is a study in contradictions. Traveling with a surfeit of indispensables, those "oppressive conveniences which burden a comfortable man" p. 269), he is condescending to and disdainful of the foreigners whose charms he has willingly sought and is eager to get to the end of a journey whose pleasures presumably were to inhere in the taking. As a result, he is rude, suspicious, boorish, detached, and "out of humor with all the world." "As this," Crayon says, "is no uncommon case with gentlemen who travel for their pleasure, it is hardly worthy of remark" (p. 356). He is the kind of English traveller who seeks the pleasures of travel but looks down "with contempt on all the world around; profoundly ignorant of the country and the people, and devoutly certain that everything not English must be wrong" (p. 308). It is he who pronounces accounts of banditti "to be mere travelers' tales, or the exaggerations of ignorant peasants, and designing innkeepers" (p. 271), only to be unwittingly both victim and hero of an attack by robbers.

If the Englishman is unimaginative in his coldness and skepticism, Alderman Popkins is equally unimaginative, but not because he is skeptical; rather, he is too ingenuous. He is one of those "well-stuffed travelers" (p. 310), so smug that any attempt to learn from traveling is merely gratuitous. He and his family travel because it is the thing their wealth and position entitle them to do rather than because they have any curiosity to satisfy. His complacency thwarts any imaginative capacity to conceive of danger en route, until, determined to walk at leisure among the bandit-infested hills, he is taught a "lesson in Italian" by the bandit chief he mistakes for an honest goatherd (p. 310).

Of other instances which seem to comment on unimaginative travelers, we might include the Uncle of the first story, a traveler so jaded that his curiosity about the ghost exists only on an intellectual level; he is interested merely in her history, not in her appearance in his chamber: "accustomed to strange adventures, he drew his nightcap resolutely over his eyes, turned his back to the door, hoisted the bed-clothes high over his shoulders, and gradually fell asleep" (p. 30).

Other travelers are mocked for the extremity of their imaginative tendencies. For example, the Misses Popkins, "quite delighted with the adventure" at the hands of the bandits, convert the experience in imagination to suit a romantic view of the world whose source lies in the novels of Mrs. Radcliffe (p. 311). Or consider the curious case of the traveling French painter mistakenly kidnapped by the banditti. His realistic assessment of the danger in which he finds himself soon gives way to his tendency to color experience with the romantic tints of the artist. No fewer than half a dozen times does he interrupt his story to describe his fascination with the "picturesque" effects of the Abruzzi landscape. Even the long-awaited meal is enjoyed more for its color and form than for its taste: "never did repast appear to me more excellent or picturesque"; "everything presented a study for a painter" (p. 337). It is this tendency of his imagination to reduce experience to its picturesque features which accounts for the failure of the Young Robber's story to affect him more than momentarily. Shortly after the telling, he can again romanticize the bandit chieftain as a "benevolent cutthroat," turn once more to the picturesque features of the landscape at nightfall, and relegate the truly powerful and distressing story to one of "the many agitations" he has experienced during the course of a wearying day (p. 350).

If Irving elsewhere celebrates the pleasant and profitable association between travel and imagination, such instances as these - with their emphasis on travelers who have too little imagination or who exercise what they have of it perversely - suggest this is not his intention here. An examination of the role of imagination in the tales travelers tell shows a similar departure.

The major stories in each section concern, to a significant extent, the effects of imagination, and the pictures they paint of it are not positive ones. We confront in an Ottavio, a Gottfried Wolfgang, a Jack Buckthorne, a Wolfert Webber, or even in the Young Robber a species of imagination portrayed as detrimental or, as Irving often labels it, "diseased." The most salient feature of Ottavio's and Wolfgang's makeup, in particular, is their susceptibility to the dangers of imagination.

The temper of the German Student's Gothic melancholy has its base in his "visionary and enthusiastic character" (p. 55), an overheated imagination exercised in an "unhealthy appetite" for abstruse theories, "decayed literature," and "reveries on forms and faces which he had seen, [for whom] his fancy would deck out images of loveliness far surpassing the reality" (p. 56). He is haunted by a dream vision of "transcendent beauty" which he projects upon the reality of a stormy night. He creates more than perceives the creature of his dream, and she becomes the fiend of his imagination.

The fate of the Young Italian, Irving's prototypical Man of Feeling, is similar. The story is a history of the shaping of his "dangerous sensibilities" (p. 83) and the consequences of their attachment to Bianca. She is a vision which his imagination seizes and elevates "into something almost more than mortal": "She seemed too exquisite for earthly use; too delicate and exalted for human attainment . . . I drank in delicious poison that made me giddy," he avows (p. 94). The consequence of his idolatry, when thwarted by Filippo's treachery, is the bloodthirsty murder and mutilation which replaces forever after the image of ideal beauty with "the horrible countenance of [his] victim" (p. 112). Here, as in "The Adventure of the German Student," an imaginative vision of ideal beauty is transmuted into a horror.

Even the Young Robber resembles his fellow young Italian in this. The image of Rosetta first entices him into the madness of love by its distinctive fairness and later arouses his imagination "almost to a fever" (p. 341) when, by his act of jealous violence, she is forbidden to his sight. Ultimately, for his complicity in her death and dishonor, it returns to haunt him "like a burning iron consuming [his] very heart" (p. 334).

All three are dark romantic figures, Byronic victims of the power of their own imaginations. The stories of Buckthorne and his compatriots, despite their difference in tone, share to a significant degree in the treacheries of imagination. Buckthorne's story is virtually an exemplum of the distresses which arise from a poetical temperament. The dangers of imagination in his case, though, consist of more physical than emotional torment. Throughout his youth and young manhood, he is repeatedly flogged for "trespassing upon Parnassus" (p. 166) and even peevishly disinherited as a consequence of his rhyming. But this veritable school of hard knocks is not without its benefits. He begins to understand "the poetical temperament working within me, and tempting me forth into a world of its own creation, which I mistook for the world of real life" (p. 173), and learns both to recognize reality and to compromise with it.

Were it not for Wolfert Webber in the fourth section of _Tales of a Traveller_, we might be inclined to read these various stories of imaginative self-deception as a commentary on the propensities of youth. The protagonists, after all, are clearly denominated "young," and

Buckthorne is permitted to outgrow his illusions and mature into a practical philosopher who "has learned to estimate the world rightly, yet good-humoredly" (p. 161). Even the Poor-Devil Author profits from a healthful dose of hard reality which, he says, "manured my mind, and brought it back to itself again" (p. 130). Irving's pun is significant and symptomatic of the ambivalence which frequently touches his portrayal of characters with imaginative inclinations. Imagination is both prized and suspect. The attitude emerges most directly in the ironic characterization of Diedrich Knickerbocker, who claims to have devoted his mature years "to diligent research after the truth of [the] strange traditions" which fascinated his imagination in boyhood (p. 367). But truth is elusive, and fable exceedingly more alluring. For every protestation of "authenticity" in Knickerbocker's histories, we learn early and automatically to read "fiction."

In the Wolfert Webber of Knickerbocker's narrative, we have no young man of poetic temperament but a middle-aged man in his plodding prosperity who is equally susceptible to the dangers of imagination. Too willingly does he allow the stories of buried treasure to take hold of his mind and instill there images of "ingots and heaps of gold" (p. 405). His golden dreams are never quite stifled by the "pinching realities" (p. 409) his family is suffered to feel. "Indeed, his infected fancy tinged everything with gold" (p. 432). Wolfert, like Buckthorne, is ultimately delivered by chance good fortune from the predicament into which his golden dreams have plunged him. He becomes a prosperous citizen once more and retires to the comfortable esteem of Raam Rapelye's chair, "where he long reigned greatly honored and respected, insomuch that he was never known to tell a story without its being believed, nor to utter a joke without its being laughed at" (p. 456).

All our carefully instilled distrust of Wolfert's imagination is brought to bear on the jest of these final lines, just as it is earlier on our appreciation of the crest with which Wolfert "commemorate[s] the origin of his greatness": "a full-blown cabbage . . . with the pithy motto alles Koff, that is to say, all head meaning thereby that he had risen by sheer head-work" (p. 456). Beyond the pun on cabbages, Irving forces us to recall the manner of head-work for which Wolfert will be remembered the hyperexcitable imagination by which, rather than making his fortune, he very nearly lost his family to poverty and his life to folly. Irving's wordplay here and in the final ironic link between the believability of a story and the humor of a joke allows us to return full-circle to Geoffrey Crayon's suggestion in his preface of the blurred distinction between what is imagined or dreamed in the course of travel and what is acquired as fact.

As motifs, travel and imagination figure significantly in Tales of a Traveller. Although they may ultimately fail to give us the comprehensive itinerary critics have sought both in Irving's time and in ours, we may nonetheless emerge from their examination with an insight into an essential ambivalence-one which bears directly on a central question in Irving scholarship: the extent to which he can be called a romantic. Irving wrote in an age and in a milieu which, both in England and on the Continent, was preoccupied with the authenticity of the imagination. He could not have been blind to this basic tenet of romanticism: that the imagination is a way of penetrating to truth, of knowing. But nowhere in Irving are we likely to find an assertion of this romantic faith. On the contrary, Irving is often preoccupied in this volume with demonstrating not so much the pleasures or truth of imagination as with asserting its follies and dangers. Likewise, we look in vain to Tales of a Traveller for a romantic portrayal of travel. If we acknowledge that romantic literature is characteristically a "literature of movement," a "circuitous journey" through alienation toward transcendent reintegration,(9) we see how short of such a fulfillment the travels of Geoffrey Crayon and those of the various protagonists of his tales fall. What Irving draws from the conventions of literary pilgrimage owes more to eighteenth-century precedents for the impulse to irony or satire than to motifs of the romantic quest.

We have in him not a traveler toward transcendence so much as one who is content to rest in that shadowy middle region where imagination is both enticingly acknowledged and playfully denied. It is a compromise position between ingrained skepticism and emergent romantic faith. That Irving never crossed the border to deal deeply and significantly with the powerful themes which fascinated other writers of his and later generations has been proposed by some to be a consequence of his lack of intellectual scope and depth, an inherited American suspicion of the imagination, or the influence of the Scottish Common Sense philosophers.(10) It is unnecessary to deny any of these propositions to recognize another which seems to me equally influential. Irving's hesitant romanticism stems not so much from a distrust of the imagination as from an intrinsic ambivalence toward his talents rooted deeply in personality.

The account he gives of himself in his letter to Sir Walter Scott in the preface to the revised edition of The Sketch Book is, by the testimony of Tales of a Traveller, no pose: "I have no command of my talents, such as they are, and have to watch the varyings of my mind as I would those of a weathercock . . . I must, therefore, keep on pretty much as I have begun; writing when I can, not when I would. I shall occasionally shift my residence and write whatever is suggested by objects before me, or whatever rises in my imagination; and hope to write better . . . by and by."(11)

Travel was an essential stimulus to his imagination. But when it became financially necessary to live by his pen, the tensions between the pleasures of imagination and the necessity of achievement became palpable. The delightful reveries and anecdotes which fill his journals are matched by evidence that he found the work of shaping his material difficult, demanding, and draining. If there is not quite an underlying doubt about the value of the creative life, there is every indication that he frequently felt the burden of his talent and the tensions between the pleasant inclinations which fostered it and the tedious necessity to demonstrate or fulfill it. There is within his temperament a distinctive vacillation between the impulse to escape into imagination and the need to employ it in the real world. The one operated as a restraint on the other. The escape never quite succeeded, so there could be no leap of faith beyond.

The product, all too often as in *Tales of a Traveller,* is a tempting but finally incomplete commingling of associations. Bound by "commonplace" necessities, never fully to explore the "shadowy grandeurs," Irving was ultimately content to relish the middle region where imagination is more reverie than revelation, at best a temporary pleasure, at worst a form of delusion. It is the ambivalence in the life that accounts for the ambivalence in the work: the ironic uncertainty, playfully maintained, between what is learned or known and what is imagined or dreamed. And it may be this which, at the core, accounts for Irving's hesitant romanticism and the lack of an itinerary in *Tales of a Traveller*.

NOTES

1. See Walter A. Reichart, *Washington Irving and Germany* (Ann Arbor: University of Michigan Press, 1957). pp. 159-64.

2. William L. Hedges, "The Way the Story is Told," in his *Washington Irving: An American Study, 1802-1832* (Baltimore: Johns Hopkins, 1965), pp. 191-235.

3. Henry A. Pochmann, "Washington Irving: Amateur or Professional?" in *Essays on American Literature in Honor of Jay B. Hubbell*, ed. Clarence Godhes (Durham: Duke University Press, 1967), p. 73.

4. Stanley T. Williams, *The Life of Washington Irving* (New York: Oxford Univ. Press, 1935), I: 217.

5. Washington Irving, "Sleepy Hollow," in *Miscellaneous Writings, 1803-1859*, ed. Wayne R. Kime (Boston: Twayne Publishers, 1981), II: 106-7.

6. Washington Irving, "The Author's Account of Himself," in *The Sketch Book of Geoffrey Crayon, Gent.*, ed. Haskell Springer (Boston: Twayne, 1978), p. 9.

7. *The Life Of Washington Irving,* p. 223.

8. Washington Irving, *Tales of a Traveller*, author's Rev. ed. (New York: Putnam, 1849), p. x. Subsequent references are cited parenthetically.

9. M. H. Abrams, *Natural Supernaturalism: Tradition and Revolution in Romantic Literature* (New York: Norton, 1971), pp. 193-94; see also chapters 3-5.

10. The first is, generally, the position of Williams. For the other factors see Terence Martin, "Rip, Ichabod, and the American Imagination," *American Literature* 30 (1959): 137-49 and Donald A. Ringe, *American Gothic: Imagination and Reason in Nineteenth-Century Fiction* (Lexington: University of Kentucky Press, 1982), ch. 5.

11. *The Sketch Book*, p. 5.

7.

Reevaluating Scott: Washington Irving's "Abbotsford"

WILLIAM OWEN

Washington Irving's relationship with Sir Walter Scott was one of the most significant and fruitful relationships between Old and New World writers. From his initial visit with Scott at Abbotsford in 1817, Irving derived significant personal, artistic, and professional benefits. Scott directed him to German folklore, which provided sources for "Rip Van Winkle" and "The Legend of Sleepy Hollow," and lent assistance in the publication of _The Sketch Book_ in 1819-20. Irving's personal letters at the time express a warm personal fondness for Scott(1) and the 1848 introduction to _The Sketch Book_ contains Irving's graceful acknowledgment of Scott's help. Viewed against this background, "Abbotsford," published in 1835, Irving's account of his four-day stay with Scott, has been regarded, not surprisingly, as a tribute to Scott, who died in 1832. Yet close attention to the narrator's perspective, his reactions to and reflections on the incidents of the narrative, reveals a critical reevaluation of the relationship. While there remains much personal regard for Scott, "Abbotsford" details a meditative scrutiny of Scott's form of romanticism. Irving, in reviewing the discovery of his own artistic direction at the time, found that his talents, interests and American origins required him to distance himself from Scott.

This interpretation of the relationship between the two writers in "Abbotsford" derives from a view of "Abbotsford" as primarily an imaginative reconstruction of Irving's mental life during the visit rather than as the essentially factual account accepted by many biographers of Scott and Irving. Retelling its anecdotes, they have given "Abbotsford" the patina of historical truth despite John Lockhart's warning(2) of its factual inaccuracies. Also affecting the evaluation of its accuracy are the circumstances of its composition. Irving could rely upon only a few journal entries in writing "Abbotsford" seventeen years after the event.(3) It is not surprising, therefore, that Dahlia Kirby Terrell has uncovered a case of cobbling from other sources.(4) Yet "Abbotsford" was a work of personal importance to Irving as his literary strategies indicate. He decided to recreate the visit within its original time context, thereby demonstrating his commitment to relive his time at Abbotsford. The presence of the narrator's perspective used to retrieve the thoughts and feelings of the visit further shows the introspective nature of the essay. Comments on Scott, which might be thought to serve as public testimonials, instead are turned inward for the narrator's private use. While Irving focuses intently on the four-day visit to explore its significance, the seventeen-year lapse means that the initial experience has been reformulated so that "Abbotsford," instead of disclosing Irving's actual thoughts in 1817, presents his conception of his state of mind at the time. Complicating the analysis of "Abbotsford" is the awareness that Irving's concerns at the time of composition-shortly after his return to America-may have had a bearing upon his view of the initial experience.

Irving's visit to Scott came at a time of personal crisis in Irving's life. In 1817 the family business was sliding into bankruptcy and he was considering the possibility of becoming a professonal writer: the meeting with Scott offered him the opportunity to evaluate an important model of the professional writer. During Irving's four days with Scott, the two went on long walks, met Scott's neighbors and retainers, inspected ruins, viewed the landscape, and engaged in rambling conversation. Evenings were pleasantly spent with the rest of Scott's family. This narrative record of incident and conversation, presented with the untroubled air of nostalgia, is the basis of the easy acceptance of "Abbotsford" as grateful tribute.

If we recognize that the narrator of the tribute may be Geoffrey Crayon, the familiar persona of _The Sketch Book_, we may come to suspect that all is not as it seems in "Abbotsford." While the narrator does not identify himself as either Crayon or Irving, "Abbotsford" was published in _The Crayon Miscellany_ and attributed to "The Author of _The Sketch Book_," thus leaving Crayon as the narrator of record. William L. Hedges, basing his judgment primarily on the voice, contends that Irving is the actual narrator in his works by 1832.(5) Certainly, the identity of the creator of Crayon was well known by this time and the narrator's reflective voice in "Abbotsford" differs from Crayon's ebullient one in _The Sketch Book_. However, if we regard the narrator as a persona, we provide a more satisfactory explanation for the fictional aspects of "Abbotsford." The persona is a suitable cover for the liberties Irving took with the facts in "Abbotsford" and for his arrangement of incident. Even in the presumably accurate presentation of feelings and attitudes, the persona is used significantly as a distancing technique. The author achieves a great degree of control over the account of the changes and development in his outlook during the four-day stay. For instance, there is no explicit mention of Irving's career subsequent to the visit. The narrator is thus a created persona, different from Irving the author; we will call the narrator "Crayon" in this essay to set him apart from the author. Since the focus in "Abbotsford" is on the period prior to _The Sketch Book_, we are involved in a curious time warp. We witness actions and listen to words supposedly occurring in 1817 though the words were actually written in 1834. The distancing is highly unusual for a tribute. As Irving may have been well aware that the conclusions he reached concerning Scott were not completely laudatory, the persona helps him deflect criticism of his reflections.

While Irving's use of the persona as narrator creates uncertainty as to his real feelings toward Scott, the opening of "Abbotsford" compounds the ambiguity, for the narrator assumes different roles in his first meeting with "The Great Unknown." While the roles suggest Irving's tentativeness with Scott, they function as controlling devices in the essay. Initially, Crayon is introduced as a traveler, ostensibly bound to see Melrose Abbey. As Scott limps down the lane to meet the narrator, the note of casual serendipity rings false when contrasted with the real determination on Irving's part, as revealed in his letters,(6) to meet Scott. It also requires the narrator to minimize the letter of introduction he has from Thomas Campbell. The distance between Irving and the narrator is at its widest in this scene, revealed in the treatment of the narrator's feelings that he is intruding upon Scott's life. To the narrator, "the noise of the chaise [is disturbing] the quiet establishment." Scott's dogs begin "a furious barking."(7) While Irving's journal records the barking dogs, the scene in "Abbotsford" accentuates the timidity and hopefulness of the narrator and above all the joyful satisfaction upon first sight of Scott. The latter's generous invitation to stay and his hearty self-confidence form a great contrast to the narrator's feelings. The nature of the relationship between the two men is indicated in Scott's insistence that the narrator stay for several days, a necessary stay for "an observant traveller." Furthermore, Scott offers the narrator the chance to be a "true and nothing doubting antiquary."(8)

These roles of traveler and antiquarian have psychological significance. The role of traveler is a trope of displacement in space. Curiously, in the text, Scott confirms the first trope and suggests another, the role of antiquarian, a trope of displacement in time. When Scott invites the narrator to adopt these roles, Irving is being asked to abandon both his contemporary time and his native place. As the displacement of the narrator from America to Britain and from present time to the past occurs, he appears willing to accept the changes. While the traveler is by definition entering a strange land, unsure of what he will find, the narrator in "Abbotsford" is reversing the usual pattern in many American novels by returning east to Britain, the known past, instead of venturing into the west, the unknown future. Yet Crayon realizes that in the offer to be an antiquarian is the opportunity to become like Scott himself, the master antiquarian. Implicitly, Irving, the novice writer, can follow in the path of the famous writer even though he may be maintaining a colonial dependency in imitating Scott, the Briton. The tropes of displacement, the traveler and antiquarian, complicate the search for identity.

When the narrator fulfills the ostensible purpose of his trip by visiting Melrose Abbey on the first day of his stay it is obvious that his real purpose as traveler has been to discover Scott. As he assumes his new role of antiquarian at the Abbey, the narrator's thoughts significantly turn to Scott and his writings, prompted by the comments of Johnny Bower, one of Scott's retainers, that the Abbey is an important locale for "Lay of the Last Minstrel." Crayon recognizes the close connection between the artifacts of Scottish history and Scott's fictions, remarking that "the fictions of Scott had become facts" with Johnny Bower.(9) Fact and fiction are interchangeable in an antiquarian environment. While the ruins of Melrose Abbey are of obvious interest to the antiquarian for their evocation of the past, the people and landscape possess the associations of folklore and legend, which similarly interest the antiquarian. And, as Johnny Bower realizes, writing gives permanence to the antiquarian subject. "Abbotsford" conveys the idea that Scott's literary talent is based on this unity of eternal landscape, present people and past ruins. As the narrator travels in the vicinity of Abbotsford, he continually discovers models for characters and settings of locales in Scott's novels. Bower, identifying himself as a typical element of the unity transferred to literature by Scott, wishes to be immortalized by Scott.(10) In writing of the aged retainer, Irving tries to fill that expected role. The narrator's attraction to the people of the area is a promising beginning for Irving's imitation of Scott.

Yet when the narrator goes on a walk with his host, he realizes he cannot share Scott's enthusiasm for the landscape featured so prominently in the Waverley novels. Taking over the role of cicerone from Bower, Scott takes the narrator to a lookout and proudly displays "Lammermuir, and Smallholm, and there you have Gallashiels, and Torwoodlie, and Gallawater: and in that direction you see Teviotdale, and the Braes of Yarrow, and Ettrick stream winding along like a silver thread, to throw itself into the Tweed."(11) The narrator confesses he gazed about for a time "with mute surprize, I may almost say with disappointment."(12) According to the narrator, the land was monotonous and "destitute of trees," and "the far famed Tweed appeared a naked stream, flowing between bare hills without a tree or a thicket on its banks."(13) The narrator's alienation from the landscape is introduced significantly at the moment of pride for Scott, who seems to be offering the narrator the opportunity to possess the territory as his own subject. Irving seems to be suggesting that he cannot follow Scott's model because of his own failure to respond to the landscape. The striking juxtaposition between the narrator's and Scott's comments is the product of literary craft rather than an accurate memory since, the actual description can be traced to notes Irving recorded in his journals before he met Scott. On the ride from Berwick to Edinburgh he observes in one notebook that the valleys are "rather destitute of trees,"(14) and in another place, "the Tweed winding between naked banks."(15) His impressions of the landscape were already formed by the time he was shown the vista by Scott. In the text he justifies his opinion by pleading that he "had been so accustomed to hills crowned with forests and streams breaking their way through a wilderness of trees that all my ideas of romantic landscape were apt to be well wooded."(16) This sentiment may have been truly felt in 1817 for it appears to be a preliminary meditation on the importance of landscape prior to the definitive statement that Geoffrey Crayon utters in "The Author's Account of Himself" in The Sketch Book: "no, never need an American look beyond his own country for the sublime and beautiful of natural scenery."(17) In preferring his own landscape, rather than Scott's, Irving shows the first signs of resisting the model set for him by Scott. To follow his own feelings for landscape, he should return home, become a native writer, not a traveler, and conquer one of the tropes of displacement.

The question of returning home to America was a significant one to Irving during the time of the visit and during the period of his composition of "Abbotsford" in 1834. In the influential North American Review from 1815 to 1850, as Darwin Shrell has shown, writers were contending that a national literature could and should be developed on the basis of the associations derived from nature.(18) Archibald Alison, in his Essays on the Nature and Principles of Taste (1790) had provided the philosophical underpinnings for this belief by asserting that one's tastes were most easily formed during youth.(19) In realizing the power of his own preference for native landscape Irving maintained the principles of Alison's associationist psychology.(20) In addition, Irving subsequently gave thought to writing on American subjects, for his notebooks of late 1817 were full of extracts from American travel books.(21) Yet Irving remained in England and Europe until 1832. That he felt uneasy about his protracted stay abroad is indicated in the introduction to A Tour on the Prairies, a tale of his first excursion to the American West. Evasive and apologetic, the introduction does not satisfactorily explain his decision to stay abroad. The persistence of the issue probably accounts for its appearance in "Abbotsford" since "Abbotsford" was begun soon after or even during the writing of A Tour on the Prairies. The link between the two works on this issue is even stronger since the notebooks used on the western tour were the same as the ones used to record his impressions of Scotland.

What is surprising in "Abbotsford" is that the implied suggestion to return home is Scott's. Following the narrator's comments on landscape, Scott remarks that his only acquaintance with American forests is in the shape of an "immense stick of timber." He speculates that the timber was "like one of the gigantic obelisks which are now and then brought from Egypt, to shame the pigmy monuments of Europe; and, in fact, these vast aboriginal trees that have sheltered the Indians before the intrusion of the white men are the monuments and antiquities of your country."(22) While these statements are attributed to Scott, they are not recorded in Irving's journal; indeed, they are more likely to have been created by Irving. In A

Tour of the Prairies, Irving often describes Indians in terms of classical images.(23) In giving words of his own making to Scott, Irving is using the character of Scott to function as a projection of his own ideas on his future. While all of Scott's dialogue cannot be presented in these terms, much of Scott's conversation can be perceived as attractive courses of action to Irving, given more authority because they are uttered by Scott. The suggestion to return home was thus difficult to resist.

While the imagery of Scott's comment suggests that Irving could remain an antiquarian if he returned home, the imagery also conveys disturbing implications about America and Irving. The image's focus on the American tree and the Egyptian obelisk, both located in England, provides a new perspective on the trope of displacement, in space introduced above. The phallic power of the tree and obelisk has been lost in the displacement for they appear in England as cut lumber or as curios. Linking the tree to the Indians and the obelisk to Egypt suggests the decline of once-strong cultures, in other words the classical theme of ubi sunt, one Irving had already taken up in his Indian essays, "Philip of Pokanoket" and "Traits of Indian Character," written in 1814, before his visit to Abbotsford.(24) Thus, Scott's suggestion seems to be one that Irving has already followed, but the comment may appear in "Abbotsford" as a self-rebuke by Irving for not continuing to write about such American subjects. The image implies, moreover, that Irving, by remaining in England, will similarly lose his power. Indeed, his regret at remaining in England was expressed in the introduction of A Tour on the Prairies. He acknowledged that by his return in 1832, writers of the "able pens,"(25) perhaps James Fenimore Cooper, had already written extensively on the Indians. The image in "Abbotsford" indirectly repeats the sentiment that his opportunity to capture the topic had passed.

Irving, however, chose to depend upon Europe's ruins and monuments for subject material rather than their American equivalents. His rationalization appears in "The Author's Account of Himself" in The Sketch Book:

> But Europe held forth the charms of storied and poetical association. There were to be seen the masterpieces of art, the refinements of highly cultivated society, the quaint peculiarities of ancient and local custom. My native country was full of youthful promise: Europe was rich in the accumulated treasures of age.(26)

"Abbotsford," we have seen, maintains enough consistency with The Sketch Book to provide illumination of the decisions recorded in "The Author's Account of Himself." In preferring the scenery and ruins of separate nations, Irving violates the logic of associationism. Unable to participate in Scott's romantic unity, Irving disconnects the elements of the unity from their sources. After recognizing that he can find pleasure in the images of setting in Scott's fiction while rejecting their sources in the actual landscape, ironically because his own native associations have produced a preference for American landscape, Irving breaks away from associationism. He concludes that the successful appeal of the images does not depend upon the reader's shared knowledge of the source of the image with the writer. Literary craft might answer the romantic claim that images must arise out of deeply rooted feeling. Irving's choice of artistic direction results as well from his own shrewd evaluation of his talents. He undoubtedly realized his literary skills led away from the romantic fictions of Scott. European ruins may be preferred because the full store of associations they already possess will serve as subject matter rather than because the ruins evoke strong personal feeling in Irving.

Persons and characters also interest Irving for they are various, complex, and abundant subject matter for his craft. Johnny Bower is an example of the rustic character who provides links with antiquarian subject matters. Irving particularly enjoyed the family scenes at Abbotsford. He prefers the sounds of the indoors, the noise of the family circle, the singing of Sophia, Scott's daughter, to the silence and quiet of the ruins and landscape. He is very conscious of being an observer but he approves of the harmonious hierarchy of the Scott family. Typically, his images are of the past for his best representation of the family is a humorous one of the "sage grimalkin" who, presiding in the manner of feudal times, "assumes a kind of ascendancy among the quadrupeds."(27) The cat, of course, is a counterpart to Scott. These scenes of family life evoke a more positive feeling in Irving, and their wholesomeness and sociability seem to have directed Irving toward the writing of similar scenes in The Sketch Book and Bracebridge Hall.

In preferring the gaiety and convivality of everyday social life, Irving has corrected but not conquered the second trope, the displacement in time. He relishes the contact with people, for his main interest in "A Tour on the Prairies" is with his fellow travelers, not the landscape. The handling of character is the best register of Irving's romanticism. He creates picturesque types, employing a charming tone. In describing character he relies on literary models to evaluate characters, thus reinforcing stereotypes, which sometimes leads him to employ double references. He calls the real-life model for Edie Ochiltree the Nestor of beggars and refers to Scott himself as Monkbarns for his antiquarian habits.(28) Because he never seems to have been able to trust his own responses, Irving was never able to create individuality to the same degree as Scott. Irving's decision to remain in England most likely related to character as much as ruins. England provided him with a range of types, easily placed and easily understood by English and American audiences alike. America offered fewer fixed types.

While the narrator's perspective on landscape, ruins, and character reveals Irving's personal preferences in relation to Scott's, there still remains the question of his own personal commitment to writing. As Scott and the narrator discuss various writers, Scott's words again become projections of Irving's own advice to himself. Scott relates an anecdote concerning the poet James Hogg and his publisher which has a relevant application to Irving. When the poet's dabbling in metaphysics brought a rebuke from his publisher, Blackwood, Hogg confessed his own bewilderment. The moral that he should be more aware of his own limitations was advice that Irving seemed to follow, as evidenced in his decisions on artistic issues. In discussing Thomas Campbell, the poet who had furnished Irving with a letter of introduction, Irving and Scott focus on the relationship between personality and artistic success. Scott comments that Campbell's early success with the poem "Gertrude of Wyoming" had proved to be a detriment to all his further effort. In a statement pointedly underlined in the text, Scott is given attribution for saying that Campbell is afraid of the shadow that his own fame casts before him.(29) The line can only have been emphasized because Irving realizes how pertinent the judgment is to his own situation. The sense of crisis in Irving's life is underlined by a gunshot interrupting the conversation. Like the single gunshot which signals the change and reality of an outside world in "The Legend of Sleepy Hollow," the gunshot serves to remind Irving of the need to come to grips with his life. Yet the gunshot in forcing reality upon Crayon pushes him away from the idyllic life Scott is leading, thoroughly immersed in his surroundings, mingling imagination with superstition, creating his dream world. The portrait of Scott is multifaceted but the predominant image of him as writer is one divorced from the realities around him. In one of the most striking incidents in "Abbotsford," Scott is disturbed to find that a favorite dog is actually a sheepkiller, a result of his master's neglect.(30) Consequently, Scott resolves to spend more time with the dog to make his concession to the practical and commonplace. Tellingly, Abbotsford itself becomes a symbol for Crayon of Scott's immersion in a romantic dream world. The expenses involved in shaping the house to his dreams are blamed for Scott's overwork and early death.(31)

If Scott's romanticism is one in which the writer becomes thoroughly immersed in a world formed by the unity of landscape, people and those evidences of a distant past-ruins, Irving offers an eclecticism that depends on the writer's craft to create unity out of diverse elements. An excellent example of Irving's method of composition is his popular tale "Rip Van Winkle." The tale is an amalgamation of different sources and techniques successfully unified by Irving's skillful manipulation of tone. The tone, however, shows Irving's distance from Scott, for Irving treats the superstition and folklore elements with playful humor, an anti-romantic attitude different from Scott's acceptance and respectful use of them in his romantic fiction. The emphasis on composition therefore marks Irving as one who still favors eighteenth-century technique,(32) though his materials may be romantic.

The revelation in "Abbotsford" of the rejection of Scott and his romanticism may be why Irving delayed so long in writing about Scott, a writer who had been personally generous and of great professional assistance to him. Significantly, when the more distinctly authorial voice emerges in the last few pages, breaking out of the 1817 time context and overpowering the narrator's perspective, a more laudatory opinion of Scott appears. The traveler is no longer a *persona* but an analogy in inflated, empty rhetoric. Irving says he has "looked forward to a new work by Scott as a traveler on a waste looks to a green spot at a distance."(33) Yet Irving has already told us of his closeup meeting with Scott from whom he now seems to recoil. The lessons he learned were very different from the ones set by Scott and his career diverged in a different direction.

The final evaluation of the relationship between Scott and Irving can be summarized in an extrapolation of the legend, mentioned in "Abbotsford," of the plans of the Pretender to set up his standard in the back settlements of America.(34) Perhaps, Irving hoped that he could be a successor to Scott and transplant the banner to America. But as things turned out, he did not succeed Scott and, to change the terms, neither did he return to America until after a lengthy absence. The Pretender is another image of displacement that is faulty in one crucial area. Irving and Scott were men from the provinces who were successful in their ambition to win literary reputations in the metropolis.

NOTES

1. Washington Irving, "Letters to Peter Irving, September 1, and September 6, 1817, in Ralph M. Aderman, Herbert L. Kleinfield and Jenifer S. Banks, eds., *"Washington Irving, Letters, 1802-1823* (Boston: Twayne Publishers, 1978), pp. 500-503.

2. John Gibson Lockhart, *Memoirs of the Life of Sir Walter Scott, Bart.*, Vol. V (Toronto: George N. Morang and Co., 1901), p. 180.

3. Walter A. Reichart and Lillian Schlissel eds., *Washington Irving, Journals and Notebooks, Volume II, 1807-1822* (Boston: Twayne Publishers., 1981), p. 117.

4. Washington Irving, *The Crayon Miscellany* ed. (Boston: Twayne Publishers, 1979), n. xxxvi.

5. William L. Hedges, *Washington Irving, An American Study, 1802-1832* (Baltimore: The Johns Hopkins University Press, 1965), p. 265.

6. Washington Irving, "Letter to Peter Irving, August 26, 1817, in *Letters, Volume I*, pp. 490-93.

7. Washington Irving, "Abbotsford," in *Crayon Miscellany*, op. cit., p. 125: compare with *Journals and Notebooks Volume II*, p. 117.

8. "Abbotsford", p. 127.

9. "Abbotsford", p. 129.

10. "Abbotsford", p. 127.

11. "Abbotsford", p. 134.

12. "Abbotsford", p. 135.

13. "Abbotsford", p. 135.

14. *Journals and Notebooks Volume II*, p. 175.

15. *Journals and Notebooks Volume II*, p. 97.

16. "Abbotsford", p. 135.

17. Washington Irving, The Sketch Book (New York and Scarborough: Signet New American Library, 1961), p. 14.

18. Darwin Shrell, "Nationalism and Aesthetics in the North American Review 1815-1850," in Studies in American Literature, ed. Waldo McNeir and Leo B. Levy, L.S.U. Studies, Humanities Series, No. 8, (Baton Rouge: L.S.O. Press, 1960), pp. 11-12

19. Archibald Alison, Essays on the Nature and Principles of Taste, 6th ed. (London: Longman, Hurst, Rees, Brown and Green, 1825), p. 10.

20. For fuller accounts of Irving's work in relation to associationism, see Donald A. Ringe, The Pictorial Mode (Lexington: University of Kentucky Press, 1971).

21. Journals and Notebooks Volume II, pp. 203-53.

22. "Abbotsford," p. 136.

23. Washington Irving, "A Tour on the Prairies," in Crayon Miscellany, op. cit., p. 20.

24. Daniel Littlefield, Jr., discusses this topic in more detail though he does not refer to "Abbotsford." Compare with "Washington Irving and the American Indian," American Indian Quarterly 5: 1979: 2. p. 141.

25. "A Tour on the Prairies," p. 9.

26. The Sketch Book, p. 14.

27. "Abbotsford," p. 138. In a letter to Peter Irving, September 6, 1817, in Letters Volume I, p. 503, Irving refers to "the cat perched on a chair." The image may also refer to Monkbarn's cat in The Antiquary.

28. "Abbotsford", p. 151. The references to Edie Ochiltree and Monkbarns are some of the many direct and indirect references to The Antiquary in "Abbotsford."

29. "Abbotsford", p. 136.

30. "Abbotsford", p. 150.

31. "Abbotsford", p. 143.

32. Irving's use of eighteenth-century technique has been discussed by Walter A. Reichart in "In England", in A Century of Commentary on the Works of Washington Irving, ed. Andrew B. Myers (Tarrytown, N.Y.: Sleepy Hollow Restorations, 1976), p. 291.

33. "Abbotsford", p. 168.

34. "Abbotsford", p. 142.

Part III

Romance, Illusion, and Craftsmanship

8.

Pushkin's Creative Assimilation of Zhukovsky and Irving

MICHAEL R. KATZ

In a lecture entitled "On the Study of Comparative Literature," one of the great Russian formalist critics, V. M. Zhirmunsky, defends the method of critical "comparison," declaring that it "has always been-and must always remain-the basic principle of historical investigation" both in literary research and in other social sciences. He concludes:

> The comparative study of . . . common trends of literary evolution leads to a comprehension of some of the general laws of literary development and of the social preconditions, and at the same time to a deeper understanding of the historical and national peculiarity of each individual literature.(1)

Zhirmunsky was interested in the concept of world or universal literature. He cites Goethe as the "most striking example of such a 'universal' poet of the new era, who was able to absorb and assimilate to his own personality and national character the multifarious traditions of world literature."(2) In his conclusion, Zhirmunsky turns his attention to Pushkin and makes the following comparison:

> Something of the same kind can be claimed for Pushkin and for his significance in the history of Russian literature. Pushkin was not only the first Russian poet who took an active and prominent individual part in the general movements and trends of European literature of his time: the universality of his genius introduced Russian literature to the great cultural heritage of world literature. He did this by means of the creative assimilation of classical, oriental, western European and Slavonic literatures and folklores, which he re-created (much as Goethe did) in new poetical compositions which were both highly personal and national in character.(3)

It is to this notion of creative assimilation in Pushkin

that I would like to address myself. In particular I will examine one of his _Tales of Belkin_ (1830), namely "The Snowstorm," as original appropriation of Vasily Zhukovsky's literary ballad "Svetlana" (1808-12) and Washington Irving's sketch "The Spectre Bridegroom" (1819-20). This investigation aims to show the intimate and complex interconnection between romanticism in the Old World and in the New-not merely the obvious one between Russian and American literature but also some of the common themes and forms in the English and German movements as well.

Our inquiry begins with the publication by Allan Ramsay of an old Scottish folk ballad, "Sweet William's Ghost," in _The Tea-Table Miscellany_ (1724-37), a collection which almost single-handedly revived awareness of Scottish national culture. True to its genre, "Sweet William's Ghost" lets the action "unfold itself in event and speech," and tells its story "objectively with little comment or intrusion of personal bias."(4)

When, one dark night, "Willie's" ghost arrives at Margret's door, he does nothing whatever to disguise his otherworldly identity:

If I should come within thy bower,
     I am no earthly man.
And should I kiss thy rose lipp,
     Thy days will not be long.(6)

My bones are buried in a kirk yard
     Afar beyond the sea,
And it is but my sprite, Margret,
     That's speaking now to thee. (9)(5)

Nevertheless the intrepid Margret is eager to be reunited with her beloved. When Willie vanishes at the cock's crowing, leaving her "all alone," Margret cries out and instantly expires.

"Sweet William's Ghost" was republished in Sir Thomas Percy's well-known collection of songs _Reliques of Ancient English Poetry_ (1765), one of the most influential works in the history of the so-called ballad revival in European romanticism. This ballad was subsequently translated into German by Johann Gottfried Herder. When in 1773 Gottfried August Burger sat down to write "Lenore," he had access both to the English (Scottish) original and to Herder's German translation.

In contrast to the genuine folk ballad, the literary ballad was conceived as a form of _Kunstpoesie_, written with deliberate and serious artistic intent. It represented the conscious choice of an individual author to imitate the techniques of folk poetry. But those techniques were subject to transformation by the canons of preromantic taste. So-called sophisticated poets had lately become interested in the causation of events, in the physical description and psychological motivation of their characters in the localization of the setting and in rich diction and dense rhythms. They sought to express their own individuality through literary style and their personal interpretation of the narrative.

Burger was concerned with the immediate emotional impact which his ballad would have on his readers. He wanted "to turn [their] flesh ice-cold," to "make their hair stand on end," to make them "start up at night in bed."(6) He warned his friends that "Lenore" would scarify them, like the ghost in Hamlet, and he recommended that they read his ballad "at twilight in a ghostly room, with a skull on the table."(7)

Indeed, Burger's contemporaries document the spine-chilling effect which the ballad produced on them. Herder, whose translation was probably one of Burger's sources, wrote, "When I read it, it took hold of me so, that that afternoon I saw naked skulls on all the church pews. The deuce of a man, to terrify people that way! Why and for what purpose?"(8) The novelty, supernatural dread, popular speech and sound effects of "Lenore" produced a literary sensation throughout Europe. At the height of his popularity the poet announced to his friends: "With trembling knees all of you shall prostrate yourselves before me, and acknowledge me as a Genghis Khan, that is, the greatest Khan of the ballad."(9) In addition to his concern for effect, Burger's ballad also conveyed an interpretation of the narrative events and an edifying moral lesson. Lenore was guilty of losing her faith and of "quarrelling" with God (hadern-to wrangle, quarrel, squabble, dispute, grumble). The poet has her punished appropriately and then pronounces the moral of the tale: "Geduld! Geduld! Wenn's Herz auch brict!/Mit Gott im Himmel hadre nicht!"(10) Thus, while Burger may have believed that originality of style was more important than that of content, his "Lenore" must still be read as a composition with a serious theme-despair, deceit, death,(11) and their antithesis-patience, endurance, faith.

As a measure of the sensation created by Burger's "Lenore," suffice it to say that in one year, 1796, seven distinct renderings into English by five different translators were published-including Sir Walter Scott's famous version, "William and Helen."(12) Twelve years later, in 1808, there appeared in Russia the first of Vasily Zhukovsky's three versions of "Lenore," catapulting its young author into the literary limelight and creating something of the same excitement in Russia that Burger's original produced in Germany.

Zhukovsky was immediately hailed as the creator of a new genre; he went on to write forty literary ballads which established the model for future Russian writers. The memoirist, F. F. Vigel, captured the novelty of this form and explained its significance:

> Nourished on the classics and on French literature . . . we saw something monstrous in his choices. Corpses, visions, demons, murders by moonlight . . . instead of Hero awaiting his drowning Leander, he presented us a madly passionate Lenore with her galloping corpse of a lover! His miraculous talent was needed to force us not only to read the ballads without repugnance, but also, finally, to fall in love

> with them. I do not know if he spoiled our taste; but at least he created new sensations, new enjoyment for us. That was the beginning of our romanticism.(13)

While "Lyudmila" (1808), Zhukovsky's first literary ballad, was a self-styled "imitation" of Burger's "Lenore," the differences are far greater than the superficial similarity in the subject. Zhukovsky's generalization of time and place, his sentimentalization of the heroine and her melancholy lover, his use of literary syntax and diction in place of colloquial language-all reveal his extensive transformation of the German source. Nevertheless, the strong emotional impact of "Lyudmila" and the author's concluding moral lesson produced a similarly strong effect on Russian readers. The literary ballad became the dominant genre of the decade with Zhukovsky as its undisputed master.

It is not, however, "Lyudmila," which interests us today; rather it is Zhukovsky's second version of Burger's "Lenore" entitled "Svetlana" (1808-12). The characters in this ballad only vaguely resemble those in "Lyudmila." Svetlana is a silent, melancholy, sentimental heroine whose acceptance of fate is a far cry from Lenore's Hader and even Lyudmila's ropot. Her lover is a pale, gloomy sentimental hero who speaks elegant romantic Russian, even when addressing his horse. However, just as Svetlana's terror reaches an emotional climax and the previously unsuspecting heroine realizes that her lover is really a corpse, she suddenly awakens. All the mystery disappears-darkness and silence are replaced by light and sound. The very next morning Svetlana's genuine flesh-and-blood lover returns and Zhukovsky describes in detail the amorous delights which await the much-relieved heroine.

In a pithy epilogue Zhukovsky places the whole subject into a commonsensical perspective: the imaginary adventure was indeed frightening (as good ballads are), but it was only her bad dream, a creation of his poetic fantasy. The nightmare has not come true; the happy ending has shown it to be false. Zhukovsky concludes with a deeply antifolkloric moral, consistent both with his own sentimental poetics and his philosophical optimism: neither fortune-telling nor dreams reveal truth. The only appropriate response to the vicissitudes of life is "belief in providence."

It has been suggested that in "Svetlana" Zhukovsky was applying the principles of parody to the poetics of the Gothic ballad.(14) It is this point which I would like to emphasize and amplify. Within the dream framework Zhukovsky manages to create the loneliness, anticipation, fear, and mystery of the ballad world; then he strips away the illusion and turns the conventions upside down. He mocks and parodies that concern for immediate sensory effect which was the hallmark of his own "Lyudmila," of Burger's "Lenore," and the ballad genre in general.

It is this idea of parody that will serve as our bridge to romanticism in the New World. In a recent study of American romance, Michael Bell argues that Washington

Irving was the single most important practitioner of gothic fiction during the 1820s'; that his lack of recognition represents a serious critical oversight; and that for later American writers, including Poe, Hawthorne, and Melville, Irving was the model to be approached and ultimately surpassed.(15)

What concerns us in this context is not Irving's gothic fiction per se, but one tale from The Sketch Book (1819-20), namely, "The Spectre Bridegroom." In it, the heroine's father, Baron Von Landshort, is initially described as a man "much given to the marvellous," a "firm believer in all those supernatural tales with which every mountain and valley in Germany abounds." When the guests are all assembled at his daughter's wedding feast (where the young Starkenfaust is awkwardly impersonating the slain bridegroom), the Baron relates all sorts of "wild tales and supernatural legends":

> and [he] . . . nearly frightened some of the ladies into hysterics with the history of the goblin horseman that carried away the fair Leonora; a dreadful story, which has since been put into excellent verse, and is read and believed by all the world.(16)

The Baron is a "true believer" and his audience shares his credulity. The enterprising hero capitalizes on their blind faith and carries off the heroine, later to return, fall at the Baron's feet, embrace his knees, explain the ruse, and beg his pardon. As Irving notes with astounding simplicity: "The mystery was soon cleared up."(17) The spectre bridegroom was not a goblin at all; the Baron's daughter was safely returned (and respectably married); he pardons the young couple on the spot; everyone lives happily ever after.

Critics have characterized Irving's treatment of the Gothic theme in this tale as "pleasant ridicule of Burger's ballad," a "gentle burlesquing of the Lenore-motif," or an example of the author's "sportive Gothic."(18) I would argue that what Irving does in "The Spectre Bridegroom" is parallel to what Zhukovsky does in "Svetlana." Irving parodies the poetics of gothic fiction, frustrates his readers' expectations, and turns the literary conventions upside down. Whereas Zhukovsky criticizes trust in fortune-telling and in dreams, and explictly advocates belief in providence, Irving criticizes faith in supernatural tales and implicitly advocates the values of common sense and perhaps also of individual initiative. The most significant difference between Zhukovsky's ballad and Irving's tale lies in the fact that the reversal in "Svetlana" occurs at a definite moment: the heroine's awakening is followed by a return to reality and by an epilogue which presents the author's interpretation of the meaning of the dream. In "The Spectre Bridegroom" the reversal is continuous from the epigraph on, including the initial footnotes explaining allusions and names, the setting in a "wild and romantic tract of Upper Germany," and so on. As Michael Bell expresses it, Irving indulges in romance in full awareness of its duplicity:

> "What distinguishes his best gothic tales is the self-consciousness with which they simultaneously exploit and burlesque the basis of their own narrative appeal."(19)

While Zhukovsky engages in the same two activities sequentially (first mystery, then parody), Irving does both simultaneously (mystery and parody). It is the second, more complex relationship to literary conventions and attitudes that attracted Pushkin's attention and shifts the focus of our inquiry back to the Old World for its final stage. American readers were unacquainted with Russian romantic literature, Russian readers were very familiar with the works of the American romantics. During the 1820s' the tales of Washington Irving and James Fenimore Cooper became the rage in Moscow and Petersburg. The writer and critic Nikolai Polevoi begins the introduction to his story based on the life of Russian peasants with the invocation: "Would that I had the pen of Washington Irving . . . "(20) "The Spectre Bridegroom" circulated in French translations as early as 1822; the first Russian translation appeared three years later in _Son of the Fatherland_.

Pushkin's name has long been connected with Washington Irving's.(21) Pushkin refers to _The Sketch Book_ in a fascinating article on John Tanner published in _The Contemporary_ in 1836. Critics such as the great comparatist M. P. Alekseev and writers including the talented Anna Akhmatova have previously examined links between the two authors.(22) A provocative hypothesis was advanced by the Soviet scholar N. Ya. Berkovsky (1962): he interprets Pushkin's story "The Snowstorm" as an ironic version of the subject of "The Spectre Bridegroom" which "polemicizes" with Irving.(23) In a recent article on the poetics of parody in _The Tales of Belkin_, David Bethea and Sergei Davydov further develop Berkovsky's suggestion; they also provided the impetus for this presentation.(24)

Pushkin begins "The Snowstorm" with an epigraph from Zhukovsky's ballad "Svetlana" (just as Irving had made explicit his debt to Burger in "The Spectre Bridegroom"). Pushkin's heroine is as pale and delicate as Zhukovsky's, but she is, in addition, _literate_. Marya Gavrilovna was "raised on French novels, and consequently, she was in love." The object of her affections is a poor army ensign; hence, her parents forbid her even to think about a match. Unlike the timid Svetlana, however, Marya is an enterprising girl. She enters into a secret correspondence with her beloved Vladimir and begins to meet him secretly, swearing vows of eternal love, complaining about her fate, and devising schemes for escape. He proposes that they elope, marry secretly, and return to throw themselves at her parents' feet and beg their forgiveness. The plan pleases Marya's "romantic imagination"; she writes two splendid farewell letters and retires early on the fateful eve. After a restless night filled with extraordinary dreams, she proceeds to the arranged rendez vous. However, as a result of a terrible snowstorm, Vladimir loses his way; when he arrives at the church, he is too late. There, we discover later, he learns the awful truth: Marya has been married off to someone else, a passing (and dashing) young Hussar.

The heroine slinks home, falls ill, and mutters Vladimir's name in her delirium. Her parents confer and resolve to accept the lad as their daughter's chosen suitor. But, when Vladimir is informed of their generous decision, he writes a mad letter, departs, and is subsequently slain in a battle. Time passes, Marya's father dies and the war ends. Suitors begin to appear. One stands out from all the rest: Burmin, a lieutenant in the Hussars, sports both a war medal and an "interesting pallor." When he arrives to declare his honorable intentions, Marya awaits him by the pond, beneath a willow, dressed all in white, book in hand, looking like "a genuine heroine of a novel." He confesses his love, quoting St. Preux from Rousseau's _Julie, ou La Nouvelle Heloise_ (perhaps the same book is in Marya's hand, for she was "raised on French novels"). Then Burmin confesses his terrible secret: he is already married! He relates the strange tale of his midnight ride past a church during a snowstorm; how he was hurried in; how he _allowed_ the priest to begin the ceremony. He attributes the extraordinary adventure to his own "incomprehensible, unforgivable frivolity (thoughtlessness)." She quickly recognizes her long-lost spouse, he throws himself at her feet and begs forgiveness.

Pushkin is clearly engaged in a very witty and sophisticated form of parody, I would argue "double parody," inasmuch as he is parodying two works which are in and of themselves already parodies of Burger's "Lenore"-Zhukovsky's "Svetlana" and Irving's "The Spectre Bridegroom."

Pushkin's epigraph from Zhukovsky is the first significant indication of that; in addition, the characters, setting, and events of "The Snowstorm" closely parallel those of a conventional literary ballad: the poor hero and pale heroine come from different social classes, parents are the primary obstacle to young love, an elopement is planned and executed at midnight, a dramatic ride is undertaken through a snowy landscape, and the heroine has terrifying, "prophetic" dreams. But just like Svetlana's nightmare, Marya's dream is not fulfilled. Svetlana's real-life lover returns and she will likely settle into a conventional marriage. Pushkin parodies the romantic disguise/recognition motif characteristic of Zhukovsky's later ballads, and, by manipulating events in the natural world, he reunites the heroine with her stranger-lover by means of a most unlikely coincidence. Pushkin's tale does have a "happy ending," but it is not the one that we were expecting. The heroine fails to recover her own true love; instead, she is provided with one who turns out to be even better-that is of higher rank, more attractive exterior, and more decorous behavior. Pushkin has engineered a brilliant ironic reversal of Zhukovsky's typical ballad conclusion.

If we turn to Irving's tale, we can see that it is there Pushkin found his _theme_, the purpose of his "double parody." The old Baron, it will be recalled, was characterized as a "firm believer" in supernatural tales; his audience was nothing if not gullible; the heroine's aunt was entranced by ghost stories and she assured one and all that her niece had been carried off by a goblin. But Irving parodies that credulity and "clears up" the mystery in a twinkle of his eye. It seems that Irving's shrewd heroine was never taken in by all those tales. When she returns with her cavalier, she has been provided with a very acceptable substitute for her affections: the hero is splendidly attired, noble in appearance, possessing the glow of youth and joy. He is clearly the equal of his unfortunate friend.

Pushkin's heroine, on the other hand, steeped in sentimental novels, is young and foolish enough to believe what she reads. She commits the most grievous Pushkinian blunder: she expects life to imitate art. Pushkin says here (and elsewhere) that it does not and that she should not expect it to. In fact, life provides Marya with a much better suitor than the romantic one whom she lost. As a result she fares considerably better than either Lenore (who gets a corpse), Svetlana (who gets her own lover back), or the Baron's daughter (who gets an equivalent).

I have described Zhukovsky's satire of Burger as sequential: first mystery, then parody; Irving's as simultaneous: both mystery and parody. Pushkin has gone one step further; he eliminates the mystery altogether. "The Snowstorm" is pure parody from epigraph to ironic reversal in the conclusion.

Burger's Gothic was justifiably perceived as genuinely terrifying; Zhukovsky's as temporarily frightening, followed by joyful relief; Irving's as slightly disconcerting and subsequently amusing; Pushkin's, however, is nonexistent. The elaborate chain of influence analyzed here, from "Sweet William's Ghost" to "Lenore," from "Lenore" to "Svetlana" and "The Spectre Bridegroom," and from those to "The Snowstorm," can thus be viewed as an indication of the rise and fall of the Gothic impulse in European and American romanticism. Pushkin's tale provides further evidence for Zhirmunsky's claim that like Goethe, its author is a striking example of a "universal" poet who absorbed and assimilated the multifarious traditions of world literature.

NOTES

1. V. M. Zhirmunsky, "On the Study of Comparative Literature," Oxford Slavonic Papers XIII (1967): p 1.

2. "On The Study of Comparative Literature", p. 11.

3. "On The Study of Comparative Literature", p. 12.

4. G. H. Gerould, The Ballad of Tradition (Oxford University Press: 1932), p. 11.

5. The Tea-Table Miscellany: A Collection of Choice Songs Scots and English, ed. Allan Ramsay (Glasgow, J. Crum Publishers: 1871), II, ps. 117-20.

6. Wm. A. Little, Gottfried August Burger (New York: Twayne Publishers: 1974), p. 105.

7. Roy Pascal, The German Sturm and Drang (Manchester: University Press 1953), p. 271.

8. Gottfried August Burger, Little, p. 106.
9. Briefe von und an G. A. Burger, ed. A. Strodtmann Gebruder Paetel (Berlin: 1874), p. 132.
10. The Penguin Book of German Verse, ed. Leonard Forster (London: Penquin Books, 1967), p. 190.
11. See Gottfried August Burger, p. 104.
12. Oliver Farrar Emerson, The Earliest English Translations of Burger's "Lenore": A Study in English and German Romanticism (Cleveland, Ohio: Case Western Reserve University Press, 1915), p. 10.
13. F. F. Vigel, Zapiski (Moscow: Russkhii Arkiv, 1891-93), III: p. 137.
14. V. A. Zhukovsky, Stikhotvoreniya, ed. by Ts. S. Vol'pe (Leningrad: Sovetskii Pisatel, 1936), I: p. xvii.
15. Michael Davitt Bell, The Development of American Romance: The Sacrifice of Relation (Chicago, The University of Chicago Press: 1980), pp. 64, 78.
16. Washington Irving, Selected Writings, ed. Saxe Commins (New York: Modern Library, 1945), p. 60.
17. Selected Writings, p. 64.
18. Henry A. Pochman, "Irving's German Sources in The Sketch Book," Studies in Philology 27 (1930): 505; and The Development of American Romance, p. 78.
19. The Development of American Romance, p. 82.
20. A. N. Nikolyukin, "K tipologii romanticheskoi povesti," in K istorii russkogo romantizma, ed. Yu. V. Mann (Moscow: Nauka, 1973), pp. 259-60.
21. During Pushkin's lifetime, Polevoi, among others, noted the influence of Irving's works on The Tales of Belkin. See A. N. Nikolyukin, Literaturnye svyazi Rossii i S. Sh. A. (Moscow: Nauka, 1981), pp. 180-255.
22. Alekseev compared Pushkin's "History of the Town of Goryuhino" (1830) with Irving's A History of New York (1809) in Pushkin Stati i materialy, Vyp. II, Odessa, 1926, pp. 70-87. Akhmatova located the source of Pushkin's "Tale of the Golden Cockerel" (1834) in Irving's "The Legend of the Arabian Astrologer" in his collection The Alhambra (1832) in Zvezda 1 (1933): ps. 161-76.
23. N. Ya. Berkovsky, "O Povestyakh Belkina," Stat'i o literature (Leningrad: Khudozhestvennaya Literatura, 1962), pp. 289-92.
24. David M. Bethea and Sergei Davydov, "Pushkin's Saturnine Cupid: The Poetics of Parody in The Tales of Belkin," PMLA 96 (1981): ps. 8-21.

9.

Irving, Chateaubriand, and the Historical Romance of Granada

JOHN FREY

The vogue for travel to unknown places in the eighteenth century signaled a shift in Western mentality which further manifested itself in the ramifications of the exotic voyage or "tour" in the romantic literature of the early nineteenth century.

European and American romantics were "on the move," and there was an urge to make contact with other societies and cultures. The British, especially Byron, Shelley, and Keats, concentrated on Italy, as did Stendhal. Chateaubriand went to America (1791), landing at Baltimore with a group of Sulpician missionaries. Alexis de Tocqueville spent nine months in the United States (1831-32). And American romantics, notably Irving and Longfellow, made the romantic pilgrimage to Europe.

Travel excited the romantic imagination and was a source for the literary development of historicism, nationalism, and of the taste for local color and the picturesque. Indeed, Madame de Stael described romanticism as a kind of cosmopolitanism in literature, and the romantic travelers made it apparent that they were usually ready to assimilate other cultures or to fuse them with their own.(1)

Spain and the Middle East played a special role in the history of romanticism, especially for the French: there is, for example, Mérimée's _Carmen_; Hugo's theatre, _Hernani_, _Ruy Blas_, his poetry, _Les Orientales_; the oriental motifs in the paintings of Delacroix; and, finally, the travels of Flaubert in quest of the Oriental woman. For the romantic generation, the Orient begins at the Pyrenees mountains. Romantic fixation on the East is referred to as orientalism, the term Edward Said employs to describe the Anglo-French-American experience of the Arabs and Islam.(2)

This study will consider Spanish or oriental materials in the writings of Irving and Chateaubriand which relate to their travels in the Iberian peninsula. Spanish-Moslem motifs as found in _The Chronicle of the Conquest of Granada_ (1829) and in _The Alhambra_ (1832) will be compared with similar motifs in _The Adventures of the Last Abencerraje_ of Chateaubriand, probably written between 1807 and 1809, but not published until 1826.(3) Prominent in comparative romanticism is a methodological controlling element whose central theme in both writers is the conflict between Christian and Islamic civilization, culminating historically in the expulsion of the Moors from Granada in 1492. This subject captivated both writers. Analyzing and comparing their work may lead to the clarification of a difficult problem in the history of romanticism, namely that of viewing it as a general Western phenomenon transcending national borders.

Irving and Chateaubriand had not only literary but also political interests in Spain. Irving made three trips to Europe, first in 1804-6, then a long residency from 1815 to 1832. In 1824 he began to study the Spanish language and Spanish history. He was in Spain from February 1826 until September 1829. It was then that he deepened his knowledge of Spanish society, history, and legend through travel, conversation, collecting oral histories, and reading in archives and libraries. Especially noteworthy is the trip from Seville to Granada in the company of Prince Dolgorouki who was attached to the Russian embassy. With extraordinary good luck began the romantic idyll of a long, warm, and intimate residency in the Alhambra itself. Irving returned to America in 1832, but was again in Spain as American minister from 1842 to 1846. These three sojourns put Irving in contact with European romanticism with a special emphasis on Spain. Charles Dudley Warner, writing in 1884, insisted that Spain is the most fruitful period of Irving's literary career, and wonders what Irving's reputation would have been without this dimension.(4)

Chateaubriand spent only five weeks in Spain and this forms the conclusion of his trip to the Middle East which he records in his _Itinerary from Paris to Jerusalem_ (1811). Landing in Algenciras at the end of March 1807, he moved rapidly across Spain, entering France at Bayonne on May 3. He spent no more than two days in Granada, but the _Itinerary_ records an affirmative romantic reaction to the Alhambra and a sharing of Irving's empathy for the Moorish lament over its loss.(5)

The trip through Spain also had a sentimental dimension in the person of Nathalie de Noailles,(6) the result being a crossing of the romance of Granada with the personal romance of Chateaubriand for this woman, which adds a biographical layer to his Moorish tale of the _The Adventures of the Last Abencerraje_.

Irving represented American political and diplomatic interests in Spain in the 1840s'. Chateaubriand made his presence similarly felt there, but in the 1820s', which places the together on the political plane, albeit in an antipathetic manner. Mary Weatherspoon Bowden in her analysis of the _Conquest_ aptly notes that Irving was aware of the similarity between the events of the late fifteenth century and what was happening in Spain during the 1820s'.(7) Thus, Irving's text could be seen as an ironic and satirical comment on the crushing of the liberal revolution in Spain by the Holy Alliance at the Conference of Verona in 1822. The role of the conservative Chateaubriand in the Bourbon Restoration is well known.(8) He was behind the French incursion at Cadiz, which fell on October 1, 1823, thus assuring the absolutism of Feridnand VII. Chateaubriand's adroit manipulations at the Congress of Verona insured this conservative victory. Two romantics therefore meet in past and present history, but with different perspectives.

The literary question, however, is primary. Therefore, we should ask what is the common denominator in Irving's and Chateaubriand's Spanish materials? The answer is found in that very difficult word, "romance," with all the etymological and semantic implications associated with its rise in describing the new European literature.

Irving's romanticism is attracted to what he called the romance of history, an aesthetic appreciation of what truly took place, and consequently it is not in need of whimsical invention and never is a product of author fantasy or wish-fulfillment. Romance thus relates to heroic deeds, courage on the battlefield, fulfilling Madame de Stael's definition of romanticism as a return to the literature of our ancestors, meaning chivalrous adventure. It is in this sense that the word "romantic" is repeatedly used: Hernan Perez del Pulgar had already won fame "by his romantic valor and daring enterprise" (Conquest, P. 308); the Abencerrajes through their "splendid chivalry" attained their "historical and romantic celebrity" (The Alhambra, p. 136); Irving states that the history of the Reconquest has excited his mind by the "romantic achievements of this war" (Conquest, note to the revised ed., p. xv). The modern sense of amorous romance is not a factor in the Conquest and where present in The Alhambra is mitigated, tempered, even neutralized by rival literary conventions. The Conquest(9) Irving's romance, is drawn from history; his Conquest is an example of romanticism as historicism.

By contrast, an opposing dimension controls the work of Chateaubriand. Islam and Christianity and the Granada wars form the contrastive cultural and political background for a love affair doomed to failure. The elements of romantic languor, ennui, and "volupte" found in the Abencerraje are part of a continuing development in French romanticism (Hugo, Delacroix, Gautier) which culminate in many of the poems of Baudelaire's The Flowers of Evil. This same dimension is present in Irving's work, but it is pushed to the background; it is tempered, submerged, as if to be avoided. Its presence, however, leads to a tentative conclusion, namely that both writers found hints of this psychology of love in the documents studied BUT each chose to treat it differently; Chateaubriand to emphasize the passive, amorous nature of romanticism, Irving to affirm a romanticism of action, the call to high deeds and arms. Both attitudes are a modern reflection of a true cultural-literary debate that took place in twelfth-century France, especially in the poem-novels of Chretien de Troyes: the reasons for fighting, in tournaments and in wars. Is such fighting for God, for country, or for women?

A description of Irving's two texts, The Conquest and Alhambra, in their general contours invites comparison with Chateaubriand. In spite of his romance of history,

Irving was not historian, but creative writer, and the texts are his in structure, style, and attitude.

Built-in documentation in the form of footnoting and textual reference is a specific technique of Irving. This is part of romanticism's "realism," appealing to the reader to believe in the authenticity of the recitation. Furthermore, the Conquest itself further insists upon turning fiction into history by adapting as its basic structure the time-bound chronicle; the day by day, month by month, year by year narrating of the closing-in on Granada-battles, advances, retreats, stratagems, forays, marauding-and the gradual whittling away of the last Moorish citadel. The imitation of history includes a consideration of the lineages of the noble combatants and the listing of noble families and relationships in the manner of the medieval epic and of medieval historical chronicles.

Aesthetically speaking, this means that Irving has opted for a narrative structure almost devoid of descriptive materials. In fact, descriptive art in this writer seems to be a subcategory of narrational art with the consequence that scenes are not created, people and things are not seen; they are simply listed in a narrative chronicle.(10)

Likewise, passages in The Alhambra suggest that Irving is aware of the psychological and visual impact of the Moorish palace and its history but believes that these are private pleasures to be reported but not to be shared with the reader through any descriptive effort.(11) Atmospheres or moods are reported almost as if they are events. Irving, like Stendhal, avoids metaphor or simile except when it enhances comic or satirical effect.

Yet, the narration can rise to dramatic proportions as Irving turns town and province into collective protagonists, not unlike a Greek Chorus, commenting and dependent upon the struggle between Moor and Christian.(12)

The Conquest and The Alhambra are typical romantic pieces by their makeup of local color, anecdote, and diverse facts, all of which satisfied the homebound romantic reader's task for customs, costumes, historical events, and happenings. This may be the singular charm of The Alhambra which psychologically joins a distant Moorish Granada with nineteenth-century Spaniards and their American romantic guest in the Alhambra. Irving makes astute Yankee Protestant comments on Catholic and Moorish cultures, both of which had to appear exotic by comparison with New York.

But there are aspects of Irving's work which seem not at all romantic, which appear as lingering vestiges of eighteenth-century stances. Irving has humor and wit and his writing is both ironic and satirical. These qualities decline in France with the advent of Rousseau and are entirely missing from the serious and at times pompous world of Chateaubriand. In spite of an apparent structure of chivalric narration, the impression is received that Irving views the Reconquest with a cynical eye. He is suspicious of motives, particularly the religious which may mask the geopolitical. In the personage of Fray

Antonio Agapida, whose chronicles we are supposedly reading, Irving has created a hilarious satire of Catholic Spain. Most events of the Reconquest are commented on by this priest and add a positive Voltairian sting to the chronicle. Agapida is a sympathetic bigot, a contentious friar recalling the spirit of Archbishop Turpin of the _Song of Roland_ or Rabelais' Fr ere Jean des Entommeures.

Chateaubriand, like Irving, relies upon documentation, but indiscriminately, thus confusing history and legend.(13) The critical commentary of Professor Letessier in the Garnier edition of the _Abencerraje_ indicates that Chateaubriand is careless about history and is more interested in legendary love intrigues. Historical distortion is joined to romantic misinterpretation of Islamic religious practices, Granada replacing Mecca as the geographical point of Islamic prayer.(14)

Irving's geography is dry but precise. Chateaubri-)and's editors make it clear that he does not know north from south, east from west, or is just indifferent to geography. Poetry and harmony take precedent; the romantic landscape of the mind rearranges the Spanish atlas.(15)

Chateaubriand's interior or poetic landscape is vitalized by musings amidst the ruins of a great civilization of the past. Here we can perceive the differences in two types of romantic imaginations. Nowhere in Irving's _Alhambra_ do I get the impression of the slum it must have been at the beginning of the nineteenth century, before the restoration. In Irving, it has the humble qualities found in the paintings of Greuze, a _genre pittoresque_ quality which enhances the idyll of his residency there, the desire for the simple life, nostalgia for plain living, and honesty which even Marie Antoinette tried to fabricate behind Versailles. Irving's mind seems not to see the slum or the ruins. His present life is charmed; his artist's eye affirms the "reality" of the historical past; his mind enthusiastically reconstructs for himself the palace as it was over 300 years before; he destroys the ruins. Chateaubriand recounts the impossible love between the last of the Abencerrajes and the descendant of the Cid. The infrequent interviews of the lovers in Granada must be seen as love among the ruins.

What is past is irretrievable, but living amidst its vestiges gives poignancy and pathos to that which has been lost. Thus Chateaubriand joins the Alhambra to his romantic tale of love denied. Aben-Hamet and Blanca stroll across the Alhambra mingling the drama of their love with the drama of sixteenth-century Moslem and Christian history. The past affects the present in a psychological manner.(16) Chateaubriand deftly joins together his motifs of love, religion, and battle: "Something voluptuous, religious, and martial seemed to breathe in this magical edifice; a kind of cloister of love, mysterious retreat where the Moorish kings tasted every pleasure or forgot all of life's duties" (_Abencerraje_, pp. 284-85).(17)

Cornellian virtues of duty, glory, and renunciation are noted throughout Irving's _Conquest_; they form the dramatic conclusion of Chateaubriand's _Abencerraje_. It is a renunciation, however, which only augments passion.

Anguish-laden hope inspires Dona Blanca to a yearly voyage to Malaga to await the Moor's return:

> Each year Blanca would go to wander on the mountains of Malaga, at that moment of the year when her lover customarily returned from Africa; she would sit on the rocks, look at the sea, the distant ships, and then return to Granada: she would spend the rest of her days among the ruins of the Alhambra. (Abencerraje, p. 329)(18)

Chateaubriand seems to be building a romantic myth from Moorish and Spanish legend. This is achieved through the presentation of personages in high dramatic pose, in rich and colorful romantic settings. This partly explains a final point, the primacy of description over narration in the work of the French writer. Chateaubriand seeks out mood pieces, and indeed the charged atmospheres of the Alhambra breathe the poetry of romanticism, a garden of exotic tales of love denied. Chateaubriand had done the same thing for America, with his exotic contrastive but false description of the two banks of the Mississippi River in the preface to Atala (1801).(19) Thus Irving differs from Chateaubriand by the absence of developed descriptive materials in his texts.(20)

Historical and thematic analogies in both writers would embrace the following: (1) utilization of the legends of Boabdil's departure from Granada, especially the celebrated sigh of lament of the Moor; (2) the profile of Boabdil's personality; and (3) the substructure in both writers of chivalric or courtly mores.

Boabdil's departure is essentially the same with both writers:

> The heart of Boabdil, softened by misfortunes and overcharged with grief, could no longer contain itself: "Allah Achbar! God is great!" said he; but the words of resignation died upon his lips and he burst into tears. His mother, the intrepid Ayxa, was indignant at his weakness: "You do well," said she, "to weep like a woman, for what you failed to defend like a man!" (Conquest, pp. 525-26)

> From this elevated site one could see the sea on which the unfortunate monarque would embark for Africa; one could also see Granada, the Vega and the Genil, on the banks of which were raised the tents of Ferdinand and Isabella. At the sight of this beautiful country and the cypresses which mark yet here and there the tombs of the musulmans, Boabdil was taken by tears. The sultana Ayxa, his mother, who was joining him in exile with those grandees who once graced his court, said to him: "Cry now like a woman for a kingdom which you never learned to defend like a man" (Abencerraje, p. 254)(21)

Boabdil's personality has a common likeness in the texts of both writers, if we keep in mind that it is more obvious, apparent in Chateaubriand than in Irving. We piece together in Irving's texts those characteristics which are emphasized in Chateaubriand, passivity, taste for luxury, idleness, sensuality, lack of comprehension of politics.(22)

Finally, both writers make elaborate display of chivalric and courtly procedures which involve ideas of codes of behavior (honor, glory, fidelity, bravery, rivalry, revenge) with personal and collective significance. There is also in Irving the dimension of Spanish sensitivity on questions of etiquette and good manners,(23) while Chateaubriand combines the troubador with the chivalric.(24) Irving's text is more complicated. A traditional chivalric structure has been embroidered on a new and enlarged courtly tradition which transforms Isabella the Catholic into the damsel in whose name all of Spain will go into combat and in which Ferdinand is transformed into the super-symbolic knight, the future _caballero cristiano_. In this regard, Irving understands that Ferdinand was more a clever renaissance prince than medieval courtly knight.(25)

The fundamental procedure with both writers has been to create antithetical systems, a typical romantic technique, through the opposition of Islamic and Christian culture in Spain at the end of the Middle Ages. Irving's _Conquest_ puts two constructions, like two knights, in defiant proximity; the new city of the Holy Faith (Santa Fe) constructed with amazing technology by the Catholic monarchs outside the walls of Granada (_Conquest_, ch. XCV, "Building of Santa Fe"). The antithesis in Chateaubriand confronts a Christian woman, descendant of the Cid, Dona Blanca, whose family name had been changed to Santa Fe because of its role in the Reconquest, with the last Abencerraje, the proud rulers of Granada. But this was a romantic confrontation of love. In Irving it is a contest of cities, the romance of history; in Chateaubriand, it is a contest of souls. The romantic pathos evident in the works of both authors comes down to the question of unnecessary alienation. Granada and Santa Fe should have been able to coexist; Aben-Hamet and Dona Blanca should have been allowed an interfaith marriage. But then, tragedy, classic or romantic, has never been built from tolerance, reason, or accommodation.

I have tried to show that despite differences of nationality and religion, the Protestant American and the French Catholic, while emphasizing different romantic procedures(26)-Irving, the role of adventure; Chateaubriand, the role of romance have, all the same, many common romantic traits. The Granada materials have provided a unique yardstick for measuring romanticism from the Old and the New Worlds.

In the instance of these writers, we see romanticism as mannered in the sense that the conventions of these stories are obviously borrowed from previous literary and cultural traditions and reworked into a new recipe.

NOTES

1. Stendhal loved Italy so much that he prepared his own epitaph to say "Enrico Beyle Milanese." Prosper Mérimée was equally enthused with Spain, Corisca, England, and even the United States. Between 1826 and 1868 Mérimée made eighteen trips to England.

2. Edward W. Said, Orientalism (New York, Panetheon Books: 1979), p. 2.

3. The following editions of Irving and Chateaubriand have been used: Washington Irving, A Chronicle of the Conquest of Granada (New York: G. P. Putnam and Co., 1856); Washington Irving, The Works of Washington Irving, vol. XV, The Alhambra (New York: G. P. Putnam and Co. 1855); Francois-René de Chateaubriand, Atala, René, Les Aventures du Dernier Abencerraje (Paris: Editions Garnier Frerés, 1958). All citations from these three works will refer to these editions and page numbers will be cited with short title (Conquest; Alhambra; Abencerraje) in the body of the text. The translations of Chateaubriand are mine and the French text will be found in the foot- +notes. Italics, unless otherwise indicated will be mine.

4. Charles Dudley Warner, Washington Irving (Boston: Houghton Mifflin, 1884, reprints, New York: Chelsea House Publishers, 1980), p. 141.

5. "The Alhambra I deemed worthy of being seen, even after the temples of Greece. The Granada valley is delicious and looks very much like that of Sparta: it is understandable that the Moors would miss such a country." "L'Alhambra me paru digne d'être regardé, même après les temples de la Grèce. La Vallée de Grenade est dèlicieuse, et ressemble beaucoup à celle de Sparte: on conçoit que les Maures regrettent un pareil pays." Fransois-René de Chateaubriand, Itinéraire de Paris à Jerusalem, in Oeuvres romanesques et voyages (Paris: Gallimard, 1969), II: 1212. The Itinerary is a fine example of the literary historicism of the romantics. Chateaubriand's trip across Spain is recorded almost exclusively in terms of literary and historical reference, the Mancha of Don Quijote, the meaning of Old Castille at the Escorial, the Romans at the aqueduct in Segovia, the Cid at Burgos.

6. The amorous motif of Abencerraje has been well documented by an older school of Positivist criticism. Marcel Duchemin's 1938 study demonstrated that the Abencerraje, while purporting to relate the love of an early sixteenth-century Moor for a Christian maiden, was veiling the Spanish fugue of Chateaubriand with Nathalie de Noailles. This is but another example of a typical romantic procedure of imposing personal contemporary psychologies on distant historical personages. Duchemin has carefully solved the mystery, and, for those interested in literary detective work, his pages devoted to the Abencerraje and the chapter entitled "Un Roman d'amour en 1807. Chateaubriand a Grenade," pp. 249-333, show the relationship of "romance" to "history." Marcel Duchemin, Chateaubriand, Essais de critique et d'histoire litteraire (Paris: Librarie Philosophique J. Vrin, 1938).

7. Mary Weatherspoon Bowden, Washington Irving

(Boston: Twayne Publishers, 1981), pp. 123-24.

8. It is fully discussed in Andre Maurois, _René ou la vie de Chateaubriand_ (Paris: Grasset, 1938), Ch. VIII, "Ascension, Vertige et Chute," pp. 315-62.

9. Irving suggests in the introduction to the _Conquest_ that the true nature of the Granada war had never been fully studied, the true history having been distorted through Florian's romance of Gonsalvo of Cordova and through the legend by Ginez Perez de la Hita, _The Civil Wars of Granada_: It had been woven over with love tales and scenes of sentimental gallantry totally opposite to its real character . . . the genuine nature of the war placed it far above the need of any amatory embellishments. It possessed sufficient interest in the striking contrast presented by the combatants, of Oriental and European creeds, costumes, and manners; and in the hardy and harebrained enterprizes, the romantic adventures, the picturesque forays through mountain regions; the daring assaults and surprisals of cliff-built castles and cragged fortresses, which succeeded each other with a variety and brilliancy beyond the scope of mere invention. (_Conquest_, p. xvi) Irving clearly is separating legend and myth from history. This distinction is sharply made in his discussion of Boabdil in _The Alhambra_. By contrast, the justification for Chateaubriand's tale of doomed love between Moor and Christian maiden is built upon a story of Boabdil's massacre of the Abencerrajes, his rage provoked by the infidelity of his queen. Irving, empathetic to Boabdil, affirms that all this is untrue, ficton, legend (_Alhambra_, pp. 128-54). Thus he will not include this false history in the _Conquest_. Irving's _Conquest_, when compared to standard histories of Spain, verifies that his narrative does not deviate from history in factual detail or in general psychological and motivational portrait. See Rhea Marsh Smith, _Spain, a Modern history_ (Ann Arbor: University of Michigan Press, 1965), pp. 106-8, and Harold Livermore, _A History of Spain_ (New York: Grove Press, 1958), pp. 192- 94.

10. He was a chronicler as can be seen in the following "relation": "We have yet another _act_ to _relate_ of this good Count de Tendilla, who was in truth a mirror of knightly virtue" (_Conquest_, p. 486). Acts here are used in the epic sense of what the French called "gestes," Description is minimized in a number of ways, by omission, abbreviation, or ellipsis. A foray against the Moors is related: "Precautions had been taken to furnish the army with _all things needful_ for its perilous inroad. . . . Isabella . . . provided six spacious tents furnished with beds and _all things needful_ for the wounded and infirm" (_Conquest_, p. 175). Such structures reveal an insouciance for description. Irving shared with French romantic writers such as Stendhal or Merimee a distaste for figuration. There is an absence of richness in imagery. Chapter LXXXIX speaks of a devastating forage of Ferdinand around Granada. Visual romantics, Hugo or Chateaubriand, would concentrate on the detail. Irving tended to be curt, elliptic: "His present forage lasted fifteen days, in the course of which almost everything that had escaped his

former desolating visit was destroyed, and _scarce a green thing or a living animal was left on the face of the land_ (_Conquest_, p. 476). Listing within a narrative structure substitutes for description as in the following "description" of the Vega where objects are listed but not located in a specific, particular topography. They become symbolic significants in a nonspecific semantic field: "The Vega was covered with beautiful vegetation, with rice and cotton, with groves of oranges, citrons, figs and mulberries, and with gardens inclosed by hedges of reeds, or aloes and the Indian fig" (_Conquest_, pp. 470-71). It might as well be California.

11. "I am prone to seek those parts of the Alhambra which are most favorable to this _phantasmagoria_ of the mind; and none are more so than the Court of Lions" (_Alhambra_, p. 128); "It needs but a slight exertion of the fancy to _picture_ some pensive beauty of the harem, loitering in these secluded haunts of Oriental luxury" (_Alhambra_, p. 129); "_I picture to myself the scene_ when this place was filled with the conquering host" (_Alhambra_, p. 129); "As I paced the gallery, my _imagination pictured_ the anxious queen leaning over the parapet, listening with the throbbings of a mother's heart to the last echoes of the horses' hoofs as her son scoured along the narrow valley of the Darro" (_Alhambra_, p. 149).

12. This structure is dependent on the lyrics of the Spanish and Moorish romances. Collective reactions to victory or defeat echo across the _Conquest_: "'All Andalusia,' says a historian of the time, 'was overwhelmed by a great affliction; there was no drying of the eyes which wept in her'" (_Conquest_, p. 99); "Thus all Granada, say the Arabian chroniclers, gave itself up to lamentation; there was nothing but the voices of wailing, from the palace to the cottage. All joined to deplore their youthful monarch, cut down in the freshness and promise of his youth" (_Conquest_, p. 124).

13. _Abencerraje_, p. 251-52.

14. _Abencerraje_, pp. 251-520

15. Chateaubriand's main sources are A. L. J. Laborde's four-volume _Voyage pittoresque et historique en Espagne_ (1807-1818), and Henry Swinburne's _Voyage in Spain_, (1779). Laborde was the brother of Nathalie de Noailles. She was in Spain at the time of Chateaubriand's visit, making pen-and-pencil sketches to illustrate her brother's travel book. Chateaubriand's geographic indifference is apparent if we compare a description of the Douro valley which he never saw with the authentic passage in Swinburne from which it was borrowed. This geography is used to backdrop the romantic promenade of his hero Aben-Hamet through the landscape of his Moorish ancestors. Chateaubriand's romantic fantasy rearranges the landscape, creating a poetic geography superior to the actual location of bridge, tower, mills, mountains, ruins. An entire generation of critics is aware of Chateaubriand's apathy for historical or geographic exactitude. The misrepresentations of Spain only echo what he had done in America (see Joseph Bedier, _Le Voyage de Chateaubriand en Amérique_, or Gilbert Chinard, _L'Exotisme américain dans l'oeuvre de Chateaubriand_). Imagination and dream are the prime ingredients according to Duchemin (p. 269). Gita

May (*Stendhal and the Age of Napoleon* [New York: Columbia University Press, 1977] p. 206), has similar things to say about the purpose of the inexactitudes in Stendhal's guidebook *Promenades dans Rome* (1829).

16. Romantic quest for identity is prone to use this structure of walking among the ruins. The young couple in Madame de Stael's novel *Corinne* incorporate their romantic soul states to their visits to Roman ruins and to their tour of Italian cities such as Naples, Florence, and Venice.

17. "Quelque chose de voluptueux, de religieux et de guerrier semblait respirer dans ce magique édifice; espèce de cloître de l'amour, retraite mystérieuse ou les rois maures goûtaient tous les plaisirs, et oubliaient tous le devoirs de la vie." Is Chateaubriand trying to complete a cycle? Legend has it that Roderick, the last Visigothic king of Spain lost Iberia to the Moors because of amorous dawdling (maybe even rape). This text of Chateaubriand suggests that the Alhambra was more interested in love than in politics, forgetting duty. Chateaubriand seems to see Boabdil more as a lover than as sovereign. Irving's texts, based in document, put this in the background but suggest docility, passivity, and materialism in the last Moorish king of Spain. Does Boabdil do for Islam what Roderick did for the Christians?

18. "Chaque année Blanca allait errer sur les montagnes de Malaga, à l'époque où son amant avait coutume de revenir d'Afrique; elle s'asseyait sur les rochers, regardait la mer, les vaisseaux lointains, et retournait ensuite à Grenade: elle passait le reste de ses jours parmi les ruines de l'Alhambra."

19. Flaubert's historical novel about Carthage and the Punic Wars, *Salammbo* (1862), is more indebted to Chateaubriand than to the more usual romantic historical writers such as Dumas Pere, precisely because of the density of descriptive materials in the imperfect tense, evoking historical mood tones in both nature and civilization. The conclusion of chapter I with the description of the sunrise over Carthage illustrates this.

20. It is not to be assumed that Irving's narrational pattern is not present in Chateaubriand. It is there (see p. 259 for examples of this) but coupled to a painterly descriptive art, resulting from the observations of Chateaubriand as romantic traveler admiring nature and ruins and knowing how to share this vision with us. A comparison of the Irving texts cited in footnote 10 with the following material from Chateaubriand would show similarities (listings) but also amplification through figuration, geographical and meteorological details which affect the human psyche, creating a pathetic fallacy: More intense emotions were awaiting the Abencerraje at the end of his route. Granada is built at the foot of the Sierra Nevada, on two high hills separated by a deep valley. The houses built on the slope of the hills, in the hollow other foot of the Sierra Nevada, on two high hills separated by a deep valley. The houses built on the slope of the hills, in the hollow of the valley, give to the city the impression and form of a half-opened pomegranate, hence

the source of its name. Two rivers, the Genil and the Douro, the one flowing with gold dust, the other with silver sands, bathe the foot of the hills, join, and meander through a charming plain called the Vega. This plain, dominated by granada is covered with vines, pomegranate trees, fig trees, mulberries, orange trees; It is surrounded by mountains admirable in both form and color. An enchanted sky, a delicious and pure air, give to the soul a secret langour which even the most casual traveler would have difficulty resisting. This country gives the impression that passions of the heart would rapidly replace the heroic ones, except that love, to be true, had need to be joined to glory." Again, Chateaubriand hits the mark. Granada is suspected by its nature of encouraging love over deeds. Is glory, "gloire" again the coincidence of the American and French romantic at Granada? "Des émotions encore plus vives attendaient l'Abencerraje au terme de sa course. Grenade est batie au pied de la Sierra Nevada, sur deux hautes collines que sépare une profonde vallée. Les maisons placées, sur la pente des coteaux, dans l'enfoncement de la vallée, donnent à la ville l'air et la forme d'une grenade entr'ouverte, d'où lui est venu son nom. Deux rivières, le Xenil et le Douro, dont l'une roule des paillettes d'or, et l'autre des sables d'argent, lavent le pied des collines, se réunissent et serpentent ensuite au milieu d'une plaine charmante appelée la Vega. Cette plaine que domine Grenade est couverte de vignes, de grenadiers, de figuiers, de muriers, d'orangers; elle est entourée par des montagnes d'une forme et d'une couleur admirables. Un ciel enchante, un air pur et delicieux, portent dans l'âme une languer secrète dont le voyageur qui ne fait que passer a même de la peine à se défendre. On sent que dans ce pays les tendres passions auraient promptement étouffe les passions héroiques, si l'amour, pour être véritable, n'avait pas toujours besoin d'être accompagne de la gloire, (*Abencerraje*, pp. 261-62)

21. "De ce lieu élevé on decouvrait la mer ou l'infortune monarque allait s'embarquer pour l'Afrique; on apercevait aussi Grenade, la Vega et le Xenil, au bord duquel s'élevaient les tentes de Ferdinand et d'Isabelle. A la vue de ce beau pays et des cypres qui marquaient encore çà et là les tombeaux des musulmans, Boabdil se prit à verser des larmes. La sultane Aixa, sa mere, qui l'accompagnait dans son exil avec les grands qui composaient jadis sa cour, lui dit: 'Pleure maintenant comme une femme un royaume que tu n'as pas su défendre comme un homme.'"

22. In Irving's *Conquest*, Boabdil is perceived as ill-fated, "El Zogoybi: (pp. 137, 138, 197, 267, 453, 515, 517, 518); politically compromising, weak, and subservient (pp. 141, 370, 519); indecisive and Hamlet-like (pp. 238, 269, 271, 406); but above all melancholic and resigned to leaving Granada (p. 524). Here Irving's Boabdil takes on the romantic *mal du siècle* aspects of Chateaubriand's Arab hero Aben-Hamet and other Moors fashioned across a Western romantic imagination as affirmed by Said's work on this subject. We learn in the opening pages of the *Abencerraje* that the African survivors of Granada spend their time in medical researches, especially with herbs that are claimed

to calm the soul of vain regrets for things now lost (Granada?) (p. 258). Boabdil's melancholic departure from Granada equals the final departure from Spain of Aben-Hamet. Both Moors have lost; the one his beloved city; the other his beloved, the Christian Dona Blanca. Both losses are the product of religious antagonisms. Aben-Hamet, like Boabdil, accepts loss as the will of God and fate, putting theological fatalism into contact with Western romantic destiny. Aben-Hamet, seeing Boabdil's name engraved in mosaic at the Alhambra (p. 286) bursts into tears.

23. Here Irving's perceptions almost appear baroque in spite of the time period, but then it has been said that Spain is eternally baroque. Chapter XXIV of the *Conquest* treats of the gradation in honors accorded by rank of importance. Should Boabdil kneel and kiss the hand of the king (p. 135)? The surrender of Granada involves a very complex procedure of horseback riding, dismantling and submission. (pp. 524-25).

24. High Corneillian honor distinguishes all of Chateaubriand's Spaniards, Moors, and Frenchmen. Blanca cannot marry Aben-Hamet, so she will never marry. The Count of Lautrec who loves Blanca will respect her love for Aben-Hamet and returns, suffering, to France (*Abencerraje*, pp. 327-29). Blanca's brother, Don Carlos, challenging Aben-Hamet to a duel, confers knighthood on the latter so that he may be fit for noble combat (*Abencerraje*, pp. 305). The basic atmosphere, however, is reminiscent of the love poetry of the Provencal poets, such as Bernart de Ventadour, in which the lover is slave, the beloved master. Dona Blanca asks Aben-Hamet by what right he assumes her devotion, with this reply: "It is true, I am only your slave; you have not chosen me to be your knight" (*Abencerraje*, p. 288). "Il est vrai, je ne suis que ton esclave; tu ne m'as pas choisi pour ton chevalier." In a cleverly constructed couplet, the dilemma of love nonfulfilled, so important to twelfth-century Provence is tied in to the idea of hostile religions separating the lovers, insuring a life-long passionate longing: "Musulman, I am your lover without hope; Christian I am your fortunate wife." "Christian I am your slave without consolation; Musulman, I am your glorious husband" (*Abencerraje*, p. 293). "Musulman, je suis ton amante sans espoir; chrétien, je suis ton épouse fortunée." "Chrétienne, je suis ton esclave désolé; musulmane, je suis ton epoux glorieux." Thus the lovers part and will suffer from this pang until death. The texts of Irving and Chateaubriand have not only debated arms versus love, they have also included the dimension found in Chrétien de Troyes of conjugal and courtly love.

25. Irving's text highlights the crossing, fusing the evolution of literary traditions in a way unique to Spain because of its Islamic-Christian conflict. Irving's works have a superficial structure derived from epic and courtly materials in romance literatures but which receive a peculiar Hispanic-Oriental orientation. The Marques of Cadiz, besieged by the Moors at Alhambra receives aid from his arch enemy, the duke of Medina-Sidonia. Why? Because the request came from a woman, the wife . . . and because he

is chivalrous, he cannot refuse. (Conquest, p. 55). More interesting are the specific roles of Ferdinand and Isabella. Ferdinand is the super-knight, the symbolic representation of Spain (Conquest, p. 282). But we are no longer in the world of knight fighting knight; it is now army fighting army. Yet, the chivalric code is maintained, as is the "courtly" code in the person of Isabella. She assumes the role of "lady," and the army, as a collective knight, goes forth to perform great deeds for the lady. Thus, the arrival of Isabella on the battlefield (Conquests, p. 427) is an encouragement to the troops, and the Moors know all is lost. This is surface chivalry, surface *courtoisie*, Spanish facade hiding renaissance stratagem. As the conquest of Granada intensifies, Ferdinand forbids the acceptance of "any individual challenges" which are "more like the stately ceremonials of tilts and tournaments" (Conquests p. 488) for he sees that this is to the advantage of the outnumbered Moors. He resorts to other tactics. War is no longer to be considered a game as Irving calls it earlier (Conquests p. 83). Any attempt to subdue the city by main force would be perilous and bloody. "Cautious in his policy, and fond of conquests gained by art rather than valor, he resorted to the plan so successful with Baza, and determined to reduce the place by famine (Conquests p. 486). This certainly indicates a shift from chivalry to modern psychological and tactical warfare, which may explain Machiavelli's admiration of Ferdinand in *The Prince*, especially chapter XXI, "How a Prince should conduct himself in order to acquire prestige." A stylistic analysis of both Irving and Chateaubriand's works on Granada would show that the tag epithet common to both writers acts as a static placer or freezer, giving both works the quality of frieze or tapestry. This static or nondynamic quality is representative of romantic imitation of medieval epic.

26. It would be worthwhile to analyze, from *The Alhambra*, the charming "Legend of Prince Ahmed Al Kamel; or The Pilgrim of Love," in the light of the discussion in this chapter. This is a love story about a young Prince of Granada who is guaranteed a prosperous reign if he can be kept from the allurements of love until a mature age (p. 202). Chateaubriand would have made this a classic case of romantic adolescence with a moody, depressed, melancholic wandering hero. But Irving encases the romance within the confines of byzantine adventure and allegory, all of which divert attention from the effects of passion. Humor is even present. Irving's tale looks a bit like such medieval romances as *Aucassin et Nicolette*.

10.

The Charm of a Golden Past: Iberia in the Writings of Washington Irving and Antonio Gonçalves Dias

LORETTA SHARON WYATT

The singular beauty and the fabulous past of the Iberian peninsula enthralled two distinguished writers from the Americas, Washington Irving of the United States and Antonio Goncalves Dias of Brazil. Although in recent times Irving has been more renowned for his short stories based on New York folklore, while Gonçalves Dias is acclaimed for his dramatic love lyrics and poems dealing with Indians, the imaginations of both these writers found equally rich subject matter in the events from 711 to 1600 which created in Spain and Portugal a unique history within Western civilization.

Irving and Gonçalves Dias arrived at their interests in Iberia by different paths. It was only when Irving actually traveled to Spain to research the life of Christopher Columbus that he became captivated by the people and customs there, so totally dissimilar to his British heritage or the Dutch remnants lingering from old New Amsterdam. The more Irving read of the history from the Dark Ages through Columbus's voyages, the more fascinated he became, and much of his writing after 1826 concerned Spanish topics. However, while Irving felt reasonably sure of the accuracy of the facts in the sources he used for the history on Columbus, the further back in time he went, the more a skeptical Irving found to question about the veracity of the chronicles he read. Irving might grant that certain events had occurred, but the truth was so interwoven with incidents of doubtful authenticity and colored by so many layers of interpretation that these purported histories struck Irving as a little less fictitious and improbable than some of the wild yarns in the Arabian Nights. Yet to strip away the legendary aspects would mean eliminating the very details that were most intriguing and charming about the stories. Irving was not willing to give up those tales full of great heroism and base treachery, of beautiful princesses and brave princes, but here as in his other writings he took scrupulous care to distance himself from the possibility of being supposed superstitious or credulous.

Irving's most famous narrative device was to introduce an intermediary to tell the story. Consequently, Fray Antonio Agapida was credited with being the author of various chronicles and legends, beginning with A Chronicle of the Conquest of Granada. Irving described Agapida as the archetype of the medieval churchman:

> one of the many indefatigable writers, who have filled the libraries of the convents and cathedrals of Spain with their tomes, without ever dreaming of bringing their labours to the press. He evidently was deeply and accurately informed of the particulars of the war between hi countrymen and the Moors, a tract of history but too much overgrown with the weeds of fable. His glowing zeal, also, in the cause of catholic faith, entitles him to be held up as a model of the good old orthodox chroniclers, who recorded with such pious exultation, the united triumphs of the cross and the sword.(1)

Agapida, then, belonged to Irving's list of overly educated but mentally sterile pedants, an intolerant cloistered being blinded to all but his own narrow interests, devoted to esoteric knowledge for its own sake, as well as totally convinced of the righteousness of his own policies.

The splendid collection known as the Tales of the Alhambra was a skillful blend of travel commmentary and description; autobiographical essay detailing Irving's adventures, the people he met, and his reactions to southern Spain; and stories resembling the A Thousand and One Nights. Irving claimed here that he was essentially repeating the information and stories he had been told by the residents in and around the old Moslem palace. Mateo Jimenez was his major source, "having the most marvellous stories to relate of every tower and vault and gateway of the fortress, in which he places the most implicit faith."(2) Irving also on occasion described a party in which fairy tales were told as part of the entertainment and which he now proposed to reconstruct in his own fashion for the same reason. And lest for all that he might be criticized, Irving reminded his readers,

> If anything in these legends should shock the faith of the over-scrupulous reader, he must remember the nature of the place and make due allowances. He must not expect here the same laws of probability that govern common-place scenes and every-day life; he must remember that he treads the halls of an enchanted palace and that all is "haunted ground."(3)

Unlike Irving, who came late to the romance of the Iberian past, Antonio Gonçalves Dias-like other Brazilians, was early imbued with the traditions and heritage of the old mother country, Portugal. Gonçalves Dias found equal magic suffusing Portuguese history, but far from disassociating himself from the myth-making aspects, the poet deliberately set out to cultivate them in his

Sextilhas de Frei Antao. As Gonçalves Dias explained in the prologue,

> I adopted as my own the ancient phrase and thought, attempting to render the style smooth and easy so as not to displease modern ears, and to impart to the thought the strong and meaning-laden color of those times, in which faith and bravery were the two cardinal virtues, or rather the only virtues. I placed myself in the midst of those days of rigid and profound beliefs -- perhaps of fanaticism -- and forced myself to simplify my thought, to feel as the men of those days felt, and to express (the thought and the feeling) in the language that could best convey them -- that of the troubadours.(4)

Gonçalves Dias also made his narrator a priest, the Dominican Frei Antao de Santa Maria de Neiva. However, Frei Antao was much more than a mere narrator in the _Sextilhas:_ he was also an active participant in many of the events. Though Gonçalves Dias began with a real person whom he discovered in the _Historia de S. Domingos_ by Fr. Luiz de Sousa, he took considerable license in developing this character, especially with regard to age. For dramatic purposes, Gonçalves Dias wanted a single person who could communicate the euphoria felt during the period of greatest glory for Portugal, when it launched the modern age of exploration and conquest beyond European shores, and the terrible bleak despair that pervaded the country in its worst period of national defeat, psychological depression, and temporary loss of independence. As this made Frei Antao well over 200 years old, matching the longovity of antediluvian patriarchs in Genesis, to avoid being accused of an unfortunate fit of inattentiveness, Gonçalves Dias in a footnote remarked that, "It is needless to say that Frei Antao must have been one of the hardiest souls who ever existed, to still be alive at that time."(5) The time element was otherwise handled by being relatively ignored with the action compressed in Frei Antao's narrative and uncluttered with such details as dates.

While Irving had to explain the background, the participants, and the events about which he was writing to his intended audience, Gonçalves Dias was able to presume his Brazilian readers were well acquainted with the specific episodes to which he was referring. Consequently, Gonçalves Dias simply plunged into the opening story, "Loa de Princeza Sancta," carrying his listeners back to the time when Christians were fighting the Moslems and the king was expected to be the active commander-in-chief. Young Portuguese princes would not settle for being granted automatic knighthood but insisted on earning their spurs by actually fighting in a war. The king therefore summoned the parliament to advise it of this decision and received the immediate united and enthusiastic support of the nation. When the campaign was over, Ceuta and Tangiers were won for Portugal. Thus, in a few brief, deft strokes, Gonçalves Dias revived the memory of John I, first of the Avis dynasty, and his oldest sons, Edward, Peter, and Henry, the future so-called Navigator, who began the great age of exploration with the conquest of Ceuta in 1415.

Nevertheless, one of the themes running through both Irving's and Gonçalves Dias's work was the inevitability of change. This theme unavoidably introduced a note of melancholy, because the change did not strike either writer as being desirable or as bringing improvement but as being a descent from a golden past. Given the circumstances in which Frei Antao lived, it was understandable that he would feel there had been a definite decline in religion, valor, and virtue. In every story, he repeated the notion that the old days were far better but expressed the idea most forcefully when contemplating the period of the revered Afonso Henriques, who founded the kingdom of Portugal in the twelfth century:

> There is nothing left of that time
> In which everything was superior!
> The actions and life and behavior
> Of this Portuguese people,
> Have been changed so completely
> That today everything is defiled.(6)

This attitude also reflected the theory generally held by the Portuguese that their country fell from greatness when it lost its original religious fervency and became more commercial and practical-minded. That Irving held much the same negative opinion about change, particularly when geared toward making what he was the first to term "the almighty dollar," is more apparent in his American-based stories, but the sentiment pervaded The Alhambra as well. The most telling examples may be found in the touching detail with which Irving described the once-glorious Alhambra, a sad ruined vestige of its former self. The sentiment is also discernible in the tales, as in the rough, yet fundamentally satisfying humorous treatment the One-Armed Governor meted out to the upstart notary who dared to infringe on rights and privileges consecrated by time and custom.

There was relatively little of the miraculous or supernatural overtly in the Sextilhas largely because the Portuguese and the Brazilians regarded their historical past fabulous enough in itself. The Alhambra, naturally, overflowed with such marvels as hidden treasures "always laid under magic spell and secured by charm and talisman,"(7) Boabdil's enchanted army, held in spellbound sus-pension until such time came for them to again conquer Granada, plus demon horses, incantations, a phantom or two, and even a flying carpet.

The loveliest enchantment of all is, of course, love, so it is hardly surprising that many of the stories told by Irving and Gonçalves Dias dealt with the effect this passion had on their protagonists and reflected much of their own susceptibility to beautiful and charming women. All these affairs began with instantaneous love at first sight because, as Irving explained, "In those days people fell in love much more suddenly than at present, as all ancient stories make manifest."(8)

Sometimes the infatuation was distinctly one-sided, particulary when the lady in question had little choice in the matter. When Christians and Moslems went out on raids against each other, their usual practice was to return with captives, both men and women. Though one is assured knights such as Goncalo Herminguez in Afonso Henriques' court were models of chivalrous conduct who would never dream of hurting a woman, carrying off a girl does not appear to have been conceived as harming her. Young Goncalo's entire courtship, as recorded in chronicles and used by Gonçalves Dias, consisted of seizing the sweet young Fatima as she fainted and fighting off dozens of furious Moslem soldiers. The dubious aspects of this story were not resolved satisfactorily by the affirmation that she was "twice conquered . . . / First by the force of arms, / Afterward by the force of love."(9)

Possibly some of such encounters resulted in happiness, but not always as Irving made clear in "The Legend of the Arabian Astrologer" and "The Legend of the Three Beautiful Princesses." In both stories rather elderly Moslem men were beguiled by lovely young Christian maidens. Irving provided his classically cool and reserved Visigothic princess in his first tale with her own magic weapon to protect her from the unwanted ardent advances of King Aben Habuz in his harem and later on, forevermore presumably, from the wizard Abu Ajub in the enchanted cavern: she simply strummed her silver lyre which had a "mystic charm in the sound"(10) that put the old men to sleep. More realistically, the Christian beauty in the power of Mohamed the Left Handed could only weep over her fate and reluctantly accept marriage as better than the alternative.

There was a sense of innocence and decorum proper to a fairy-tale atmosphere that pervailed at all times in Irving, but Gonçalves Dias infused many of his characters with a more passionate nature. Frei Antao among other traits discovered a deeply sensuous side to his nature when he first laid eyes on the gorgeous Gulnare, one of the Moslem slaves Afonso V brought back from his African conquests as a gift to his daughter Joanna. For all his faults, at least Frei Antao was no hypocrite. However much he admired honorable and saintly virtues, he did not pretend to be better than he really was. "Gulnare and Mustapha" was the lengthy confession of his fall into temptation and forbidden love. Poor Frei Antao was so be-witched that he was even subjected to the ritual of exorcism by his amazed and exasperated superior, though ex-orcism turned out to have no power to break the spell of love whatever it might be able to do about demon possession. Only the fortunate appearance of Gulnare's lost lover Mustapha at the last moment saved both the girl and the priest, and it obviously did not behoove the reader to quibble about coincidences in Portuguese palaces any more than to worry about laws of probability in Spanish ones.

A recovered Frei Antao probably would have agreed

with Irving's comparison of love to an attack by an enemy, albeit a pleasing enemy, who could overwhelm the greatest warrior or wisest man. That was why the marvelous weathercock, the bronze figure of a warrior, took up its aggressive warning stance when it became aware of the Visigothic princess, reacting exactly as if she were an invading army. Certainly her arrival had devastating consequences on the kingdom with the rupture of friendly relations between the king and the magician as well as the depleting of the treasury.

Irving also described exquisitely the awakening of a lonely sheltered youth to love in "The Legend of Prince Ahmed al Kamel or the Pilgrim of Love," as well as in the story of the three princesses, and in "The Legend of the Rose of the Alhambra; or the Page and the Ger-Falcon." Ahmed certainly fulfilled the prophecy that his amorous temperament would lead him into many dangerous adventures. He finally won the woman he loved with the help of several birds whose languages he spoke, an enchanted Moslem warhorse and suit of armor that made the peaceful youth invincible in battle, and a carpet on which to fly away with his beloved Aldegonda. Irving may well have found inspiration in the incident in the life of the tenth-century Count of Castile Fernan Gonzalez for his view that women, and men as well, will usually abandon parental and other old ties for love. When the count went to Navarre, he was imprisoned by its king. The king's sister, Sancha, visited Fernan in his prison, fell in love with him, and not only helped him to escape but also went with him to live reasonably happily ever after. Not only is the _Chronicle of Fernan Gonzalez_ one of Irving's best, but he liked this particular motif so much he used it in Ahmed and two other variations as well, the three beautiful princesses, and "Governor Manco and the Soldier." Not everyone is brave enough, or wise enough, however, to seize the golden opportunity. The soft, timid Zorahayda hesitated to escape with her handsome prince and flung away her single chance for happiness. The rest of her brief unhappy life was spent lamenting her fatal choice, the memory of which haunted her rooms in the Alhambra.

The story of the three princesses was remarkable in including an extraordinary character in Irving's work, an unusually strong but rather ambiguous woman with a forceful, fun-loving personality. Kadiga may well have been suggested by several of the women residents in the Alhambra such as Reyna Coquina, who had lost five husbands but not her humor, as well as that baudy old reprobate matchmaker Celestina from the classic Spanish play of the same name. The discreet Kadiga's role was to act as the catalyst for the plot's progress. As the _duena_ or companion-chaperone for the Christian captive of Mohamed, Kadiga persuaded her to marry him, even if he was the enemy (a Moslem), and old as well, through such pithy logic as, "When in the hands of a robber, it is better to sell one's merchandise for a fair price than to have it taken by main force."(11) Ever practical, Kadiga even converted to Islam in order to keep her position, as many people did during the long Reconquest, and was prepared to convert back to Christianity if need arose. As _duena_ for Mohamed's daughters, she comprehended their emotional state before they did and actively promoted their romances with the three handsome Christian cavaliers, but she so skillfully and subtly stage-managed the whole affair that the girls never realized how she was manipulating them. She joined her wards in the escape, planning to marry the renegade guard Hussein Baba, but Irving apparently was not comfortable with giving such a suspect character a happy ending. He had her swept away in a river, though he turned out to be equally unwilling to consign her to a watery grave and allowed her to be hauled to safety in a fisherman's net and disappear into an unknown future, still discreet, and always a survivor.

Washington Irving and Antonio Gonçalves Dias were not alone in being receptive to the magic and charm inherent in the past and in the people of the Iberian peninsula. The writer and the poet, however, shared a gift few had for extracting the distinctive character and flavor from both the true and the mythical Iberian past to use as the bases for their stories. One of the recommendations for writing a story well is to construct the environment as convincingly as possible and to keep the characters and plot consistent with that background. Irving and Gonçalves Dias must have wondered what better locale could be found for stories dealing with larger-than-life personalities and fantastic, thrilling adventures than Granada and Portugal, where extraordinary people and actions seemed merely commonplace.

NOTES

1. _A Chronicle of the Conquest of Granada_, in _The Works of Washington Irving_ (New York: P. F. Collier and Son, 1904), 3: p. 3.
2. Washington, Irving, _Tales of the Alhambra_ (Granada: Editorial Padre Suarez, 1960), p. 65.
3. _Alhambra_, p. 131.
4. Antonio, Gonçalves Dias, _Poesias_ (_Nova edicao organizada e revista por J. Norberto de Souza Silva e precedida de uma noticia sobre o autor e suas obras pelo Conego Doutor Fernandes Pinheiro_, Rio de Janeiro: Livraria Garnier, 1919), 1: 13. All the translations are mine.
5. _Poesias_, 2: 335.
6. _Poesias_, 2: 282.
7. _Alhambra_, p. 130 passim.
8. _Alhambra_, p. 171.
9. _Poesias_, 2: 300.
10. _Alhambra_, p. 147.
11. _Alhambra_, p. 163.

11.

Washington Irving's *Tales of the Alhambra* and Early Photography in Spain

LEE FONTANELLA

When Washington Irving published his book on the Alhambra in 1832, photography as we know it was not yet a reality. (It did not become one until 1839.) Instead, the lithograph, and sometimes even the cruder woodcut, was the pictorial medium which competed informationally with the descriptive word. Although lithography was at a relatively advanced stage, as soon as the daguerreotype became available in 1839, photographers went to the noteworthy monuments of the world to gather what they considered to be concrete visual records of current realities, which in turn reflected truths about the past.(1) For many, the monument acquired a life through the photograph, which prompted psychological transport to the scene depicted in the visual image, so that the image came to suffice for the experience of the place itself. This was surely the idea behind the publication of the *Excursions Daguerriennes*, by Lerebours of Paris. Between 1840 and 1842, Lerebours sent daguerreotypists to various countries to collect characteristic views, in order to publish them in the form of engravings, based on the original daguerreotypes. Accompanying each view in the publication was a brief text. By this arrangement, Lerébours published two views of Granada and one of Seville, to cover the general topic of Spain. By his choices, he forecast the affinities of future photographers in Spain: probably no place in Spain was as photographed in the nineteenth century as the Alhambra and, especially, the Court of the Lions.

Generally speaking, lithography -- at least the pictorial style which developed along with it -- abetted, more than did subsequent photography, the artistic aims of writers such as Washington Irving. Lithography allowed for exaggerations of Gothic proportions and for enhancement of the gracefulness of Moorish architecture, whereas photography, relatively speaking, tended to normalize these qualities by presenting them more matter-of-factly. Photography tended to render a scientific report concerning actuality more often than did lithography, and, in so doing, it departed from romanticism. The mimetic potential of the photograph, in comparison to the lithograph, seemed to contradict the significance of the Alhambra, which lent itself to romanticizing. Irving sensed immediately this quality of the Alhambra, and he was haunted by this throughout his book. That (merely) "Moorish pile," as he called it, became "that extraordinary pile"(2) toward the end of the book, almost as a sign that Irving himself had moved from a state of matter-of-factness to oneAlhambra,Alhambra, of marvel, rapture, and fantasy in the course of his experience. This is not the customary direction of nineteenth-century photography in its earliest years. The earliest purpose of photography was quite the opposite; it was rather scientific.

Beginning around 1860, twenty-five to thirty years after Washington Irving's sojourn in the Alhambra, the British, French, and Spanish, more than photographers of any other countries, started making views of the Moorish site. We could point to such names as the British Petit, George Washington Wilson, and Charles Clifford; the French Laurent; and the Spaniards Puig and Senan y Gonzalez. Granted that span of years (twenty-five to thirty years), it is conceivable that the fashion, or the psychological willingness, to romanticize reality, in the way that Irving did, was passing. Nevertheless, with the exception of some details here and there (such as the disappearance of the Frenchified gardens in the Court of the Lions, which Irving deplored), the Alhambra probably retained in 1860 the appearance it had when Irving took up lodgings in it. I do not mean to reduce the charm of Irving's depictions by associating them tightly with these photographic renderings. On the contrary, I feel that an insight into the reality behind his visit might allow us to appreciate better his temptations into fanciful musings or his journeys into realms of legend and history.

Irving's first view of the Alhambra embraced the Torres Bermejos, and his entrance was through the magnificent Gate of Justice, which surprised him for the height of its arch. In the course of the first tour through the palace of the Alhambra, in which his self-appointed guide, Mateo Jimenez, assisted, Irving passed through the Court of the Alberca, otherwise called the Court of Myrtles, and he ended up in the Court of the Lions.

It is tempting to think that the man whom Clifford photographed sitting at the base of the temple in this Court might have been Mateo's son Jose, who, years after Washington Irving, might have posed for the photographer, since we know that Jose did offer his services to visitors; or perhaps it was Dona Antonia's nephew Manuel, some twenty-five years after Irving had seen him receive his medical diploma. In fact, another photographer from Britain, named Napper, who began to take photographs in Spain in the charge of the enterprising photographer Francis Frith, did a great many genre portraits of human types in Andalusia, and it is tempting also to see in Napper's excellent portraits the imagined faces of Irving's own characters.

However facile this projection into enchanting old photographs may be, the question arises as to whether or not this is legitimate procedure -- not only from the point of view of criticism but also because of the nature of Irving's book. Do the photographs destroy the romance of the book, as the guide Mateo destroyed "the romance of the name" (p. 51) of the Hall of the Two Sisters? Dolores preferred to retain the romantic interpretation of the beautiful hall by relating a narration to it, rather than attributing its name to the two slabs of alabaster which constituted its floor, as Mateo preferred. In this instance, although not on most, Mateo saw the Hall of the Two Sisters as the earliest photographers did; that is, rather prosaically, without romanticizing it. Dolores, on the other hand, viewed it as Irving would have done -- fancifully.

On most other occasions, Irving listened to Mateo with what he termed "easy faith" (p. 49) or, on another occasion, "easy credulity" (p. 50), which led to Irving's artistic formulation of legend. As he listened to the splash from the basin in the Garden of Lindaraja, he felt the "early associations of Arabian romance" (p. 52). Irving was functioning within what some critics have called "l'esthetique de la rupture," namely, a creative, artistic response to the ancient monument, as opposed to the early eighteenth-century response to ancient ruins and monuments, which was a contemplation of the vanity of man's political endeavor.(3)

Photography tested the limits of the two modalities of vision which are represented by the little disagreement between Dolores and Mateo regarding the naming of the Hall of the Two Sisters: the romanticizing on the basis of the ancient monument, on the one hand, and the analytic factuality of the monument, on the other. Laurent executed a detailed, straightforward view of a portal in the Hall of Lindaraja, but he also made one of the Mirador (Balcony) de Lindaraja, which conceivably contrasts with the first. The photograph of the Mirador de Lindaraja could be understood in the same way as the first: a straightforward statement about the architecture of one of the most eye-catching portions of the Moorish palace. It could also be taken as an appeal to romantic musings. Just as Irving would project the character of Lindaraja into the balcony scene, so too the photographer may have meant for us to do the same. In a much more subtle way, Clifford's photograph of the monumental tree in the Alhambra walkways is intended to strike up for the viewer those "associations of Arabian romance"; this is a fact of photographic history. But it is also true that the tree is photographed for itself, as a kind of wonder of natural science, without any implications of romance.

Irving played with the labyrinthine structure of the Alhambra palace in two ways: to draw the reader in toward Gothic mystery, for which purpose he associated physical enclosure with psychological enclosure. He was often imaginatively enticed by the mysteries behind closed doors: for example, the door to the Hall of Justice. In contrast, he used other portions of the Alhambra to prompt his contemplation outward, at which times he achieved knowledge about a peopled, actual world. We could take the photograph of the Mirador de Lindaraja as a point of departure: we are enticed into it by virtue of the photographer's vantage point, but association of the view with the legend about it recalls for us the story of Lindaraja pining away, her imaginary sights on the lover in the outside world. The balcony in the Hall of the Ambassadors is the vantage point from which Washington Irving contemplated his outside world: "It served as a kind of observatory, where I used often to take my seat, and consider not merely the heaven above but the earth beneath" (p. 108). He even used a telescope (an analog for the camera) to:

> sweep the regions below and bring the countenances of the motley groups so close as almost, at times, to make me think I could divine their conversation by the play and expression of their features. I was thus, in a manner, an invisible observer, and, without quitting my solitude, could throw myself in an instant into the midst of society, -- a rare advantage to one of somewhat shy and quiet habits, and found, like myself, of observing the drama of life without becoming an actor in the scene. (p. 109)

Perhaps he saw scenes similar to the many photographic views of the rooftops of the city, as he looked from the Hall of the Ambassadors toward the Albaicin. Or he may have been able to focus on individuals similar to those whom Napper photographed in Andalusia: a *majo* in holiday dress, a more humble collection of Andalusian gypsies, and so on. The meaning of the view from the balcony of the Hall of the Ambassadors is objectivity; legendary transport is only incidental here. This is why his imaginative spying on the novice nun is undercut by Mateo and leveled to reality on the spot.

Outside the Alhambra, Irving found "forlorn realities" (p. 55), such as the Spanish *posada* in which he was supposed to stay at the beginning of his book, or, we may suppose, the gypsy dwellings on Sacromonte. To these realities, he preferred the "mysterious chambers" (p. 89) of the Italianate Tocador de la Reina, where in the beginning he took up lodgings for a while. From time to time, he tempered his natural inclination toward romance by frequenting the library of the Jesuits, where he could fulfill his social duty as historian by unearthing and transmitting the information gleaned from its parchments but even on these occasions, he sometimes ended by transforming history into legend. To temper fantasy, he also joined in extroverted musical revelry within the Alhambra walls, although even this revelry was infused with current-day remnants of Moorish culture, just as in the photograph by Clifford, of gypsies dancing in the Court of the Lions.

Irving's account of his stay at the Alhambra exhibits a range of modalities. He has a yearning to live out the childhood fantasies which he derived from readings of Gines Perez de Hita on the banks of the Hudson, and, to tell the truth, this is the principal substance of his book. But he also wanted to right the historiographic wrongs of Perez de Hita, and this is ostensibly his reason for cultivating the resources at the library of the Jesuits. (In the same vein, he said he had to keep his eye on Tio Polo for his readings in Feijoo's book on superstions [Feijoo was the eighteenth-century rationalist voice, righting his people's superstitious wrongs.]

Clearly, Irving's bent is usually in the direction of romance (he himself uses the term in the traditional sense of "imaginative narration"). Romance was, after all, his purpose for residing in the Alhambra, instead of in the stark reality of the posada. This stance of the writer in 1830 seems not to be that of the photographer later on (but still in photographic infancy), although it was more so that of the lithographer who translated daguerreotypes into a more manual, less "scientifically accurate" pictorial form, which -- at least in photography's earliest years -- was customarily more imaginative. Partly because Irving opted for the viewpoint of the Alhambra from within, for his own artistic purposes, his vision often differed from that of the photographer of 1860, who many times stood apart from the "extraordinary pile": beneath it in awe of it. Frequent views of the Alhambra from San Nicolas, from El Chapiz, or views of the palace from across the upper gardens, all indicate a disengaged, rerily more imaginative. Partly because Irving opted for the viewpoint of the Alhambra from within, for his own artistic purposes, his vision often differed from that of the photographer of 1860, who many times stood apart from the "extraordinary pile": beneath it in awe of it. Frequent views of the Alhambra from San Nicolas, from El Chapiz, or views of the palace from across the upper gardens, all indicate a disengaged, respectful vision of the palace as intangible-in a word, not the approach of Washington Irving. The photographer viewed the beautiful Torre de los Picos, or the Tower of Comares in his own, comparably distant way, more often than he used the towers in the way that Irving did; that is, sitting atop them and using them as catalysts for recollections of historical anecdotes: for example, the anecdote that Irving recalled from atop the Comares Tower (that of the son of Don Juan, who requested that the Moorish king allow him to retrieve the body of his father, who had aggressed against the Moors). Perhaps still more telling in this regard is a photographic view by Laurent of the Alhambra from the Hill of the Martyrs. Irving, in contrast, retraced the steps of the departing Boabdil from the Alhamb not, and it is only by accident that a corner of it peeks through the arch of the Wine Tower -- almost as if to depict it as intrusive. Just as it was brushed over by Washington Irving, whose sensibilities for things Moorish were offended by it, was photographically neglected until some years later. So, too, the romance of the Alhambra must have died out considerably in the nineteeth century, some years after the period 1830-1860, although the Alhambra still possesses some of those "witching charms" (p. 57) for us today. Over half a century after Irving, views of the Alhambra could be purchased in the form of a commercial, touristic, photographic resume, that is, in a series of photographic fold-outs. And by 1890, the photographer Senan y Gonzalez could make light of the Court of the Lions in his delightful scene of a party of men sitting on the lions. This unassuming photograph is important, in the sense that it prompts us to measure the distance between Irving's Alhambra and the Alhambra at the end of the century: here, the lions are not a supposedly Christian imposition into a graceful Moorish atmosphere, as Irving assumed they were; they become, instead, comical, accepted fixtures out of which to make further comedy. By the end of the century, this most photographed portion of the Alhambra was encountered by the modernist sensibility, not at all by the romanticized one of Washington Irving. At least, we can take some comfort in the fact that the Frenchified gardens-which Irving ridiculed and which were still there at the time of Lerebours (1840) -- remained repaved in 1890, in the original Moorish style.

The Alhambra from the Albaicín. Etching from the original daguerrotype. *Lerebours, ca. 1840.*

Court of the Lions and the frenchified Gardens which Irving deplored. Etching from the original daguerrotype. *Lerebours, ca. 1840.*

Court of Lions and Alhambra resident. *Clifford, 1862.*

The Gardens of Lindaraja. *Señán y González.*

El Mirador de Lindaraja. *Clifford.*

El Tocador de la Reina, Irving's lodgings. *Laurent*.

Gypsies dancing in the Court of the Lions. *Clifford, 1862.*

The Alhambra from El Chapiz. *Laurent.*

The Wine Tower (Torre del Vino) from the exterior, and the intrusive corner of the palace of Charles V.

Four men sporting in the Court of the Lions. *Señán y González, 1890.*

NOTES

1. This paper was originally deliverd with forty-three photographic views of the era. The number has been shortened greatly here for purposes of publication, and the text has been altered slightly to accommodate this change.

2. All references are to *The Alhambra*, ed., Alfred M. Hitchcock (New York: Macmillan Co., 1928); here, pp. 70 and 391. Subsequent page references appear parenthetically in the text.

3. See Roland Mortier, "Deux Poetes des Ruines au XVIIIe Siecle," *Etudes sur le XVIIIe Siecle* (Bruxelles: Universite de Bruxelles, 1974), I:39-47.

12.

The Romantic Lie: Irving's "A Tour on the Prairies" and Stendhal's *Promenades dans Rome*

JOHN JOSEPH

> These things are almost romantique and yet true.
>
> Pepys, Diary, March 10, 1667

On May 21, 1832, Washington Irving returned to his native America after seventeen years in Europe. He had left the United States at the age of 32, neglected as an author and frustrated as a magazine editor; he returned at 49, celebrated on both continents. Yet the adjustment from so long an expatriacy was a difficult one, not unlike Rip Van Winkle's awakening to a strange, changed homeland.(1) His letters, and the recollections of his friend the actress Fanny Kemble, record the search to rediscover his American "identity."(2) In early July, just over a month after his return, he set off West with two companions he had met on the crossing, an Englishman named Charles Joseph Latrobe, and the Count de Pourtales, a high-spirited 21-year-old Swiss noble. After a tour of upstate New York, they took a Lake Erie boat from Buffalo to Detroit. On it they made the acquaintance of Henry Leavitt Ellsworth, one of three commissioners appointed by President Andrew Jackson to undertake the relocation of certain native American tribes from the southern states to the Indian territory. Ellsworth was en route to a congress of tribes at Fort Gibson, Arkansas. When he heard the trio's plans for exploring the western frontier, he suggested they accompany him. They accepted at once, Irving even agreeing to serve as official secretary of the expedition.(3) After reaching Fort Gibson on October 8, they set off with a colorful pair of buffalo hunters on a four-week expedition through the largely unexplored region that is now known as Oklahoma.

It was early the following year, back home in New York, when Irving realized that his journal entries from this expedition furnished the raw materials for a book on a truly American topic, one that might attenuate the nationality crisis he was suffering both internally and, it seemed, in the minds of many of his readers in the United States who suspected him of cultural treason. Also, despite his fame, his financial assets were somewhat in need of a boost.

When Irving's account of the voyage, modestly entitled "A Tour on the Prairies", finally appeared in 1835 as the first of three sections of The Crayon Miscellany,(4) it was a success both here and in Britain and helped to quell fears that its author had "gone European."(5) It is a curious book, to which Irving attached a more curious preface:

> Having, since my return to the United States, made a wide and varied tour, for the gratification of my curiosity, it has been supposed that I did it for the purpose of writing a book; and it has more than once been intimated in the papers, that such a work was actually in the press, containing scenes and sketches of the Far West.
>
> These announcements, gratuitously made for me, before I had put pen to paper, or even contemplated any thing of the kind, have embarrassed me exceedingly. I have been like a poor actor, who finds himself announced for a part he had no thought of playing. . . .
>
> I have always had a repugnance, amounting almost to disability, to write in the face of expectation; and, in the present instance, I was expected to write about a region fruitful of wonders and adventures, and which had already been made the theme of spirit-stirring narratives from able pens; yet about which I had nothing wonderful or adventurous to offer.
>
> Since such, however, seems to be the desire of the public . . . I have hastened . . . to meet in some degree, the expectation which others have excited. . . . As such, I offer it to the public, with great diffidence. It is a simple narrative of every day occurrences; such as happen to every one who travels the prairies. I have no wonders to describe, nor any moving accidents by flood or field to narrate.(6)

Thereupon follows an account filled with memorable depictions and dramatic incidents at every turn. Irving summoned his full stylistic powers to vivify characters and events which command rather less attention in Latrobe's,(7) Ellsworth's,(8) and Pourtales' accounts,(9) in direct contradiction to Irving's prefaced apology. What is more, the Count de Pourtales wrote to his mother on September 26, that "Mr. Irving will publish two works on this summer's trip. He has spoken to us of the plan and the form of the work and has told us, in confidence, some of the anecdotes which he will include."(10) I shall return to these matters momentarily.

Early in 1828, Romain Colomb left on a trip to Italy for health reasons, carrying with him a thirty-seven-page itinerary dictated by his cousin, Henri Beyle, himself ill with fever at the time.(11) Colomb returned to find Beyle penniless, stranded in Paris, near suicide. He was 45, and his first novel, _Armance_, had appeared and failed the previous year. Colomb, already intending to pen a book on his travels, saw what straits Henri was in and offered to let him share the labor and profits. Beyle set to work enthusiastically, taking over the project in fact, so that Colomb was reduced to the rank of very crucial research assistant.(12) After months of preparatory reading at the Bibliotheque Nationale, followed by a further period of composition in a hotel room close by, Beyle finished the book in March 1829, and it went to press that September under his pen name, Stendhal. It purports to be a diary of the author's personal voyage to Rome -- it was written entirely in Paris. He gives eyewitness accounts of historical events he could only have read about in newspapers. And in truth, many of his descriptions and stories are not simply derived but clearly plagiarized from other guidebooks and histories. Says Haakon Chevalier, "He pilfered the most readily available books quite shamelessly -- Nebly and Lalande, the two leading guides, whole pages out of Sismondi's _Italian Republics in the Middle Ages_ and Potter's _Spirit of the Church_. . . He carefully read and culled passages out of President de Brosses's classic _Voyage_, out of Pizarotti, Carlo Verri, Guidi, Duclos, Lullin de Chateauvieux, Misson . . .Fea, Petit-Radel and Creuxe de Lesser."(13) Stendhal's preface to the work states:

> The author entered Rome for the first time in 1802. Three years previously it had been a republic. The thought of this still troubled all minds, and as a consequence of it our small company was provided with an escort of two observers who did not leave us during our entire sojourn. . . .
>
> He saw Rome again in 1811; there were no more priests in the streets, and the Civil Code ruled; it was no longer Rome.
>
> . . . Everything had changed in 1828. . . .
> All the anecdotes contained in this volume are true, or at least the author believes them to be so. (14)

The real truth is that Stendhal first entered Rome in 1811, not 1802, and his firsthand acquaintance with the city was far less profound than his writing would give to believe.(15) Although he assembled the book for mercenary motives, it was no slapdash, cut-and-paste affair. His prospective readers were not fools, just foolish enough, he hoped, as he applied the camouflage, adapting the borrowed passages to his personal sytle, often to his own literary vision.

Two authors were caught, it would seem, in two very different lies. To be sure, plagiarism dates almost to the day the second human being incised flint into rock, and untruthful premises preface many a work of the eighteenth century and before, though in almost every case it is a declaration of _truth_ attached to a work of _fiction_. Fiction is, by definition, founded upon an illusion, an essential metaphor, and an opening, "The story you are about to hear is true," is an accepted element of the magic-making apparatus. With a nonfiction work, however, fraud is considered criminal and spurious modesty attendant upon somewhat freehanded dramatization of events more than borders on deception. As for plagiarism, if disguised stylistically it should be less easy to detect (all other things being equal) in a piece of descriptive nonfiction, where the subject matter is a given, than in a fiction or a treatise outlining original thought, where the subject is itself a facet of the creation. Yet one wonders whether these works by Irving and Stendhal could have achieved such success prior to the Romantic era, when the aesthetic of "complete expressiveness," as Jacques Barzun terms it,(16) came to engage the artist's creative faculty at all costs, promoting it to a position of supremacy and giving it rein to replace previously accepted notions of truth just as, early on, it had refashioned the tenets of beauty.(17)

Of course, Washington Irving's reputation was as a writer both of fictional tales and of historical accounts and travel sketches, serious and jocular. By the time Stendhal's "lies" were found out, he had established himself as one of Europe's great novelists; indeed, it was because of his importance as a novelist that scholars turned their concentrated attention to his travel writings, in search of source material or evidence of style development, and detected the borrowings and untruths. Appreciation of both men's power of invention has been enough to spare them any charge of dishonest conduct. Dishonesty happens to have been their forte, the heart of their contribution. Do not the untruths, after all, begin on the title page, where both authors signed a name that is not their given, legal name, but a conscious literary creation? "A Tour on the Prairies" appeared as the work of "Crayon," Geoffrey Crayon, alter ego of Diedrich Knickerbocker. Stendhal is one of over _fifty_ noms de plume employed by Henri Beyle in his writings.(18) The pseudonym, once the refuge of anonymity for writers fearing political reprisal, poor critical reception, or other disaster, had become for Irving and Beyle an integral element of the literary artifice, as in the commedia del l'arte tradition -- a recognition that for them even the narratorial "I" is a contrived persona, shaped to the exigencies of maximum expressiveness. The Crayon or Stendhal on the cover stood as an unintentional (or at best, subliminal) _caveat emptor_: if you really want a factual, objective account, look elsewhere! Consider too the titles: _Promenades dans Rome_, implying that the following journal entries were composed _en pleine marche_, when in truth the author's only promenades were through his memory, or across the street to the library to pilfer others' memories. "A Tour on the Prairies" is an utterly bland title, suspiciously modest, as though the author dared not oversell the shamelessly dramatized pages within. Two more lies are apparent, then, in title choice, Stendhal committing the sin of excess, Irving the sin of penury. An anonymous contemporary critic writing in the _Monthly Review_, a British magazine, was sensitive to the latter: he or she described "A Tour" as "possessed of singular charms, and greatly beyond what the writer claims for it."(19) Even Stanley Williams, who takes Irving's preface to "A Tour" at face value, comments at length on the process of romanticizing:

> [O]ne can . . . perceive how, as a natural stylist, he warmed to his task; how more and more he appreciated the richness of his materials; how easily the romantic glow, which the everyday citizen also craved, was diffused over the pages of his narrative.
>
> . . . Western meadows, of course, like the Spanish vega or the English countryside, are "enamelled" Ellsworth observed that Irving described at a distance "a perfect resemblance of an old moorish castle in ruins. . . ." Indeed, we soon wearily concede the resemblance between forest glades and cathedral naves and between Andalusian ponies and Indian steeds(20)

As Wayne Kime notes, such ways of seeing in "A Tour" have earned Irving the disdain of modern critics:

> Irving's use of historical and literary allusions in the work has been attacked by John F rancis McDermott, Robert Edson Lee, and others, as revealing his constitutional unpreparedess to describe Western life as it actually was. According to this generally accepted view, Irving's comparisons of an Indian brave to Adonis, a half-breed cook to Gil Blas, or the prairie terrain to a landscape by Claude Lorraine, are all bogus and misleading because they fail to represent these personages and places in immediacy, relying instead on stereotyped, derivative models.(21)
>
> The notion that Irving was unable to perceive or portray the West except in false terms is virtually universal in the rather scarce published discussions of "A Tour".(22)

Kime does not contest the falseness, but argues that because "almost without exception these fillips of style appear only in the first one-third of "A Tour"," their presence and gradual disappearance effectively chart the elevation of Irving's consciousness in this encounter between himself and the West.(23)

To understand the nature of the authorial force we are discussing, I propose to examine the bee hunt of 13 October as related in all four surviving narratives of the expedition. Pourtales, as usual, is laconic:

> Our hunters chopped down about ten trees in which there were bees. We, therefore, had an enormous quantity of honey. This previous product made us appreciate and admire even more this 'campement de miel' or honey cam

Latrobe, in the only other contemporary published account, says merely:

> The bee-hunters also had been on the alert, and eighteen bee-trees were discovered, cut down, and rifled of their hoard of sweets . . . .(25)

Ellsworth's letter-journal contains a much longer version detailing the locating and chopping of the trees and smoking out of the bees.(26) Then:

> The tree fell with a tremendous crash -- the hive broke nearly in the middle -- the bees poured out . . . and they soon became "good natured" -- they surrendered the fortress at discretion, and abandoned their winter residence, and gathered their little republic or kingdom, on the tree adjoining, where they were, when we left them, settling matters of state.(27)

Ellsworth is a great dramatizer, though the effusiveness of his language usually undercuts him. It is interesting how he expands the episode by interpreting the bees' activities in terms of human actions and reactions. Irving takes a similar approach but develops it to a vastly higher degree, imputing to the insects not only human reactions but also a wide gamut of human emotions. The bee hunt occupies an entire chapter of "A Tour",(28) of which I shall give but brief excerpts:

> The jarring blows of the axe seemed to have no effect in alarming or disturbing this most industrious community. They continued to ply at their usual occupations, some arriving full freighted into port, others sallying forth on new expeditions, like so many merchantmen in a money making metropolis, little suspicious of impending bankruptcy and downfall. . . .
>
> [The bees] made no attack and sought no refuge; they seemed stupified by the catastrophe and unsuspicious of its cause.
>
> . . . [A]s if the bees would carry through the similitude of their habits with those of laborious and gainful men, I beheld numbers from rival hives, arriving on eager wing, to enrich themselves with the ruins of their neighbors. . . . As to the poor proprietors of the ruin they seemed to have no heart to do any thing, not even to taste the nectar that flowed around them; but crawled backwards and forwards, in vacant desolation, as I have seen a poor fellow with his hands in his breeches pocket, whistling vacantly and despondingly about the ruins of his house that had been burnt.(29)

This is literary art -- not simply a more masterly management of words but a wholly different way of seeing. The reading public buys the writings of an Irving in order to share in that vision. Other dynamics are also at play: the public wants the prairies to be as exciting, dramatic a place as possible, within the bounds of inhabitability. It wants to find adventure in reading of lands and ways of life altogether different from its own, a locus for dreams. For a small number of readers, such tales will make them grow even more restless with their daily existence, until they wave it all goodbye from the back of a covered wagon. But for the majority, paradoxically, this reading leaves them _more_ content to go on with the next day's routine. Apparently the hunger for adventure is not unlike the need for other pleasurable quantities; most of us require small doses at regular intervals, which leave us temporarily sated and content; while a few persons with addictive personalities find that each dosage leaves them hungering for more.

The prospective reader of "A Tour" could anticipate adventure not simply from the description of the unknown prairies and their riches and dangers but also from sharing a great American writer's vision of them. And Irving's reputation promised the savory adventure of his wordsmith's and storyteller's crafts. As in the epics of old, realism serves as a necessary frame of reference without which the sensational and the miraculous would not stand out with so much force. Except for persons unfamiliar with the name Crayon, would anyone have purchased the book hoping for the sort of account advertised in the preface? In an established stylist's report of his voyage, writing is foregrounded as a corollary of reputation. For a straightforward description, the anonymous guidebook serves better.

For a tourist of the romantic period, the worst disappointment might be to visit an exotic locale and not be moved to thundering, weeping paroxysms of soul and emotion. Yet few persons genuinely possess such deep sensibilities. Of those few, still fewer are able to transform the emotions, meaning intact, to words; only a handful can do this in a readable, truly poetic way, where the written account actually transcends the emotion of the moment and carries it to a universal level.

Now, if Average Intelligent/Sensitive Reader _X_ familiarizes him or herself with Great Writer _Y_'s account of Locus _A_ before he or she (_X_) travels there, he or she in all probability will see _A_ much as _Y_ saw it (or claims to have seen it), particularly if he or she (_X_) wants to see it that way. Writer _Y_, of course, was committed _not_ to see _A_ as _X_ would otherwise have seen it, if indeed _Y_ is worthy of his or her literary credentials. Thus is the "lie" institutionalized into nonfiction travel literature of the romantic period, almost as deeply as into fiction. And it represents precisely the "constructive," "creative," "solving" kind of romanticism that Barzun hypothesized.(30)

In _Promenades dans Rome_, Stendhal makes this aesthetic of subjective, creative vision quite explicit:

GROTTAFERRATA, Aug. 25 Except on days of vivid

> emotion, when the imagination is creative and yields sensations even in connection with a mediocre work, my friends look at a painting only when it is attributed to one of . . . twenty-nine painters.(31)

Later he complains of the obstructive effect memory and knowledge have on the romantic vision and when, quite astoundingly, he impugns reading, he veers awfully close to insulting his audience and pulling down his own house:

> I should like to find in Naples, after having seen Italy, the Lethean waters that would make me forget everything, and then begin my travel over again . . . ; every new voyage that one makes to this country has its character, and a little science unfortunately enters into the sixth. Instead of admiring the ruins of the temple of Jupiter Tonans as I did twenty-six years ago, my imagination is shackled by all the stupidities I have read about it.(32)

But the less sensitive reader, who does need the book, is less sensitive to the hint as well. He or she does not toss the volume out but goes on reading and even feels a sense of sharing with Stendhal's superior sensitivity and vision.

A fascinating example of such reader reaction may be found in Jean Dutourd's _L'Ame sensible_, a rather presumptuous meditation over Stendhal and over Prosper Merimee's essay on him. Says Dutourd, "One of the charms of reading Stendhal is that one never finds what one expects" --(33)the adventure motif. Describing Stendhal's _Memoires d'un touriste_, the 1839 Account of the travels through France of a fictionalized French narrator,(34) Dutourd writes:

> He looked at France, which was his native land, where he had lived since birth, through the eyes of an Iroquois or a Huron and, what is still more remarkable, _without doing this on purpose_.
>
> I read _Les Memoires d'un Touriste_ when I was about 18. The truth about dozens of little things appeared naked before me. . . . _The scales fell from my eyes_.(35)

It may be that Dutourd says "_without doing this on purpose_" in order to distinguish Stendhal's approach from the broad "how-others-see-us" satire found in Montesquieu's _Lettres persanes_ and elsewhere. Stendhal's "clear vision" in this later work is never gratuitous, nor even foregrounded. If, however, Dutourd means to assert that Stendhal achieved this condition without conscious planning, I would first inquire on what basis he claims to know; then, I would have to admit that my own intuitive guess is exactly the opposite. In any case, it would do all the more honor to Stendhal the writer to credit him with such ability to sell the "lie" that even a sensitive, admiring reader cannot believe him capable of it.

Finally, I would like to couple this question of sincerity with a consideration of the profundity of the inherent untruth in Stendhal's _Promenades_ and Irving's _Tour_. Stendhal starts from a foundation in the lie of plagiarism, one we are wont to consider a crime against our profession and utter dissimulation regarding the circumstances of the book's composition. Irving begins with a truth -- "I have no wonders to describe" -- for the actual journey may have yielded little raw material in the way of "wonders" -- and he proceeds to turn it into a lie by the rightful exercise of his romantic authorial invention, without which the book might have appealed to a few historical specialists but certainly not to the wide audience of readers it has attracted and pleased on two continents in two centuries.

It is in part _because_ Irving left the prairies without a wealth of immediately appealing material and was compelled to apply his powers of imagination to come up with a tale worthy of his pen that "A Tour" is superior to _Promenades_ as an embodiment of the romantic spirit. Since Irving left the "no wonders to describe" preface stand even after he had nullified its veracity, the reader may take the lie either as an escape clause, in case the author's inventive powers had not proved sufficient to the task or as a very clever bit of misdirection to be appreciated after one has finished the book or as both. There is even the possibility that it represents an uncharacteristic show of modesty.

On the other hand, when one asks which of the books gives the more honest, accurate portrayal of the place it promises to portray, it is surely the _Promenades dans Rome_. Stendhal did his plagiarizing and lying thoroughly and effectively, and prospective tourists found themselves, and still find themselves, well served by it. Treating a city rich and filled with wonders from several epochs, he was not under such a compulsion to create from naught. His lie about the 1802 visit to Rome was written simply to establish a consistent, interesting framework for the presentation of historical facts, for which his readers are that much more knowledgeable.

The ultimate irony, I think, is that if at the time _Promenades_ was published Stendhal had already been established as a writer of fiction, the book might not have succeeded; for then his readers' expectations would, like Irving's readers', have been quite otherwise, and his painstakingly researched accuracy would amount to a disappointment. For when fashion and circumstances lead the public to demand the lie, accuracy can only be seen as a deception.

NOTES

1. Cf. Johanna Johnston, _The Heart That Would Not Hold_ (New York: Evans, 1971), pp. 317-18.
2. Stanley T. Williams, _The Life of Washington Irving_ (New York: Oxford University Press, 1935), 2: 27-37.

3. Letter from Ellsworth to the secretary of war, dated Fort Gibson, November 18, 1832 (Office of Indian Affairs, National Archives, Washington, D.C.).
4. Washington Irving, The Crayon Miscellany, ed. Dahlia Kirby Terrell (Boston: Twayne Publishers, 1979), pp. 1-22.
5. Martha Dula, "Audience Response to "A Tour on the Prairies" in 1835," Western American Literature 8 (1973): 67-70.
6. Crayon Miscellany, pp. 8-9.
7. Charles Joseph Latrobe, The Rambler in Oklahoma, ed. Muriel H. Wright and George H. Shirk (Oklahoma City, Chattanooga: Harlow, 1955).
8. Henry Leavitt Ellsworth, Washington Irving on thePrairie, ed. Stanley T. Williams and Barbara D. Simison (New York: American Book Co., 1937).
9. Count de Pourtales, On the Western Tour with Washington Irving, ed. George F. Spaulding, tr. Seymour Feiler (Norman: University of Oklahoma Press, 1968).
10. On the Western Tour, Pourtales, pp. 35-36.
11. Stendhal, Petit guide d'Italie, publ. Robert d'Illiers (Paris: Le Divan, 1951).
12. He eventually published his own memoirs of the trip: R[omain] C[olomb], Journal d'un voyage en Italie et en Suisse, pendant l'annee 1828 (Paris: Vediere, 1833).
13. Stendhal, A Roman Journal [Promenades dans Rome], ed. and tr. Haakon Chevalier (New York: Orion, 1957), pp. xix-xx (editor's preface).
14. Roman Journal, pp. 1-2.
15. Roman Journal, p. xix (editor's preface).
16. Jacques Barzun, Classic, Romantic and Modern, 2 ed. (New York: Doubleday/Anchor, 1961), p. 72.
17. Compare Mario Praz, The Romantic Agony, 2 ed. (Cleveland and New York: Meridian, 1956), pp. 25-50.
18. Stendhal, Memoirs of a Tourist [Memoires d'un touriste], ed. and tr. Allan Seager (Evanston, Ohio: Northwestern University Press, 1962), p. ix (translator's preface).
19. [Anonymous], "A Tour on the Prairies". By the Author of 'The Sketch Book,'" Monthly Review, 1, 4, Art. 4 (April 1835): 468.
20. The Life of Washington IrvingWilliams, vol. 2, pp. 80-81.
21. Wayne R. Kime, "The Completeness of Washington Irving's "A Tour" on the Prairies," Western American Literature 8 (1973):55-56.
22. "Completeness of Irving's A Tour", Kime, p. 56, n. 2.
23. "Completeness of Irving's A Tour",Kime, p. 56.
24. On the Western Tour, Pourtales, p. 50.
25. Rambler, Latrobe, p. 37.
26. Irving on the Prairie, Ellsworth, pp. 29-31.
27. Irving on the PrairieEllsworth, p. 30.
28. Crayon Miscellany, Irving, pp. 29-32.
29. Crayon Miscellany, Irving, pp. 30-32.
30. Classic, Romantic and Modern, Barzun, p. 14.
31. Roman Journal, p. 27.
32. Roman Journal, p. 96.
33. Jean Dutourd, The Man of Sensibility [L'Ame sensible], tr. Robin Chancellor (New York: Simon & Schuster, 1961), p. 190.

34. See note 18 above; see also Bernard Delvaille, "Un commis-voyageur nomme H.B.," *Magazine Litteraire,* no. 191 (janvier, 1983):26-28.

35. *Man of Sensibility*, Dutourd, p. 190.

13.

A Quaint, Picturesque Little Pile: Architecture and the Past in Washington Irving

DAVID R. ANDERSON

When in 1856 an essayist for Harper's New Monthly Magazine wrote about "Sunnyside," Washington Irving's home near Tarrytown, New York, he gave an account so meticulously detailed thats the modern reader wonders that the general public could have had so avid an interest in the minutiae of Irving's domestic arrangements. Although accounts of celebrities' houses are no oddity to the modern reader of Architectural Digest or to the devotees of Barbara Walters' televised intrusions into people's lives, we are struck by the reverent tone with which T. Addison Richards portrays Sunnyside and its environs. More striking than lists of trees in the extensively landscaped gardens or descriptions of neighbors' villas or their occupations (the banks of the Hudson were populated by a bevy of painters, sculptors, and writers) are some of the assumptions about Irving and his house which are made by the visiting journalist. Sunnyside is no ordinary house, as Richards points out:

> The cottage, with its crowstepped gables and weathercocks overrun with honey suckle and eglantine, with the rose-vine and the clinging ivy is a wonderfully unique little edifice, totally unlike anything else in our land, but always calling up remembrances of our fancies of merrie rural England, with a hint here and there of its old Dutch leaven.(1)

The reporter has perceived what Irving was trying to achieve in designing and rebuilding the simple cottage he had bought in 1835, twenty years before the article was published. Irving and his contemporaries in the Knickerbocker Club were painfully aware of the newness of America at a time when their European brethren had discovered the potent analogy of the Middle Ages for the emotional, dark, mysterious side of the human psyche. European romantics had rejected the bright rationality of the eighteenth century in favor of irrationalitz and vision as sources of art. Instead of using classical precedent as a social measure, medieval and nationalistic examples became desirable in literature and art.

Americans, ever wont to ape the fashions of their foreign counterparts, had a crucial dilemma. The romantic landscape that afforded Europeans the raw material for their works was lacking in raw, young America. After Hawthorne's death, the American novelist Henry James "enumerate[d] the items of high civilization . . . which are absent from the texture of American life"; there are, he laments,

> no aristocracy, no church, no clergy, no army, no diplomatic service, no country gentlemen, no palaces, no castles, nor manors, nor old country houses, nor parsonages, nor thatched cottages, nor ivied ruins; no cathedrals, nor abbeys, nor little Norman churches.(2)

Although not born until after the American Revolution, Irving bore as his Christian name the family name of the hero who proclaimed America as new. From the advent of romanticism as an aesthetic movement, American artists were forced to find a way around the newness represented by Washington and his generation in order to find a usable past that would be the equivalent of European antiquity.

In 1807-8, under the collective pseudonym "Launcelot Langstaff, Esq.," Irving, his brother William, and James Kirke Paulding (Knickerbockers all) published twenty satirical pamphlets entitled _Salmagundi_. One of the most imaginative, "Cockloft Hall," attributed to Washington Irving, illustrates his budding romantic prejudice for the old over the new:

> Modern _style_ has always been an object of great annoyance to Christopher, and is ever treated by him with sovereign contempt, as an upstart intruder. It is a common observation of his, that your old-fashioned substantial furniture bespeaks the respectability of one's ancestors, and indicates that the family has been used to hold up its head for more than the present generation; whereas the fragile appendages of modern style seemed to be emblems of mushroom gentility. . . .(Salmagundi, 267)

Hardly had the hostilities surrounding the War of 1812 diminished than Irving was wandering around England, notebook in hand, capturing the romantic qualities he sensed in the English romantics, particularly in the atmospheric novels of Sir Walter Scott. In "The Author's Account of Himself," a youthful Irving wrote:

> My native country was full of native promise: Europe was rich in the accumulated treasures of age. Her very ruins told the history of time gone by, and every mouldering stone was a chronicle. I longed to wander over the scenes of renowned achievement -- 'to tread as it were, in the footsteps of antiquity -- to loiter about the ruined castle -- to meditate on the fallen tower to escape, in short, from the commonplace

> realities of the present, and lose myself among the shadowy grandeurs of the past.(The Sketch-book, 744)

His yearning for mildew is palpable! In the years before buying the Tarrytown cottage, Irving's essays and sketches increasingly reflected the values of antique surroundings which he felt he could convey to fellow Americans. He was particularly impressed by the sense that domestic English dwellings had an influence on the people who lived in them and that the appearance of a manor or hall revealed things about its inhabitants. He perceived a correspondence between the homes of the english gentry and personal characteristics -- which he sometimes viewed with ironic whimsy -- that distinguished them from Americans.

From William Wordsworth in England to William Cullen Bryant in America, romantic poets had preached the quite modern sounding doctrine that the environment is a primary influence on the developing character. For Irving - as for many of his contemporaries, including Andrew Jackson Downing -- there was only a short step from the influence of nature on the individual to the influence of the created environment.

In a series of essays collected under the title Bracebridge Hall, Irving creates a charming fictional portrait of English life. His narrator (and pseudonym) Geoffrey Crayon begins the essay "Family Relics" by declaring that "an old English family mansion is a fertile subject for study." "An old manor house, and an old family of this kind are rarely met with at the present day," he adds in "The Hall." As he leads the reader through the house and the variety both of daily routine and holiday celebration, Irving's narrator intends more than a record of Old World customs. Ambling through the Hall and into the Portrait Gallery, Crayon suggests that the English manor is not just atmospheric machinery but the prototype of a rambling approach to literature as well. "I would have it understood," he writes,

> that I am not writing a novel, and have nothing of intricate plot nor marvelous adventure, to promise the reader. The Hall of which I treat has, for aught I know, neither trap-door nor sliding-pannel, nor donjon-keep; and indeed appears to have no mystery about it.(Bracebridge Hall, 8)

Crayon, in The Sketch Book in the essay "John Bull," provides the prototype for the rambling, romantic structure that fascinates him in his writing as well as finally in the building of his own house. The balance and symmetry of neoclassicism are abandoned in favor of

> an old castellated manor-house, gray with age, and of a most venerable though weather-beaten appearance. It has been built upon no regular plan, but is a vast accumulation of parts, erected in various tastes and ages. . . . Like

> all the relics of that style, it is full of obscure passages, intricate mazes and dusky chambers.(The Sketch Book, 1032-3)

Crayon, like Irving his creator, is drawn to Bull's admiration for the old manor and finally fears lest modern times tamper with it and spoil it. He strikes out at modern taste:

> There is something, too, in the appearance of his old family mansion that is extremely poetical and picturesque; and as long as it can be rendered comfortably habitable, I should almost tremble to see it meddled with, during the present conflict of tastes and opinions. Some of his advisors are no doubt good architects, that might be of service;
> but many, I fear, are mere levelers who, when they had once got to work with their mattocks on this venerable edifice, would never stop until they had brought it to the ground, and perhaps buried themselves among the ruins.(The Sketch Book, 1038-39)

When Irving stayed at Barlborough Hall in 1831 (the owner of which insisted it had been the prototype for Bracebridge Hall), he was intrigued by the eccentricities of his host, the Rev. C. R. Reatson Rodes. "Such a character and such a Mansion as you may easily suppose, furnish me much food for amusing speculation," he wrote to his sister.(3)

Irving was ambivalent about adopting the English manner/manor for home use. His familiar ironic attitude is to be found in the architectural simile which describes the eccentric squire of Bracebridge:

> His mind is like modern Gothic, where plain brick-work is set off with pointed arches and quaint tracery. Though the main groundwork of his opinions is correct, yet he has a thousand little notions, picked up from old books which stand out whimsically on the surface of his mind.(4)

For Irving, the manor can be looked on as the structure by which he hopes to imply the correspondence between ancient structures -- the romantic associations that accompany them -- and their inhabitants which will become a part of American literary life as it is in England. An architectural metaphor for literature had already suggested itself when he was preparing the manuscript for The Sketch Book in 1817. He observes:

> In literature Poetry is like classical architecture -- should be formed of the finest materials -- we build temples with the choicest marbles. Who would build a temple with brick & Hunt a mason with dirty apron and trowel.(5)

In some ways it is an eighteenth-century commonplace, but that he turns so soon afterward to Bracebridge Hall suggests it as a harbinger of Irving's fascination with architecture throughout his work.

Although English manors dominate his architectural fantasy; Irving was also drawn to the Dutch tradition which had contributed to the picturesque ambience of the Hudson River valley. The sense of history linked with picturesque tradition that is so much a part of "The Legend of Sleepy Hollow" and "Rip Van Winkle" is also reflected in the essay "Communipaw" in the Book of the Hudson. As so often in Irving's writing, his contemporary viewpoint places an antique residence in romantic perspective. He describes Garret van Horne's "House of the Four Chimneys":

> Here are to be seen articles of furniture which came over with the first settlers from Holland; ancient chests of drawers, and massive clothes presses, quaintly carved, and waxed and polished until they shine like mirrors.
>
> In this house the primitive Dutch Holy Days of Paas and Pinxter, are faithfully kept up, and New Year celebrated with cookies and cherry bounce; nor is the festival of the good St. Nicholas forgotten; . . . it is said that at the founding of the house St. Nicholas took it under his protection.

He tries to recreate the manor of European and English tradition which America has so far failed to produce. If Americans cannot actually live at Bracebridge Hall, they can through Irving's writing at least vicariously absorb the qualities contained within it. Irving brazenly creates a past for Americans in Knickerbocker's History of New York or wittily suggests New World antiquity in "Rip Van Winkle." He wrote real history in his biographies of Columbus, Washington, and Mohammed, but atmospheric history -- whether American or Spanish or whatever -- was more to his liking. It is as a writer and a builder, rather than as a historian, that his reputation remains current.

Architecture represented for Irving the link with the past. And America, despite its novelty, could recognize or even forge new links through architecture. He warns Americans to avoid the metropolis which reeks too powerfully of "white clapboard palaces, and Grecian temples, studded with 'academies,' 'seminaries,' and 'institutes'" which are "strongholds of Yankee usurpation;" far better if

> [the American]haply light upon some rough, rambling road [with] . . . here and there a low, red-roofed whitewashed farmhouse, cowering among apple and cherry trees; an old stone church, with elms and willows, and button-wood, as old looking as itself, and tombstones almost buried in their graves. . . [then] he has found one of the . . . haunts of poetry and romance.(6)

This is what Irving recreated at Sunnyside, for the American -- if he could not find antiquity at home -- had to recreate it himself, so that the solid virtues and literary associations found among Europeans would grow in new soil. Geoffrey Crayon in "Rural Life in England" states the value of English landscape in the strongest terms:

> The old church of remote architecture . . . the parsonage, a quaint irregular pile, partly antiquated . . . the neighboring village with its venerable cottages . . . the antique family mansion . . . all these common features of English landscape evince a calm and settled security and hereditary transmission of homebred virtues and local attachments, that speak deeply and touchingly to the moral character of the nation.)The Sketch Book, 800)

The last twenty-four years of his life, Irving, working with his artist friend George Harvey (neither of them trained architects), created a neo-Gothic "snuggery," to use Irving's term, that became for many the prototype of an American romantic literary fantasy transformed into wood and stone.(7) He was determined to create the illusion of an American past in his house that would be the equivalent of Sir Walter Scott's fictional portrayal of a stable feudal society. He had visited Scott's home "Abbotsford," itself a bogus medieval castle erected at the beginning of the nineteenth century. Writing to his brother after his first visit there in 1817, he remarked, "The few days I passed there were among the most delightful of my life, and worth as many years of ordinary existence."(8) The famous lithograph, "Scott and His Literary Friends at Abbotsford" hung in the study at Sunnyside to remind him of Scott's place, literally and figuratively, in literature.

In the essay "Abbotsford," collected in The Crayon Miscellany, Irving recalls a visit with Scott when Abbotsford was just under construction with materials derived from the ruins of Melrose Abbey. Irving was impressed with Scott's undertaking; his understanding of the building of Abbotsford and its connection with the creation of a new kind of literature is illuminating. Irving quotes Scott's conversation(The Crayon Miscellany, 144):

> There is no telling what treasures are hid in that glorious old pile. It is a famous place for antiquarian plunder. There are such rich bits of oldtime sculpture for the architect, and old time story for the poet. There is as rare picking in it as in a Stilton cheese, and in the same taste -- the moldier the better.

His reminiscence of Scott is echoed in a letter to his brother Peter at the same time that the initial work on

Sunnyside was nearly completed:

> I have just returned from a visit of two or three days to Tarrytown, to take a look at my cottage. . . It has risen from the foundation since my previous visit . . . and promises to be a quaint picturesque little pile. I intend to write a legend or two about it and its vicinity, by way of making it pay for itself.(9)

Later, Irving planted slips of ivy and eglantine procured from Abbotsford around the door at Sunnyside which have survived to this day.

Irving and Harvey consciously created an American version of a European house at Sunnyside, striving always for quaint and picturesque effect -- a literary legend in stone -- rather than a new or original structure. The mixture of styles was eclectic; over the door was engraved, in Dutch, "Boumeester" (architect) after Harvey's name, and Irving's letters are filled with sketches and suggestions about details of the house for Harvey to pass on to the workmen. "I have seen an irregular attic room managed that way in France with a very pretty effect. The very irregularity became a source of ornament," he writes in November 1835.(10)

That he was consciously apeing Scott while building Sunnyside is evident in a letter in 1852 to his friend William Preston; he recollected that "you warned me to take care that I did not outbuild my means, as poor Scott did at Abbotsford. I never did a more fortunate thing in my life. It completely anchored me and secured for me a delightful home."(11)

In 1855, four years before his death, he published _Wolfert's Roost_ (that is "Wolfert's Place of Rest," in corrupt Dutch) in which he fabricates a whimsical history for Sunnyside, with enough tongue-in-cheek to be recognized as gentle mockery of his own historical bent.

> It is said to have been modeled after the cocked hat of Peter the Headstrong, as the Escurial [_sic_] was modeled after the gridiron of the blessed St. Lawrence. Though but of small dimensions, yet like many people, it is of mighty spirit, and values itself greatly on the antiquity being one of the oldest edifices, for its size, in the whole country.

The ingenuous equivocation of the statement illustrates Irving's consciousness of the American romantic predicament as well as the self-deprecating humor that pervades many of the sketches.

The success of Irving's efforts can be measured by T. Addison Richards' observation that there exists an almost organic correspondence between Sunnyside and its inhabitant:

> There is about the cottage, as about himself, an air of reserve, without coldness, which while cordially inviting approach, creates instinc-

> tively and willingly a respectful deference. The sweet sunny sentiment of his home is ever seen in his genial smile, and his kindly and benevolent nature in its aspect of cheerfulness and benignity; while its odd twists, and turns, and unexpected vagaries speak of the quaint and whimsical, yet refined and delicate humor of his character.(12)

The confusion of pronouns here, so that references to Irving must be sorted out from references to his house, is a conscious literary device. We are not meant to differentiate house from houseman; they are, finally, one and the same. Richards is not alone in acknowledging Irving's domestic accomplishment; the poet, H. T. Tuckerman, writing in 1853 for Putnam's Houses of American Authors, characterized Sunnyside in language usually reserved for describing personality: "It is difficult to imagine what moral attraction it possesses to the kindred and friends who there habitually enjoy such genial companionship and frank hospitality."(13)

Throughout Irving's career a certain melancholy pervades his work that seemed to underscore his conservative bent, particularly as he grew older. He comes not only to yearn for the older European ways but to see all change -- certainly in architecture -- as an emblem of decline. In the last essay of Bracebridge Hall, "The Wedding," he anticipates the passing of the old order which gives meaning to his work:

> A little while hence, and all these will probably have passed away. Ready-Money Jack will sleep with his fathers; the good Squire, and all his peculiarities will be buried in the neighboring church. The old Hall will be modernized into a fashionable country seat, or peradventure, a manufactory. The park will be cut up into petty farms and kitchen gardens.

And in the nostalgic essay "The Legend of Sleepy Hollow," Irving captures the poignant contrast between his "mystic and dreamy" boyhood memory of the region and the adult writer's apprehension that "the dream of youth was at an end; the spell of Sleepy Hollow was broken!" The church, above all, has suffered "the hands of improvement":

> The pulpit, fabricated in Holland, had been superseded by one of modern construction, and the front of the semi-Gothic edifice was decorated by a semi-Grecian portico. Fortunately, the two weathercocks remained undisturbed on their perches, at each end of the church, and still kept up a diametrical opposition to each other on all points of windy doctrine.

For several pages he documents the loss of quaint, picturesque tradition in the village, finally departing "with the sad conviction that I had beheld the last of the good old Dutch times in this once favored region."

In 1846, having returned to Sunnyside from another European sojourn -- this time as minister to Spain -- he embarked on yet another picturesque building plan for expanding Sunnyside, as though to create a bulwark against currents in American letters that were already leaving him behind. The architecture of the Alhambra in Spain had been the inspiration for a popular series of essays both on the legends associated with it as well as the influence which "this Moslem pile in the midst of a Christian land" had on him. in the essay, "important negotiations," he speaks of the power which the alhambra has over him:

> I tread haunted ground, and am surrounded by romantic associations. From earliest childhood, when, on the banks of the Hudson, I first pored over the pages of old Ginez Perez de Hytas' apocryphal but chivalresque history of the civil wars of Granada . . . that city has ever been a subject of my waking dreams; and often have I trod in fancy the romantic halls of the Alhambra. Behold for once a day-dream realized.

This, his last project at Sunnyside, was a romantic tower, often referred to as the "Pagoda," though it is architecturally more related to the tower of Comares in whose shadow he slept in the Alhambra. His work on the house very nearly threatened his literary pursuits, as he points out in a letter to Sabina O'Shea:

> I was pretty much my own architect; projector and landscape gardener, and had but rough hands to work under me, I have been kept busy out of doors from morning until night and from months end to months end until within a week or two past when I brought my labors to a close. . . . I have now returned to my books and my study, and taken up my long neglected pen; and hope to go on according to my old habitudes.(14)

Irving's joining of elegant architecture and belles lettres at Sunnyside created a precedent which recurs frequently in nineteenth-century America. Romantics have traditionally been supporters of revolution against the ancien regime. American romantics were placed in the peculiar position of rejecting as their regime the generation of the Revolution! To search for useful historical parallels in European romanticism, particularly in neomedievalism, implied the denial of democratic in favor of aristocratic institutions. James Fenimore Cooper, Irving's contemporary, espoused just such a shift not only in his Leatherstocking tales, but in his less-known novels as well. He modeled much of his fiction on the aristocratic ideals which inhered in the Cooper ancestral mansion, Otsego Hall, in Cooperstown, New York.

It seems particularly fitting that at the memorial for Cooper on February 25, 1852, Irving described him as "a very castle of a man."(15) It is an appropriate met-

metaphor for both of these American literary pioneers who wished to construct the proper house for the mind which might elevate the spirit of Americans. By both writing about and building houses, they set a precedent that is reflected in a significant series of real and literary nineteenth-century structures: in Emerson, Thoreau, Hawthorne, Melville, Twain, and Harriet Beecher Stowe.(16) Because Irv_ing believed that America lacked the right kind of house for the indwelling of spirit, it was incumbent on him to create it -- in his fiction first of all, and then in his private dwelling.

NOTES

1. Addison Richards, "Sunnyside: The Home of Washington Irving," Harper's New Monthly Magazine (December 1856), p. 7.
2. Henry James, "Hawthorne (1879)," in The Shock of Recognition, ed. Edmund Wilson, (New York: Octogon Books, 1975), I:459-60. All references to Salmagunie and The Sketch Book will be from Washington Irving, History, Tale and Sketches, ed., James W. Tutleton (New York:The Library of America, 1983). Reference to Bracebridge Hall will be to: Bracebridge Hall, ed., Herbert F. Smith (Boston:Twayne Publishers, 1977); also, Washington Irving, The Crayon Miscellany, ed., Dahlia Kirby Terrel (Boston:Twayne Publishers, 1979).
3. Ralph M. Aderman, Herbert L. Kleinfeld, and Jennifer S. Banks, eds. Washington Irving, Letters, Volume II, 1823-1838 (Boston: Twayne Publishers, 1979), pp. 843-44.
4. I am indebted to G. Thomas Couser of Hofstra University for this reference which is cited in his unpublished essay "Washington Irving and Andrew Jackson Downing: An Ignored Relationship."
5. Washington Irving, Notes While Preparing Sketch Book & c. 1817, ed. Stanley T. Williams (New Haven: Yale University Press, 1927), p. 27. Williams points out that the reference is a criticism of Leigh Hunt.
6. Washington Irving, Book of the Hudson, collected from the various works of Diedrich Knickerbocker, ed. Geoffrey Crayon (New York: G. P. Putnam and Co., 1849), p. 12.
7. Harold Dean Cater in his "Washington Irving and Sunnyside," New York History (April 1957), has already suggested that Sunnyside "was a finely studied and polished miniature that had been created exactly as Irving the writer created" (p. 184).
8. Ralph M. Aderman, Herbert L. Kleinfield, and Jenifer S. Banks, eds., Washington Irving, Letters, Volume I, 1802-1823 (Boston: Twayne Publishers, 1978), pp. 502-3.
9. Letters, Volume II, pp. 842-44.
10. Letters, Volume II, p. 845. This letter is also quoted in Joseph T. Butler, Washington Irving's Sunnyside (Tarrytown, N.Y.: Sleepy Hollow Restorations, 1974).
11. Ralph M. Aderman, Herbert L. Kleinfield, and Jenifer S. Banks, eds., Washington Irving, Letters, Volume IV, 1846-1859 (Boston: Twayne Publishers, 1982), p. 313.
12. "Sunnysider," p. 12.

13. H. T. Tuckerman, *Homes of American Authors* (New York: G. P. Putnam and Co., 1853), p. 294.
14. *Letters, Volume IV*, p. 151.
15. *Fenimore Cooper: The Critical Heritage*, ed. George Dekker and John P. McWilliams (London and Boston: Routledge and Kegan Paul, 1973), p. 245.
16. For example, Emerson's home in Concord and the essays on "Domestic Life"; Thoreau's literary structure at Walden Pond; Melville's Berkshire home reflected in *Pierre*, "I and My Chimney," and a series of poems; Hawthorne's *House of the Seven Gables* and his lifelong fascination with his own dwellings; Twain's criticism of excesses in architecture culminating in the house at Nook Farm in Hartford; Stowe's fictional architecture in *Uncle Tom's Cabin*, her collaboration with her sister in a series of domestic advice books, and the building of her own splendid home in the same subdivision as Twain's.

Part IV

An Afterthought

14. *The Knickerbocker History* as Knickerbocker's "History"

WILLIAM L. HEDGES

The self-mockery of the book which Washington Irving published in 1809 in the name of Diedrich Knickerbocker starts with its hyperbolic title, A History of New York, From the Beginning of the World to the End of the Dutch Dynasty. It continues with the title-page summary of contents, which promises that "the Unutterable Ponderings of WALTER THE DOUBTER" will be uttered and touts the book as "the only Authentic History of the Times that ever hath been, or ever will be Published." The oddity, for Anglo-American ears, of the supposed author's name also gives us pause.(1) Beyond the title page, Knickerbocker's solemn dedication of his opus to the New York Historical Society (p. 366) makes us wonder if the history may not prove to be genuinely historical after all, but the peculiarities ascribed to him in the "Account of the Author," written by his former landlord, Seth Handaside (another dubious name) deepen our suspicions. And the "author" himself begins undermining his authority in his flagrantly self-contradictory preface, "To the Public."

On the one hand he presents himself as the humble antiquarian trying to unearth scraps of an almost totally forgotten past, a writer bound to "dull matter of fact" by his commitment to "faithful veracity" and his determination to appeal to the "judgment, rather than to [the] imagination" of his readers. On the other hand, he promises them the "sentiment" of Tacitus, the "dignity, the grandeur and magnificence of Livy," and the "bold excursive manner" of Herodotus; he aims to lay the "foundation" of a history of New York that will one day be as monumental as "Gibbon's Rome"; and in an outburst of megalomania he declares that "cities, empires, plots conspiracies, wars, havock and desolation, are ordained by providence only as food for this historian." Indeed, "The world - the world, is nothing without the historian!" (pp. 377-81).

Since 1848 most readers have known Irving's burlesque history only through the often reprinted "Author's Revised Edition," prior acquaintance with which seems to have made it difficult for scholars and critics to come to terms with the original Knickerbocker of 1809. What became for Irving a lifelong project of making the book more acceptable to the growing middle-class audience started early. Beginning with the second edition in 1812, for instance, he made substantial cuts in "To the Public." Among them are the climactic assertions just quoted which subordinate the world to the historian. He also deleted the final paragraph of the preface, in which Knickerbocker, after having a moment earlier referred to himself with excessive humility as "little I," turns on the "small fry of literature" and promises, if they insult his book, to "sweep" up "half a hundred" in a "scoop net" and "roast" them for "breakfast" (p. 381).

Two omissions as substantial as these within a page of each other make the self-contradictoriness of "To the Public" appreciably less blatant and thereby diminish the "dizzying" effect on the reader which Martin Roth has observed to be characteristic of Irving's early humor. It is a characteristic also, Roth maintains, of much post-Augustan burlesque, particularly when it involves a "whimsical" narrator, like Tristram Shandy, and a "self-conscious" interplay between two strands of narrative. *Knickerbocker* of course features both, the interplay being between the so-called history of New York, which roth calls the "primary fiction," and Diedrich's running account (the "secondary fiction") of the "creation" of the narrative.(2) If anything, I suspect, *Knickerbocker* makes us dizzier than most such "self-conscious" fiction because so often we cannot be sure to what extent the "historian" is involved in Irving's facetiousness.

For instance, do we read Knickerbocker's self-contradictions in "To the Public" as deliberate or inadvertent? Is he consciously pulling our leg or spoofing the classic historians -- or both? Or is the irony dramatic, an indication of the antiquarian's feeble intellect or distracted imagination? Our not knowing how to take Knickerbocker here typifies the dilemma that the narrative again and again places us in. Such disorientation is basic to the excitement of the book - at least in its original version. Initially I find myself taking Irving's persona, in the moment of what I have perhaps too hastily called his megalomania, as meaning what he says (why, I shall explain shortly). While he sounds quite mad, his paradoxical rant makes a weird sense. Yet at almost the same time I am conscious of a secondary reaction, namely that the passage mocks the pride of historians in claiming for themselves the right to award historical personages "the meed of immortality" (p. 380). So there is confusion: if Knickerbocker is at this point sincere but deluded, he cannot be aware of the satire that Irving is voicing through him. Yet maybe he *is* aware, maybe he is not mad but very cunning; maybe the irony is not dramatic but, for the persona himself, intentional. Furthermore, whether the passage is satire or crazy metaphysics or both, its conclusion ("the world is nothing without the historian") has a mind-blowing boldness.

The "Account of the Author" has prepared us for a book written by a man who, though "a little queer in his ways" (p. 373), a bit out of touch with reality, like an absent-minded professor, nonetheless has scholarly credentials. If he loses some of his credibility in "To the Public," the unflagging passion with which he throws himself into his work and promotes himself as historian in the grand tradition makes it difficult to give up on him altogether. His style itself, its range and suppleness -- high-flown Latinate eloquence one moment, free-swinging Anglo-Saxon obstreperousness the next -- its constant aural appeal and command of metaphor and allusion -- carries authority even apart from what the words themsleves say. The uncertainty and tension persist throughout the book. In the devastating satire of the famous set piece in which Knickerbocker justifies European atrocities against the Indians on the grounds that the native Americans are subhuman (pp. 412-24), we can be virtually certain by the end that he, as well as Irving, is being facetious. Yet, if his narrative has induced in us a tendency to believe that he -- we may find ourselves struggling for quite a while to take his defense of the white man at face value. Or later on we may actually doubt whether he recognizes his low burlesque account of the military encounter between the Swedes and the Dutch at Fort Christina, "the most horrible battle ever recorded in poetry or prose" (p. 648), as the travesty of epic depictions of warfare that we take it to be. But no matter how absurd he becomes -- and whether he intends the absurdity (as satire) or not -- he keeps redeeming himself by lapsing into passages of considerable length which, taken at face value, make almost perfect sense. Implausibilities, exaggerations, incongruities, and digressions fade for a time from the reader's memory, until, without our quite seeing it happen, clarity transforms itself back into nonsense, or a sudden shift of tone or a violent nonsequitur once more jolts our complacency. So in the final chapter: "Thus died Peter Stuyvesant, a valiant soldier -- a loyal subject -- an upright governor, and an honest Dutchman -- who wanted only a few empires to desolate, to have been immortalized as a hero" (p. 726).

If I seem to belabor ambiguity and contradiction, it is to call attention to the colossal nonsense of which Irving's *History* largely consists -- inspired nonsense, certainly, but nonsense nonetheless. Literary historians and critics have been reluctant to surrender fully to the self-contradictoriness which is the work's mushy core. The image, as Roth suggests, of "study gone mad," a literary descendant of the conventional "burlesque narrator," whose head, "stuffed with a vast amount of learning," is "in a continous turmoil,"(3) Knickerbocker is essentially a joke as a historian, but the joke remains only partially laughed at.

For readers can, and apparently often do, read the *History* with only minimal awareness of Knickerbocker himself, except when he intrudes on the narrative with the story of his researching and writing it. A strong sense of the erratic voice in the *History* as his (rather than Irving's) is by no means essential to getting through the book. Presumably most readers recognize him quite early as an embodiment of pretentiousness and pedantry. As a travesty, Diedrich is easily laughed at -- and then, perhaps, easily forgotten, allowed (or forced) for the most part to recede into the background as a nominal presence. With the narrator more or less out of the way, the reader, responding pleasurably to satire, humorous portraiture, and now and then unexpectedly astute perception and comment, is free to concentrate on the main narrative, to try to pick up a thread of truth amid the everlasting distortions, alert at the same time perhaps to the possibility that some general theme will emerge to give the short-lived Dutch colonial enterprise in North America a larger significance.

To unearth such significance readers often try to cut through irony and inconsistency with commonsense judgments as to what Irving really had in mind. Wanting the book to "mean" something, ultimately uneasy with -- or intolerant of -- the ambiguity or nonsense generated by Knickerbocker's verbal eccentricity, this kind of approach at some point unconsciously resists the disorientation which the *History* in its original version is so beautifully contrived to induce. Simultaneously it must deny the reality of Knickerbocker as a character is his own story.

Of course there is a certain logic in the denial: if he is a travesty, we need not take him very seriously. But if we give him half a chance, if we identify the urgent, irrepressible albeit distracted voice as completely his, not Irving's, Knickerbocker becomes the dominant presence and takes over the book. Mad, unbelievable, he is nonetheless real. If he all but falls apart as a character from time to time, the illusion of his reality keeps resuscitating itself as long as we are not inadvertently blocking it out. This is part of the book's dizzying effect. Unfortunately, most of us, including Roth, as we shall see, have trouble resisting the urge to try to tease something more than passing sense out of the nonsense. We are not always able to laugh at *ourselves* when meanings that here and there begin to develop in the book are suddenly subverted.(4)

Most commonly perhaps, *Knickerbocker* is taken as more or less bona fide history tricked out in a quaint or cute form. Faith in the book's historical legitimacy dies hard -- and not just among sub-sub-librarians who catalog it as history rather than literature. We have by now a very complete understanding of Irving's misuse, abuse, and neglect of history; of how extensively he embroidered on what his remarkably few sources told him; and how he fabricated actors, events, and historical explanations when it suited him.(5) The "Stuyvesant manuscript," to which Knickerbocker repeatedly refers, is obviously a fiction, as apparently are most of the "well authenticated traditions" he claims to have gathered from "divers excellent old ladies" (p. 378).(6) Clearly old Diedrich's Herculean labor (as he sees it) of immortalizing his ancestors is historical only in the most general or trivial sense. Nevertheless, although major research exposing the *History*'s spuriousness as history dates back to 1927, experts on Irving have often felt compelled to praise him for "scholarly regard for sources" or to call *Knickerbocker* "tolerably authentic history" or "a respectable piece of historiography."(7) In a doctoral dissertation completed as recently as 1970 we find a scholar working assiduously to show that there is here and there unexpected authenticity in Knickerbocker's "image" of the New Netherlanders, as well as a basis in history for many aspects of his depiction of the colony, no matter how much it may distort the reality.(8)

Irving's own contention in 1848 that he had tried in *Knickerbocker* to promote "good humor and good fellowship" by embodying "the traditions of our city in an amusing form"(9) has probably contributed to the persistent effort to see the *History* as history. Ironically, however, the scholar whose conception of the book most resembles the one offered in the 1848 statement of purpose is Helen Loschky, who has ably demonstrated that Irving's "description of the pattern of life in New Netherland" is a "great untruth." What he was trying to do, she maintains, was "create . . . a sentimental picture about a happier, simpler past of the Dutch." Loschky categorizes *Knickerbocker* as "folk history" rather than as history proper. Not that she attempts to show that the "folk" ever held the view which she finds embodied in the book. Scholarship, as she is quite aware, has as yet been unable to identify specific folk sources for more than a few of the stories and anecdotes incorporated into the narrative. What she means by a "folk" history is a work which presents a legendary or mythical past.(10)

She has avoided the trap of taking *Knickerbocker* for legitimate history and yet managed to square her view with that of Irving in 1848. Internal evidence from successive editions, however, suggests that he arrived at his conception only after revisions had toned down burlesque humor and ridicule and somewhat sentimentalized the text, adding to its stock of legends and other folklike materials. The 1848 statement of purpose does not fit the *Knickerbocker* of 1809. Many of Irving's original inventions -- tall tales, whimsical etymologies, and peculiar names, customs, and traditions -- are so absurd that they rend the folk -- or fake-loric fabric of which, according to Loschky, the narrative consists. In one of the more ludicrous stretchers reported by Knickerbocker, for instance, a group of New Jersey Indians on the shore of the Hudson, hearing for the first time the "tremendous and uncouth sound of the low dutch language," take flight and scamper "over the Bergen hills" to the marshes beyond, where, burying themselves "head and ears," they perish, so numerous a throng apparently that the subsequent piling up of their bones makes an Indian mound large enough to pass for a wellknown hill near Newark (p. 436). A tall tale indeed-though soberly offered by Knickerbocker as a tradition handed down in his family. Nonsense of this sort suggests that if "folk history" is truly a literary form, Irving in 1809 must have been mocking it.

And if he was trying to comfort New Yorkers by giving them a "pretty" past to look back on,(11) he was sadly misinterpreted by those Dutch-Americans who believed he was ridiculing their ancestors. One of them, his friend Gulian Verplanck, characterizing *Knickerbocker* as "burlesque history," complained of its "coarse caricature" and "ungrateful theme." Irving, he said, had perpetrated a "gross . . . national injustice".(12) Indeed it is hard to see how nineteenth-century New York's civic self-esteem or sense of well-being was to have been enhanced by a depiction of the New Netherlanders as, in Loschky's own words, "rather childlike and loveable, albeit foolish and frequently misguided".(13)

There are, as we shall see, political implications in the mythical history that Loschky argues Irving has created in *Knickerbocker* -- which is not surprising, since scholars, whether or not they take the book for genuine history, are very prone to read it as political satire or partially disguised political discourse. This is an approach which dates back at least as far as a well known article by John Neal in *Blackwood's* in 1825.(14) It is encouraged by the overt political moralizing in the final chapter of the versions of *Knickerbocker* that have long been most generally available to the reading public. Irving added four paragraphs of "reflections," on Van Twiller, Kieft, Stuyvesant, and "intemperate" political rhetoric, to the second edition in 1812, and they remained a part of the final revision.(15) What is significant about these paragraphs is not the nature of the "fruitful . . . instruction" they draw from the "history" of New Netherland but the absolutely earnest manner of presentation. Such sobriety, such total lack of humor or irony, is scarcely to be encountered elsewhere in the book. For Knickerbocker to moralize in a way that does not suggest that didacticism itself is at least in part being parodied is a rude violation of the spirit of the original *History*.

Some political readings, including Neal's, go so far as to transform the book into allegory. Loschky, for instance, argues that *Knickerbocker* "exhibits" the "brief tenure of the Dutch" in New Netherland "as a curve, beginning in simplicity and plenty and ending in the wrong kind of political sophistication and disaster." The narrative, "which is largely sentimental and nostalgic,. . . illustrates perfectly Irving's political sentiments."(16) Such a reading grows out of the now generally accepted perception that in the figure of Wilhelmus Kieft, Knickerbocker's villain, Irving has quite consciously satirized Thomas Jefferson.(17) For some readers it then follows that Peter Stuyvesant is James Madison and Wouter Van Twiller is John Adams, although these likenesses are far from obvious. As Loschky sees it, the myth or allegory carries the message that if Americans do not "learn to obey an enlightened, strong president (Madison), they, like the Dutch [may] be in danger of losing their new country to the English".(18)

Less intricate and involved than this, most political interpretations do not go much further than arguing that the *History* embodies the pro-Federalist stance that Irving is known to have taken in the *Salmagundi*-*Knickerbocker* period, 1806-9. This posture is most visible in Knickerbocker's hostility toward the economy-minded Kieft, who fights wars by proclamation, and in the antiquarian's unwavering loyalty to the feisty, high-handed Stuyvesant. Diedrich's partisanship makes itself felt persistently in spite of being undercut again and again by contradiction and irony. That the History in its original version is mildly pro-Federalist can hardly be denied. But it is easy to forget that all his life Irving's party affiliations were marginal and that Federalists, like Republicans, often differed among themselves on ideology or particular issues. By 1812, for instance, he was supporting a war with Great Britain that was anathema to many Federalists. If one disregards Knickerbocker's basic antipathy to moralizing, the political "wisdom"(19) added to the final chapter in later editions can reasonably be adduced from a commonsense reading of the original History. Wouter's tenure is seen as a warning against complacency and insufficient vigilance in the face of threats to the state; Kieft's against, among other things, pandering to the masses. Stuyvesant represents strong, courageous leadership, but also the danger of insensitivity to popular feeling. To make much more of the book politically, however, means either disregarding its complexity and ambiguity or becoming entangled in them.

The political innuendos, murky and confusing as they are, hardly offer a firm foundation for efforts to construe the text as a comprehensive statement on American politics or the nature of a good or just society. Irving's satire, for instance, is directed almost as much at factionalism in general, at unthinking attachment to party positions and automatic submission to the dictates of party bosses (including Stuyvesant [see p. 707]), as it is against Jeffersonianism or the popular faction. Indeed, the book fundamentally sabotages its own Federalist leanings by using Knickerbocker to voice them. For with his crotchety sentimentalizing of the past, his disdain for the "greasy mob" or "swinish multitude" (pp. 523, 670), and his preference for strong authoritarian government, he is surely in part the image of a distracted conservatism. Applying the party designations invented by Irving for the 1809 test (and subsequently discarded), one can classify Knickerbocker, like his idol Stuyvesant, as a "Square head," that is, in effect, one of the brainless, who are opposed by the "Platter breech" faction, those wanting in "courage, or good bottom" (p. 548). Robert Wess has pointed out that Knickerbocker curiously misinterprets Stuyvesant's nickname, "PETER THE HEADSTRONG," taking it as "a great compliment" to his hero's "understanding" (p. 567).(20) Much of the irony in the second half of the book derives from the fact that as far as the face value of what Knickerbocker says is concerned, valiant Peter can do no wrong. While never wasting an opportunity to condemn pothouse politicians, Diedrich "details Stuyvesant's flaws without" -- apparrently -- "realizing their significance."(21) That he actually may be aware of them that the irony may be, for him as well as for Irving, intentional, is often a possibility. But on the surface Knickerbocker seems almost totally blind to the dangers of hotheaded patriotism. Robert Ferguson puts it well when he says, "Chauvinism always confuses in A History of New York and at every level. Knickerbocker's 'old "seventy six" of a governor' . . . is also an 'imp of fame and prowess' whose search for glory unwittingly compounds the 'valour of tongue' and 'gallant vapouring' that replace common sense and probity in New Amsterdam."(22)

As Ferguson sees it, the basic motive behind Knickerbocker is Irving's total disgust at the domination of early American culture by legal, commercial, and political deviousness, self-serving, and hypocrisy. The book thus becomes a virtual prophecy by Irving of the eventual failure of republicanism in America, a prophecy indebted intellectually to the classic critique of "republicanism by political theorists from Plato to Montesquieu."(23) Ferguson's interpretation has much in common with Roth's. For both, the drowsy regime of Wouter Van Twiller is of central importance. Roth discovers in the "comic utopia" of Van Twiller's "golden reign" (p. 461) a myth of America as a New World release from the discontents of civilization. He regrets, moreover, that Irving could not sustain the hedonistic vision, that the History ends in defeat rather than in a reaffirmation of the value of feeling, emotion, whimsy and imagination over the work ethic attached to what is more customarily seen as the American dream.(24) Likewise for Ferguson, the eating, drinking, smoking, sleeping, and good humor under "Wouter the Doubter" represent a primitive age of "simplicity and virtue," which is destroyed by an Enlightenment-like determination to create a government of laws rather than of men.(25)

The major difference between Roth and Ferguson is that the latter sees Knickerbocker fulfilling itself artistically at the end, as the political order which succeeds the golden age, racked by litigiousness and political discord, reaches its destined demise, going the way of all republics. Both his reading and Roth's are high-level criticism, opening up new dimensions in the History. In their determination to allegorize, however, it seems to me that each misses the pointlessness which may finally be the point -- if the book has one. The hedonism of what Roth sees as a vision of a truly New World under Wouter undoubtedly has its appeal, but the grotesqueness of that world reads too easily as a trivialization of life and an avoidance of reality. The vision seems hardly substantial enough for the burden of implication that the critic puts upon it. In any case, the reign of indolence, appetite, and unconcern in Irving's low Dutch lubbers' paradise is the happy creation of the book's verbal and imaginative exuberance. The narrative lunacy, possibly more liberating for the reader than the depiction of golden age torpor, survives both the death of Wouter and the defeat of hardheaded Peter. This is something of a triumph. As for Ferguson's explication, the book is doubtless in part a critique of the republican vision of the founding fathers, but one that is often confusingly inscribed, tangled in with a host of other motifs. Neither Knickerbocker nor Irving, for instance, lets us forget that empires and kingdoms fall as inevitably as republics, that life itself is profoundly unstable, and particularly that a small nation or colony facing a large power determined to swallow it up has little chance of surviving, whatever its form of government.

And are we not subject to the author's posthumous laughter for our willingness to discuss such matters so seriously? In the end, the History undercuts the notion that the Dutch defeat had any significance. Diedrich informs us that nothing changed for the New Netherlanders themselves except "the name of the province and its metropolis", additionally, "in a private meeting of the leading citizens, it was unanimously determined never to ask any of their conquerors to dinner" (p. 721). In addition the book -- though only in the original edition and not in later editions -- mocks in advance its final melancholy rumination on "the ruins of departed greatness" by comparing the "woe begone historian" to "your well disciplined funeral orator, whose feelings are properly tutored to ebb and flow, . . . who had reduced his impetuous grief to a kind of manual" (p. 718). Irving astutely observed in 1848 that the brief "rise, progress, and decline" of New Netherland had provided him with the structural principle of his work,(26) that is, of what Roth calls the primary fiction. For what Irving wanted to make of Knickerbocker (or Knickerbocker) he did not need much more real history. He had a sketchy knowledge of Van Twiller and Kieft, a bit more of Stuyvesant and his governorship. The rest he could invent himself -- or let Knickerbocker invent. For the key to the book is that it is Knickerbocker's, not Irving's, "history." Knickerbocker's inability to detach himself from his narrative makes it a very personal history, one which becomes on one level (the secondary fiction) a grotesque account of the joys and sorrows of authorship. His mission to save New Netherland from the "wide-spread, insatiable maw of oblivion" (p. 381) is a major driving force, one that intensifies the books mock-historical humor, its satire of historians an historical writing. And the seeming meagerness of the Dutch achievement in North America -- ironic in the context -- provides Irving with images of failure and inadequacy which he uses as reflections of the shortcomings of his own society. The burlesque history turns every so often into a mock-jeremiad -- or are we to read it as, for Irving, half--serious lamentation.

It is in the gap between word and deed, the tension between desires for glory and fears of insignificance that much of the power of the original History lies. Literally, the narrative exposes the emptiness of political and chauvinistic pretensions in the New Netherland that old Diedrich seeks to celebrate; by analogy it "ridicules," as Ferguson says, "the high seriousness" of the "republican mythmakers of post-Revolutionary America".(27) The narrative voice also backs up analogy with direct contemporary allusion, as when Knickerbocker observes "how much my beloved country" owes "to a praise-worthy figure in rhetoric, generally cultivated by your little great men, called hyperbole" (p. 534).

Knickerbocker's confusions give us the image of an early American writer driven to distraction by his need, as Roth suggests, to believe in the greatness or uniqueness of the new country with which he wants to identify, when secretly he knows it is no better than it should be.(28) More generally, the text suggests a love of words, "a sense of high style in search of a subject."(29) Diedrich's story essentially resolves itself into a sustained comic improvisation, a tall tale of the gloriously ignoble Dutch venture in the New World, which he seems to deliver under the illusion that he is creating a great history -- except in those occasional moments when he rudely sweeps aside the illusion. Following "To the Public," for instance, he says that the "idle reader may totally overlook" Book I, which is, "like all introductions to American histories, very learned, sagacious, and nothing at all to the purpose" (p. 383).(30) Suddenly, Knickerbocker seems sane, a fully conscious ironist: the book may be _his_, as much as Irving's burlesque. But that illusion will not sustain itself either. The historian's commitment to the genuineness of his story reasserts itself, and his running off at the mouth or the pen runs away with the book. He says whatever pops into his mind in whatever style or fashion suits him, going through violent mood swings in the process, alternately entertaining and abusing his readers with his strong feelings and directly or indirectly making his prejudices known on virtually every topic he broaches.

The _History_ soars to the heights at times -- in its cumbersome fashion -- on one or another of the themes of great literature, only to descend before long to ribaldry or scatology. The phallic prowess of large-nosed Anthony the Trumpeter is an obvious source of humor, as is the overfeeding of hugh Dutch appetites, especially in the Wouterian utopia. By contrast, elimination is less prominently featured in the comedy of bodily functions. It is true that at the Battle of Fort Christina the surrounding hills, "terrified even unto an incontinence of water" by the noise of war, gave vent to fresh "springs" (p. 651). And later when Stuyvesant, forced by the populace of New Amsterdam to surrender to the British, denounces the "rabble" as "degenerate platter breeches," they take "incontinently. . . to their heels; even the Burgomasters [are] not slow in evacuating the premises" (p. 717). But such jokes are infrequent. What is more suggestive is Knickerbocker's near-addiction to the adverb "incontinently" when he is talking about headlong, rash, precipitate action or behavior. The habit becomes a joke in itself, and a particularly telling one, given the verbal incontinence -- his and Irving's -- that at times seems both the form and substance of the fiction.

To suggest the tall tales as a model for reading _Knickerbocker_ is not to try to make a southwestern humorist out of Irving. True, he did create an early frontier "vagrant" in Dirk Schuiler, and he knew about the flamboyant boasting of the "back-wood-men of Kentucky." In his brief observation that such men "are styled half man, half horse and half alligator" he actually mimics (at the same time mocking) their hyperbolic compulsions (p. 617). His early humor, however, is too involved with books and enamored of literary language to give itself much to the vernacular. The *History* betrays a deep attachment to eloquence and the poetic, even as it parodies elegance and high style or occasionally undercuts them with brusque directness or plainness. Still, Knickerbocker's loquacity at times suggests the garrulousness of the tall tale. Turned loose by Irving to tell his story in his own inimitably irresponsible way, he digresses, confuses, ignores the truth, and gets carried away by his own rhetoric in something like the droll manner, if not the language, of a Mark Twain storyteller.

For all the literary overtones of the language, one senses in Irving's improvisations a native freedom and spontaneity. Roth's contention that *Knickerbocker* is a "seminal work" in American romanticism" may be an overstatement, but perhaps only to the extent that it implies an actual influence of Irving's burlesque history on certain later American texts. Certainly it is not farfetched to compare *Knickerbocker* to other American "works whose sprawling, often inchoate, form seems to defy generic classification." Fondness for self-conscious play" and indulgence in a "capriciousness that extends to a delight in contradictions" do seem links between the early Irving and "works like *Walden,* `Song of Myself,' *Moby Dick,* and even *Nature.*"(31)

With its remarkable slipperiness of tone and viewpoint, *Knickerbocker* firmly resists being defined as the coherently developed expression or elaboration of any topic, idea, or conviction. Sustaining itself as neither history nor allegory, it is held together only by its contradictions. The confused and confusing Diedrich is one of the great contrivances of American fictions, an almost totally unreliable narrator whom we yet keep trying one way or another to rely on. It is highly ironic that this achievement is largely unappreciated, especially at a time when criticism seems caught up in the process of calling into question the authority of heretofore supposedly dependable narrators in fiction.

Frustration of the reader's expectations is *Knickerbocker'*a fundamental tactic. It teases us with the prospect of meaning, here and there dazzling us unexpectedly, cutting through the verbiage with odd clarity. But if we keep trying to read between the lines, hoping to match up pronouncements in the *History,* no matter how overstated, distorted, or contradictory they may be, with what we think we know about Irving's attitudes and beliefs, we ultimately find ourselves stranded or duped into imposing order on a resistant text.

It is not that Irving has no personal involvement in his book. His hostility to lawyers and the law is fully apparent, as is his disgust at the sordidness of local politics, into which he had been drawn by family ties. If biography is to be invoked, however, in an effort to "explain" *Knickerbocker,* we could probably get further by looking into the ambiguities of Irving's relationship with Matilda Hoffman, to whom he was engaged while he worked -- in secret -- on the book. She died before he finished it. It may well be that Diedrich's contradictions are in large part a projection of Irving's immediate emotional turmoil and anguish.(32) Still we do not, even on that hypothesis, account for the pleasurable excitement that we experience in being thrown into confusion. Read for its dizziness, Knickerbocker seems a very modern text. Its humor verges on the absurd at times, but the book is having too much fun with itself to tempt us to philosophical despair. At the end, Stuyvesant and New Netherland are defeated, but does anyone really care at this point, even Knickerbocker? He has finished his "history," completed his life's work. IrviNg meanwhile has had an exhilarating flirtation with the irrational. In Addisonian terms he would "qualify . . . for Bedlam" for having fathered a "monstrous infant" called "False Humour," related through "Frenzy" and "Laughter" to "Nonsense" and "Falsehood." But by letting himself be "ludicrous only for the sake of being so," he has created a world of endless ambiguity and contradiction and invited the imagination to lose -- and find -- itself therein.(33) The pity is that this provincial American did not realize the power that he had unlocked with this laudable new-world brashness and that, as he went on with his literary career, he tensed up with worry about how the Old World was going to read him.

NOTES

1. A History of New York . . . by Diedrich Knickerbocker, in Washington Irving, History, Tales and Sketches, ed. James W. Tuttleton (n.p.: The Library of America, 1983), p. 363. Subsequent citations of this reprint of the original (1809) edition of The Knickerbocker History (or Knickerbocker's History or Knickerbocker or simply the History) are given parenthetically in the text.
2. Martin Roth, Comedy and America: The Lost World of Washington Irving (Port Washington, N.Y.: Kennikat Press, 1976), pp. 43, 40.
3. Comedy and America, p. 10.
4. I include myself in this criticism. My early readings of Knickerbocker strain unduly to find in it a coherent conception of history and its significance. See "Knickerbocker, Bolingbroke, and the Fiction of History," Journal of the History of Ideas XX (1959):317-28 and Washington Irving: An American Study, 1802-1832 (Baltimore: John Hopkins University Press, 1965), ch. 3.
5. Major investigations of Knickerbocker's relation to historical source materials are Stanley T. Williams and Tremaine McDowell, eds., Diedrich Knickerbocker's A History of New York (New York: Harcourt Brace, 1927), introduction; Robert Osborne, "A Study of Washington Irving's Development as a Man of Letters to 1825," Ph.D. diss. (University of North Carolina, 1947), pp. 177-95; Michael Black, "Washington Irving's A History of New York with Emphasis on the 1848 Revision," Ph.D. diss. (Columbia University, 1967), passim (but see especially pp. 77-86); Helen M. Loschky, "Washington Irving's Knickerbocker's History of New York: Folk History as Literary Form," Ph.D. diss. (Brown University, 1970), passim.
6. Presumably the "elaborate manuscript . . . found in

the archives of the Stuyvesant family" (p. 378) is the "Stuyvesant manuscript" referred to at least nine times, beginning p. 543.

7. Peter K. McCarter, "The Literary, Political, and Social Theories of Washington Irving," Ph.d. diss. (University of Wisconsin, 1939), p. 56; Williams and McDowell, p. 11; Black, p. 52.

8. Robert C. Wess, "The Image and Use of the Dutch in the Literary Works of Washington Irving," Ph.d. diss. (Notre Dame, 1970), pp. 139-45.

9. A History of New York, ed.Michael L. and Nancy B. Black, The Complete Works of Washington Irving, VII (Boston: Twayne Publishers, 1984), This text is hereafter referred to as "A History (1984)"

10. Loschky, pp. 9, 5-6, 42, 101-219 passim. See also Robert C. Wess, "The Use of the Hudson Valley Traditions in Washington Irving's Knickerbocker History," New York Folklore Quarterly XXX (1974):212-25. In the words of Edwin T. Bowden, whom Loschky cites (p. 11), Irving's History is a "deliberately conceived myth"; see Bowden's introduction to A History of New York (New Haven: College and University Press, 1964), pp. 25-26.

11. Loschky, p. 41.

12. Gulian C. Verplanck, "An Anniversary Discourse Delivered before the New York Historical Society, December 7, 1818," Collections of the New York Historical Society III (1821):88. See also Stanley T. Williams, The Life of Washington Irving, 2 vols. (New York: Oxford University Press, 1935), II:274-75.

13. Loschky, p. 8.

14. "American Writers, No. IV," Blackwood's Edinburgh Magazine XVII (1825):62.

15. Irving, A History, (1984), VII, 291-92.

16. Loschky, p. 42. This is the substance of the legendary or mythical past which Loschky sees as the structural basis of Knickerbocker.

17. See Edwin Greenlaw, "Washington Irving's Comedy of Politics," The Texas Review I (1915): 290-306; also see Williams and McDowell, pp. lx-lxxiii.

18. Loschky, p. 45. Loschky works primarily with the 1812 edition of the History. By March 1812, when this new version was published, Madison was showing his determination to stand up to Great Britain unless the orders in council were repealed. But the situation of the United States in 1812, facing two belligerent nations which for years had been flagrantly disrespectful of American neutrality, was far more complex than that of Knickerbocker's New Netherland in its final hour. The war hawks in his own party considered Madison too cautious in his dealings with Britain, and the Federalists believed that in standing up to the British he was being duped by France.

19. Irving, A History, (1984), VII, 29

20. Wess, "The Image," p. 132. Of course if the historian is conscious of the irony, he is satirizing the governor he supposedly idolizes.

21. Robert A. Ferguson, "'Hunting Down a Nation': Irving's A History of New York," Nineteenth-Century Fiction

36 (1981):35.
22. Ferguson, "Hunting Down a Nation ...", p. 35.
23. Ferguson, "Hunting Down a Nation ...", p. 34
24. Roth, pp. 156, 114-54.
25. Ferguson, p. 33.
26. Irving, _A History_, (1984), VII, 291.
27. Ferguson, p. 30; see also p. 40.
28. Roth, pp. 34-35.
29. I quote myself here; see "The Old World Yet: Writers and Writing in Post-Revolutionary America," _Early American Literature_ 16 (1981):16.
30. This and a similar passage in which the mask of earnestness is dropped -- the first paragraph of the fourth chapter of Book I (p. 405) -- were eliminated in subsequent editions.
31. Roth, pp. 96, 44; see also pp. 37, 42.
32. See Hedges, _Washington Irving_, pp. 9-11.
33. I have used these quotations (from _Spectator_, no. 35) previously in discussing Irving's nonsense humor; see _Washington Irving_, pp. 31-32.

Romanticism in the Old and New World

INTERNATIONAL CONFERENCE
IN CELEBRATION OF

Washington Irving

Stendhal

Vasilii Andreevich Zhukovskii

Shad Fishermen on the Shore of the Hudson River,
Pavel Petrovich Svinin (1787-1839)

HOFSTRA UNIVERSITY
HEMPSTEAD, NEW YORK 11550

OCTOBER 13, 14, 15, 1983

HOFSTRA CULTURAL CENTER

Director: Joseph G. Astman

Associate Director: Peter D'Albert

Music Coordinator: Paul Hefner

Secretary: Mary Eichelberger

GALLERIES:

David Filderman Gallery

Marguerite M. Regan
Assistant to the Dean of Library Services

Nancy E. Herb

Emily Lowe Gallery

Gail Gelburd
Director

Mary Wakeford
Directorial Assistant

MUSICAL ORGANIZATIONS:

American Chamber Ensemble

Blanche Abram
Naomi Drucker
Directors

Hofstra String Quartet

Seymour Benstock
Artistic Coordinator

HOFSTRA CULTURAL CENTER

UNIVERSITY CENTER FOR CULTURAL & INTERCULTURAL STUDIES

Assistant Directors and Conference Coordinators:	Natalie Datlof Alexej Ugrinsky
Secretary:	Marilyn Seidman
Assistants:	Karin Barnaby Jo-Ann Graziano Michael E. Hurley Doris Keane Nel Panzeca Sinaida U. Weber

The continuous assistance by the following student organizations is greatly appreciated:

The French Club

President:	Gina Giuffre
Vice President:	Palmira Cricenti
Treasurer:	Crescenza Carone
Secretary:	Judy Sawyer

The German Club

President	Michael Jakob
Vice President:	Ron Junda
Secretaries:	Patricia Beck Stephanie Dana
Treasurer:	Tina Tersigni

ROMANTICISM in the OLD and the NEW WORLD

International Conference in Celebration of the Bicentennial of the Births of:

Vasilii Andreevich Zhukovskii
(1783-1852)

Stendhal
(1783-1842)

Washington Irving
(1783-1859)

Conference Directors:

Washington Irving Section: Stanley Brodwin

Stendhal Section: Avriel Goldberger

Zhukovskii Section: Valija Ozolins

Thursday, October 13, 1983

Conference Opening:

10:00 - 11:00 A.M.

Registration David Filderman Gallery
Department of Special Collections
Hofstra University Library - 9th floor

Greetings from the Hofstra University Community

Sanford S. Hammer
Provost and Dean of Faculties

Joseph G. Astman
Director
Hofstra Cultural Center
Professor of Comparative Literature & Languages

11:00 A.M.

Opening Address: Henri Peyre
Professor Emeritus
The Graduate Center/CUNY
New York, NY

"1783-1983: Romanticism Then and Now"

Opening of Conference Exhibit: "Romantic Rebels"

Reception

12:00 Noon

Lunch: Student Center Cafeteria/The Netherlands

1:30 P.M.

WASHINGTON IRVING SECTION - Dining Rooms ABC, Student Center

Introductions:

Stanley Brodwin
Department of English
Director: Washington Irving Section

Special Address: Andrew B. Myers
Department of English
Fordham University, Bronx, NY
President, Washington Irving Society
Tarrytown, NY

"Washington Irving's Relations with Key Contemporary Romantic Writers"

Thursday, October 13, 1983 (cont'd.) | Dining Rooms ABC, Student Center

2:00 P.M.

PANEL I - WASHINGTON IRVING AS A ROMANTIC

Moderator: Ruth Prigozy
Department of English
Hofstra University

"Washington Irving as a Purveyor of Old and New World Romanticism"
Ralph M. Aderman
University of Wisconsin-Milwaukee

"Washington Irving as an American Romantic"
Jeffrey Rubin-Dorsky
University of California at Los Angeles

3:30 P.M.

Special Address: Joy Kasson
American Studies Curriculum
University of North Carolina at Chapel Hill

"Washington Irving: The Growth of a Romantic Writer"

4:00 P.M.

V. A. ZHUKOVSKII SECTION

Valija K. Ozolins
Department of Comparative Literature & Languages
Director: V. A. Zhukovskii Section

"Zhukovskii: A Tribute"

PANEL II - ZHUKOVSKII AND RUSSIAN ROMANTICISM

Moderator: Kaleria Javorsky
Department of Foreign Languages
C. W. Post Center of Long Island University
Greenvale, NY

"Zhukovskii on the Death of Pushkin"
Stephanie Sandler
Amherst College, Amherst, MA

"Pushkin's Creative Assimilation of Zhukovskii and Irving"
Michael R. Katz
Williams College, Williamstown, MA

5:30 P.M.

Dinner: Student Center Cafeteria/The Netherlands

Thursday, October 13, 1983 (cont'd.) Dining Rooms ABC, Student Center

7:00 P.M. WASHINGTON IRVING SECTION

PANEL III - ROMANTIC THEMES

Moderator: William L. Hedges
Department of English
Goucher College
Towson, MD

"Irving's *Tales of the Alhambra* and Early Photography in Spain" (Slide Illustrations)
Lee Fontanella
University of Texas at Austin

"A Quaint, Picturesque Little Pile: Architecture and the Past in Washington Irving"
David R. Anderson
Hiram College, Hiram, OH

"Washington Irving and the Romance of Travel: Is There an Itinerary in *Tales of a Traveller*?"
Judith Brazinsky
University of North Carolina at Chapel Hill

"Washington Irving and the Denial of the Fantastic"
Peter G. Christensen
SUNY at Binghamton, Binghamton, NY

Reception: Wine and Cheese

Friday, October 14, 1983 — Dining Rooms ABC, Student Center

9:30 A.M. — WASHINGTON IRVING SECTION

Stanley Brodwin, Director

PANEL IV - ROMANTICISM: COMPARATIVE ASPECTS

Moderator: Nora de Marval McNair
Chair, Department of Spanish
Hofstra University

"Irving, Chateaubriand and the Historical Romance of Granada"
John A. Frey
George Washington University, Washington, D.C.

"The Romantic Lie: Irving's A Tour on the Prairies/Stendhal's Promenades dans Rome"
John Joseph
Oklahoma State University, Stillwater, OK

"Re-Evaluating Scott: Washington Irving's 'Abbotsford'"
William Owen
Ryerson Polytechnical Institute, Toronto, Canada

"The Charm of a Golden Past: Iberia in the Writings of Washington Irving and Antônio Goncalves Dias"
Loretta Sharon Wyatt
Montclair State College, Upper Montclair, NJ

11:30 A.M. — Lunch: Student Center Cafeteria/The Netherlands

1:15 P.M. — STENDHAL SECTION - Dining Rooms ABC, Student Center

Introductions:

Avriel Goldberger
Department of French
Director: Stendhal Section

Special Address: Victor Brombert
Henry Putnam University Professor
of Romance and Comparative Literatures
Department of Romance Languages & Literatures
Princeton University
Princeton, NJ

"Stendhal 1983"

Friday, October 14, 1983 (cont'd.) — Dining Rooms ABC, Student Center

2:00 P.M. — PANEL V - STENDHAL: SPACE AND TIME

Moderator: Denis-Jacques Jean
Chair, Department of French
Hofstra University

"Fathers and Sons: The Case of François Leuwen"
Marcel Gutwirth
Jaan and John Whitehead Professor of French
Haverford College, Haverford, PA

"Stendhal and the Departure Figure"
Hugues de Kerret
Cultural Attaché
Cultural Services of the French Embassy
New York, NY

"From Beyle to Stendhal: Literary Vocation in *La Vie de Henri Brulard*"
Isabelle Naginski
Bard College, Annandale-on-Hudson, NY
Mellon Fellow in the Humanities, University of Pennsylvania

3:45 P.M. — David Filderman Gallery - Hofstra University Library - 9th floor

Special Addresses: Contemporary Biographers

Moderator: Edwin L. Dunbaugh
Department of History
Hofstra University

Armand Hoog
Pyne Professor of French Literature Emeritus
Princeton University
Princeton, NJ

"Stendhal: Biographie et Mythologie"

Gita May
Department of French & Romance Philology
Columbia University
New York, NY

"Stendhal and the Biographer's Challenge"

5:00 P.M. — Champagne Reception

Friday, October 14, 1983 (cont'd.) David Filderman Gallery - Library - 9th floor

5:30 P.M.

A Reading of French Romantic Poetry

Françoise Gilot
Paris, France
New York, NY

Alex Szogyi
Department of French
Hunter College and The Graduate Center/CUNY
New York, NY

6:30 P.M. Cash Bar — Dining Rooms ABC, Student Center

ROMANTICISM CONFERENCE BANQUET

Greetings: Robert A. Davison
Acting Dean, Hofstra College of Liberal Arts & Sciences

8:30 P.M. CONCERT: John Cranford Adams Playhouse

Hugo's Romantic followers fighting jeering Classicists at the first performance of Hugo's Hernani, 1830.
J.I.I. Grandville (1803-1847)

Friday, October 14, 1983 (cont'd.) John Cranford Adams Playhouse, South Campus

The American Chamber Ensemble

Directors: Blanche Abram and Naomi Drucker

In Residence at Hofstra University

Blanche Abram, piano

Naomi Drucker, clarinet

Judy Geist, viola

Ruth Waterman, violin

William Grubb, cello

THE ROMANTIC SPIRIT

Bruch ....THREE PIECES opus 83 for viola, clarinet, piano

Mendelssohn ....TRIO in d minor for violin, cello, piano

Brahms ....TRIO opus 114 for clarinet, cello, piano

The audience is invited to join the artists for after-concert dessert and coffee in the Playhouse Lounge.

The American Chamber Ensemble is a group of distinguished musicians exploring the varied literature for clarinet and piano in combination with strings, woodwinds and voice. The performers include winners of major competitions such as the Moscow Tschaikovsky Competition and the International Bach Competition. They have also performed in festivals throughout the world. The Ensemble which is in residence at Hofstra University has won wide acclaim and is assisted by funds from the New York State Council on the Arts, Hofstra University, the Nassau County Office of Cultural Development, the Vally Weigl Performance and Recording Award Fund, the Chase Manhattan Bank, and private contributors.

Saturday, October 15, 1983	David Filderman Gallery Exhibit: "Romantic Rebels" 11:00 A.M. - 3:00 P.M. -- Special Hours
8:00 A.M.	Continental Breakfast Dining Rooms ABC, Student Center
9:00 A.M.	STENDHAL SECTION

Avriel Goldberger, Director

PANEL VI - STENDHAL AND THE WOMAN QUESTION

Moderator: Judith L. Johnston
Department of English
Rider College
Lawrenceville, NJ

"Stendhal as a Reader of George Sand"
Marie-Jacques Hoog
Rutgers University, New Brunswick, NJ

"Images et mythe de la femme chez Stendhal"
Simone Vierne
Centre de Recherche sur l'Imaginaire
Université de Grenoble 3, Grenoble, France

"Epistolary Communication in Stendhal's Le Rouge et le Noir: Masculinity and Femininity of the Scriptors"
Sylvie Charron Witkin
University of Wisconsin at Madison

10:45 A.M. PANEL VII - STENDHALIAN PERSPECTIVES

Moderator: William L. Shiver
Department of French
Hofstra University

"Perspectivism in Stendhal: Mirrors and Crystals and Turtledoves"
Michael Vande Berg
University of Illinois at Urbana-Champaign

"Littérature et idéologie: Le Rouge et le noir, chronique de 1830"
Serge Bokobza
University of Alabama, Birmingham, AL

"Aristarchus: Stendhal's Outlook on Literature and Journalism in Romantic Italy"
Carolina Donadio Lawson
Kent State University, Kent, OH

"Two Romantic Models of Octave de Malivert"
George M. Rosa
Tulane University, New Orleans, LA

12:45 P.M. Complimentary Brunch

GREETINGS

" . . . I send you all good wishes for the success of 'Romanticism in the Old and New World.'"

Jacques Barzun
New York, NY

"With my warmest wishes for the conference."

Anatoli N. Shoustov
Academy of Sciences of the USSR
Division of Literature & Language
Leningrad, USSR

Cooperating Institutions:

Cultural Services of the French Embassy
New York, NY

Hempstead Plaza Hotel
Hempstead, NY

Nassau County Office of Cultural Development
Roslyn, NY

Nassau Library System
Uniondale, NY

New York Public Library
New York, NY

Sleepy Hollow Restoration
Tarrytown, NY

Suffolk Cooperative Library System
Bellport, NY

Kindred Spirits: William Cullen Bryant during an Outing in the Catskills, Asher B. Durand (1796-1886)

PERFORMANCE NOTES

THE HOFSTRA STRING QUARTET

GALA TWENTIETH ANNIVERSARY SEASON

The Hofstra Quartet, the Island's first professional quartet and oldest continuous chamber music group celebrates its twentieth anniversary with a series of two Sunday afternoon concerts (Oct. 9th and Feb. 26th) and two Friday concerts (Nov. 11th and April 6th) at the John Cranford Adams Playhouse.

Founded in 1963, the Quartet has established itself as one of the leading chamber music ensembles in the metropolitan area, with a repertoire of over 200 works. They have been heard in public over 300 times as an ensemble and have recorded for Paganiniana Records, Ziff Davis, and recently completed an album for LaTrec Records. Its four artist-teacher members (Harry Glickman and Ray Kunicki, violins; Harry Zaratzian, viola; and Seymour Benstock, 'cello) have been associated with the WQXR, BowArt, Composers, and Kohon Quartets, and have occupied first chair positions in the NBC Symphony, Toledo Orchestra, Philadelphia Orchestra, and Symphony of the Air under such eminent conductors as Toscanini, Stokowski, Bernstein, and Ormandy.

The opening concert on October 9th will feature guests bassist Carolyn Davis and pianist Abba Bogin in a performance of Schubert's "Trout Quintet." In addition, members of the quartet will be heard in the duet for cello and bass by Rossini and the Serenade, Op. 8 of Beethoven.

For ticket information: (516) 560-5669/5670

HOFSTRA CULTURAL CENTER

CONFERENCES AT HOFSTRA UNIVERSITY

George Sand Centennial - November 1976

Heinrich von Kleist Bicentennial - November 1977

The Chinese Woman - December 1977

George Sand: Her Life, Her Works, Her Influence - April 1978

William Cullen Bryant and His America - October 1978

The Trotsky-Stalin Conflict in the 1920's - March 1979

Albert Einstein Centennial - November 1979

Renaissance Venice Symposium - March 1980

Sean O'Casey - March 1980

Walt Whitman - April 1980

Nineteenth-Century Women Writers - November 1980

Fedor Dostoevski - April 1981

Gotthold Ephraim Lessing - November 1981

Franklin Delano Roosevelt - March 1982

Johann Wolfgang von Goethe - April 1982

James Joyce - October 1982

Twentieth-Century Women Writers - November 1982

Harry S. Truman: The Man from Independence - April 14-16, 1983

John Maynard Keynes - September 22-24, 1983

HOFSTRA CULTURAL CENTER

CONFERENCES AT HOFSTRA UNIVERSITY

Romanticism in the Old and the New World - Washington Irving, Stendhal, and Zhukovskii - October 13-15, 1983

Espectador Universal: José Ortega y Gasset - November 10-12, 1983

Dwight D. Eisenhower - March 29-31, 1984

George Orwell - October 11-13, 1984

Friedrich von Schiller - November 8-10, 1984

Harlem Renaissance - February 28-March 2, 1985

John F. Kennedy - March 28-30, 1985

Conference on Higher Education - April 1985

Eighteenth-Century Women Writers - October 10-12, 1985

Avant Garde Art and Literature - November 14-16, 1985

Lyndon B. Johnson - April 1986

Carl Gustav Jung - October 1986

George Sand: Her Life, Her Works, Her Influence - November 1986

Richard M. Nixon - Spring 1987

Bicentennial of the United States Constitution - Fall 1987

Gerald R. Ford - Spring 1988

Jimmy Carter - Spring 1989

Bicentennial of the French Revolution - Fall 1989

Ronald Reagan - Spring 1990

"Calls for Papers" available

CREDIT for the success of this Conference goes to more people than can be named in the program, but those below deserve a special vote of thanks:

HOFSTRA UNIVERSITY OFFICERS: James M. Shuart, President
Sanford S. Hammer, Provost & Dean of Faculties
Robert A. Davison, Acting Dean, Hofstra College of Liberal Arts & Sciences

ARA SLATER: Tony Internicola, Director, Dining Services

DAVID FILDERMAN GALLERY: Marguerite M. Regan, Assistant to the Dean of Library Services
Nancy E. Herb
Anne Rubino

DEPARTMENT OF COMPARATIVE LITERATURE & LANGUAGES: Helene C. Waysek, Chair
Maria Cappadocia, Secretary

DEPARTMENT OF ENGLISH: Robert N. Keane, Chair
Barbara Strohschnitter, Secretary

DEPARTMENT OF FRENCH: Denis-Jacques Jean, Chair
Colette R. Bailey, Secretary

DEPARTMENT OF MUSIC: Edgar Dittemore, Chair
Eleanor Geddes, Secretary

HOFSTRA UNIVERSITY LIBRARY: Charles R. Andrews, Dean

OFFICE OF THE SECRETARY: Robert D. Noble, Secretary
Margaret Mirabella
Stella Sinicki, Supervisor, Special Secretarial Services
Jack Ruegamer, Director, Art & Printing Production
Veronica Fitzwilliam
Doris Brown & Staff

OPERATIONAL SERVICES: James Fellman, Director

PUBLIC SAFETY AND TELECOMMUNICATIONS: Robert Crowley, Director
John Fitzgerald, Deputy Director

SCHEDULING OFFICE: Charles L. Churchill, Assistant Facilities Manager
Dorothy Fetherston, Director

TECHNICAL AND MEDIA SERVICES: Robert J. Kleinhans, Director
Albert Nowicki and Staff

UNIVERSITY RELATIONS: Harold A. Klein, Director
James Merritt, Assistant Director
M.F. Klerk, Editor/Writer
Frances B. Jacobsen, Administrative Assistant

Forthcoming:

ESPECTADOR UNIVERSAL

1883 - 1955

International Interdisciplinary Conference in Celebration of the 100th Anniversary of the birth of

JOSE ORTEGA Y GASSET

Director:

Nora de Marval McNair
Chair, Department of Spanish

Thursday, Friday, Saturday, November 10, 11, 12, 1983

Registration Programs available at the Conference desk.

NOTES

Index

About the Contributors

RALPH M. ADERMAN is Professor Emeritus of English at the University of Wisconsin-Milwaukee, where he spent his entire academic career. His specialty is American literature of the Romantic period, and his research has focused on fiction of the early and mid-nineteenth century. He is senior editor of *The Letters of Washington Irving* (4 vols.), and he also edited *The Letters of James Kirke Paulding.*

DAVID R. ANDERSON is Associate Professor of English at Hiram College, Hiram, Ohio and Chairman of the Department. His principal areas of teaching and research are in English Renaissance Literature and American Literature, particularly nineteenth century Romanticism. He was the recipient of N.E.H. grants for "Architecture and History in the Undergraduate Curriculum," and "Regionalism in the Humanities."

PETER G. CHRISTENSEN teaches English at Broome Community College and the State University of New York at Binghamton. His specialty is in comparative literature and film studies. He is the author of articles on George Sand, John Dos Passos, and Marguerite Yourcenar, and of forthcoming essays on Jown Cowper Powys, Lawrence Durrell, Jean-Luc Godard, Italo Calvino, and Paul Nizan.

LEE FONTANELLA is Professor of Spanish at the University of Texas, Austin, where he also teaches comparative literature and photohistory. Among his books are *La historia de la fotografía en España desde sus orígenes hasta 1900* and *La imprenta y las letras en la España romántica*, and he has written numerous articles on Spanish photography and Hispanic literature, with concentration in the nineteenth century.

JOHN A. FREY is Professor and Chairman of the Department of Romance Languages of The George Washington University. He has authored articles on Baudelaire, Marie de France, and other figures of French literature. He is the author of *Motif Symbolism in the Disciples of Mallarmé*, *The Aesthetics of the Rougon-Macquart*, and has recently completed *Hugo's Contemplations—The Ash Wednesday Liturgy*. He is presently working on a critical translation of Ernest Renan's *Souvenir d'Enfance et de Jeunesse.*

JUDITH G. HAIG is Assistant Professor of English at the University of South Carolina at Columbia. She has published articles on nineteenth- and twentieth-century American fiction and has edited the critical edition of Washington Irving's *Tales of a Traveller* (in press) for *The Complete Works of Washington Irving.*

WILLIAM L. HEDGES is Professor of English and Chair of American Studies at Goucher College. He has published *Washington Irving: An American Study, 1802-1832* as well as numerous articles on Irving and other figures and topics in American literature, particularly in the period of the early Republic. He is also co-author/editor of *Land and Imagination: The Rural Dream in America.*

JOHN EARL JOSEPH is Assistant Professor of French and Italian at the University of Maryland. He is the author of *Eloquence and Power: The Rise of Language Standards and Standard Languages* (London: Frances Pinter, 1987), the editor of *Applied Language Study: New Objectives, New Methods* (University Press of America, 1984), and has published numerous articles in journals of linguistics and literary criticism.

JOY S. KASSON is Associate Professor of American Studies at the University of North Carolina at Chapel Hill. Her research interests focus on nineteenth-century American literature, art, and cultural history. She is the author of *Artistic Voyagers: Europe and the American Imagination in the Works of Irving, Cooper, Hawthorne, Allston, and Cole.*

MICHAEL R. KATZ is Professor of Russian and Chairman of the Department of Slavic Languages at the University of Texas at Austin. He taught Russian previously at Williams College. He is the author of *Dreams and the Unconscious in Nineteenth-Century Russian Literature* and has also translated Alexander Herzen's novel *Who is to Blame?* into English.

WILIAM OWEN is Professor of English at Ryerson Polytechnical Institute in Toronto, Ontario and teaches Utopian and American literature. He has published on James Fenimore Cooper and Charles G. D. Roberts and is continuing research work on Cooper's later novels.

JEFFREY RUBIN-DORSKY is Assistant Professor of English at the University of California, Los Angeles. He specializes in nineteenth-century

American literature and has published several articles on Washington Irving. He has just completed a book-length manuscript entitled "Representative American: Washington Irving as Psychological Pilgrim."

LORETTA SHARON WYATT is Associate Professor of Latin American History and Portuguese Language at Montclair State College in New Jersey. With her extensive academic and research background in literature and history, she has become a recognized authority on both Brazilian and Spanish American topics, including transcultural comparisons with American themes. She has published several articles on different facets of Latin American culture and history.

Hofstra University's
Cultural and Intercultural Studies
Coordinating Editor, Alexej Ugrinsky

George Sand Papers: Conference Proceedings, 1976
(Editorial Board: Natalie Datlof, Edwin L. Dunbaugh, Frank S. Lambasa, Gabrielle Savet, William C. Shiver, Alex Szogyi)

George Sand Papers: Conference Proceedings, 1978
(Editorial Board: Natalie Datlof, Edwin L. Dunbaugh, Frank S. Lambasa, Gabrielle Savet, William C. Shiver, Alex Szogyi)

Heinrich von Kleist Studies
(Editorial Board: Alexej Ugrinsky, Frederick J. Churchill, Frank S. Lambasa, Robert F. von Berg)

William Cullen Bryant Studies
(Editors: Stanley Brodwin, Michael D'Innocenzo)

*Walt Whitman: Here and Now
(Editor: Joann P. Krieg)

*Harry S. Truman: The Man from Independence
(Editor: William F. Levantrosser)

*Nineteenth-Century Women Writers of the English-Speaking World
(Editor: Rhoda B. Nathan)

*Lessing and the Enlightenment
(Editor: Alexej Ugrinsky)

*Dostoeveski and the Human Condition After a Century
(Editors: Alexej Ugrinsky, Frank S. Lambasa, and Valija K. Ozolins)

**Available from Greenwood Press*

About the Editor

STANLEY BRODWIN is Professor of English at Hofstra University. He has published articles in a variety of journals including *PMLA, American Literature, Journal of Black Studies,* and the *Journal of the History of Ideas.*